The Niagara Companion

*Explorers, Artists, and
Writers at the Falls,
from Discovery through
the Twentieth Century*

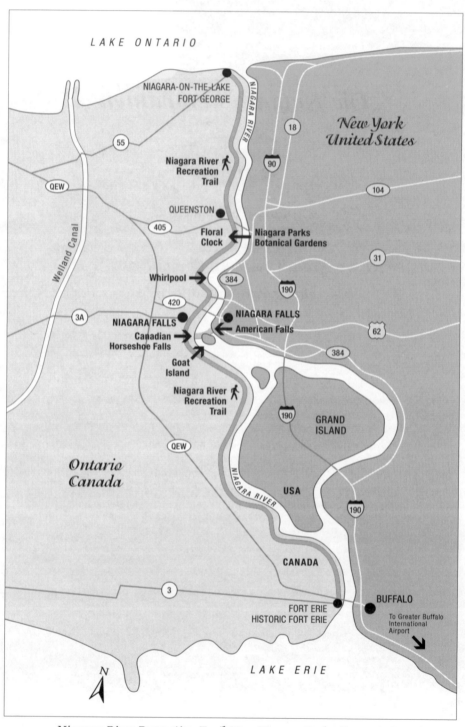

Niagara River Recreation Trail Map. Niagara Parks Commission.

The Niagara Companion

Explorers, Artists, and
Writers at the Falls,
from Discovery through
the Twentieth Century

Linda L. Revie

Wilfrid Laurier University Press

This book has been published with the help of a grant from the Canadian Federation for the Humanities and Social Sciences, through the Aid to Scholarly Publications Programme, using funds provided by the Social Sciences and Humanities Research Council of Canada. We acknowledge the financial support of the Government of Canada through the Book Publishing Industry Development Program for our publishing activities.

National Library of Canada Cataloguing in Publication

Revie, Linda L. (Linda Lee)
      The Niagara companion: explorers, artists, and writers at the Falls, from discovery through the twentieth century / Linda L. Revie.

Includes bibliographical references and index.
ISBN 0-88920-433-0

      1. Niagara Falls (Ont.)—Description and travel. 2. Niagara Falls (Ont.)—In art. 3. Niagara Falls (Ont.)—In literature. 4. Niagara Falls (Ont.)—History. 5. Niagara Falls Region (N.Y. and Ont.)—Description and travel. 6. Niagara Falls Region (N.Y. and Ont.)—History. I. Title.

FC3095.N5R477 2003   971.3'39   C2003-904095-X

© 2003 Wilfrid Laurier University Press
Waterloo, Ontario, Canada N2L 3C5
www.wlupress.wlu.ca

Cover design by Leslie Macredie, using a painting by Isabella Stefanescu; text design by P.J. Woodland.

Every reasonable effort has been made to acquire permission for copyright material used in this text, and to acknowledge all such indebtedness accurately. Any errors and omissions called to the publisher's attention will be corrected in future printings.

∞
Printed in Canada

Contents

Acknowledgments

WHILE THIS BOOK GREW OUT OF MY PH.D. dissertation at Boston College, it has deep roots in annual childhood pilgrimages to Niagara Falls (always on the Victoria Day weekend). For those early encounters, I thank my parents, Ronald and Doreen Revie. Graduate fellowships at Boston College gave me the opportunity to carry out work on the thesis. And, at Boston College, my former supervisor, Rosemarie Bodenheimer, saw me through the years of research, writing, and rewriting.

At Wilfrid Laurier University Press, thanks go to Sandra Woolfrey for instructive comments on an early draft, and to Brian Henderson, Carroll Klein, Jenny Wilson, Leslie Macredie, Pam Woodland, and Elin Edwards for advice and encouragement.

I am grateful to the three formal reviewers (all anonymous) from the Aid to Scholarly Publications Programme for detailed and thoughtful readings.

Finally, I owe very sincere appreciation to Mary MacDonald, Angela Caretta, and Jeffery Donaldson; to Isabella Stefanescu for painting Niagara; and to Karen Dubinsky for all her insightful processing.

List of Figures

Introduction

ECENTLY, A PARTY OF WRITERS on a day trip from the International Festival of Authors in Toronto gathered behind the railings at Niagara and contemplated the Horseshoe Falls. William Gass, Isabel Colegate, and Al Purdy offered no yelps of surprise; instead, they gravely reflected on the "architectural boils"—the fast-food outlets and gift shops—that ruined their view. But one writer in their midst, South African novelist André Brink, moved beyond his initial reaction to the garish spectacle and claimed that Niagara was "impressive." Brink went on to contemplate: "What impresses one is that despite all the efforts to spoil it, the real power of nature remains untamed."[1] Brink's use of words like "power" and "untamed," and the way in which his disapproval was succeeded by satisfaction echo centuries of responses at Niagara. The seventeenth-century European discoverer of the cataract, Louis Hennepin, expatiated on the wonders of the scene and on his own inadequacy, as if he did not have the power to describe such an awesome view; in the nineteenth century, writers, stunned by Niagara's sublimity, protested the impossibility of language, as if their civilized discourse could not account for the "untamed" experience of Niagara; and our twentieth-century authors from the International Festival complained about the sordid landscape and contemplated a "wilder" vision, as if they could get past the accumulated evidence of centuries of industry, commerce, and tourism to some once-pure nature, whose true form existed prior to the state of contamination. The way in which commentators at Niagara write about power and, conversely, deficiency—or wildness and sordidness—connects them through the centuries.

NIAGARA FALLS WAS KNOWN about before the *Mayflower* landed.
Samuel de Champlain, one of the first European explorers in Canada,
alluded to a large waterfall as early as 1603, yet the name did not
appear on maps until 1641.[2] The Neutral Nation, an Iroquoian tribe living in villages in the Niagara area from approximately AD 1300 to 1643,
gave us the name "Niagara" ("Thunder of the Waters").[3] It is reported
by Champlain that those Neutrals who lived along the Niagara River
were called *Onguiaronon* ("People of the Thundering Waters"). While
other variations of the Iroquoian word handed down to us include
Ongiarah, Ouinagarah, and *Ongniaraha,* it was later anglicized as
"Nee-ah-guh-ah."

In 1678, the first party of Europeans explored the place that Champlain had only heard about. When Louis Hennepin wrote about
Onguiaahra—his version of the word "Niagara"—he described an
"incredible Cataract…which has no equal."[4] According to Hennepin,
the deep, rapid river split into three waterfalls, each of which plunged
down 600 feet. His account served as the foundation for a 1697 illustration—also the first picture of Niagara. That view contains two very
tall, very broad sheets of water, a steep, thin cascade and, in the distance, a chain of high mountains. These latter features suggest that Niagara was seen as a gateway to some other place. Even though this
description and drawing were idealized, later writers and painters were
willing to follow Hennepin in his choice of viewpoint.

For the next wave of Europeans—French and British militia—the
great waterfalls were obstacles that had to be circumvented, but the
river, a channel for boats and people, allowed access to the rich
resources of the New World's interior.[5] Later in the eighteenth century, wars between the First Nations, French, and British, followed by
Indian-European alliances and inter-tribal conflicts, resulted in the
Treaty of Paris (1783), which established the Niagara River as a dividing line between British North America and the United States of America. Once a conduit for people and goods, the river was now a border
between nations. The successive wars, charters, and treaties, followed
by waves of immigration, influenced settlement and travel around the
Niagara River and had impacts on both culture and development.

While stationed at the Falls, some eighteenth-century military gentlemen sketched and described a Niagara that was implausible even by

Hennepin's standards. Then, immediately before and after the American Revolution, Niagara became popular among a different group of people—European travellers, entrepreneurs, and natural historians. They came to the Falls to "size it up" for themselves and, in the process, challenged or, in some cases, furthered the exaggerated descriptions. After the War of 1812, Niagara was added to the itinerary of the popular Northern Tour taken by Americans. Wars with France meant that the British cancelled their European grand tours in favour of trips to the Falls.[6] Early in the 1820s, thousands of genteel travellers went to Niagara. They demanded services and accommodation to suit their station; as a consequence, the Niagara tourist industry began. The first hotel along the river was established in 1822 on the Canadian side, at the site of a primitive log hostel.[7] William Forsyth, a Loyalist descendant and entrepreneur, erected the grand, three-storey Pavilion Hotel, which had the capacity to house and feed 100 guests. (Forsyth also built stairs, ramps, walkways, and railings around his property, all of which made Niagara more accessible—and more expensive.) Along with proper accommodation, tourists demanded convenient travel to and from the Falls. A stagecoach began running three times a week from the head of Lake Ontario—Hamilton—to Niagara.[8] After the Erie Canal was completed in 1825, linking Buffalo with the Atlantic Ocean, and the Welland Canal opened in 1829, linking Lake Ontario and Lake Erie, more people arrived at Niagara. "Canalling" on either side of the border was an inexpensive and frequent method of travel, replacing the steamboat and stagecoach. When the first railroad in Upper Canada began operating in the Niagara region in 1839, more sightseers were able to make the journey in safety and comfort. By 1845, close to 50,000 people visited the site annually, a figure that had doubled in just five years.[9]

Women began to go to the Falls as it gradually became more accessible. While their written records from the eighteenth century are extremely rare, women's accounts of travel to Niagara peaked during the early 1830s. The numerous wars on the frontier, the difficulties and inconveniences of travel, the barely serviceable accommodations, and the fact that women did not fight wars or generally undertake inconvenient journeys account for the scarcity of late eighteenth- and early nineteenth-century women travellers. My extensive survey of literary and painterly excursionists to Niagara yielded only two women from the early period—Ann Powell (1789) and Elizabeth Simcoe (1792). But, as Niagara became more "touristy," women flocked to the popular spot. For the years between 1830 and 1850, Charles Mason Dow's

Anthology and Bibliography of Niagara Falls (1921), the best source for Niagara representations from the seventeenth century to the early twentieth, contains more than thirteen lengthy entries by well-known women writers.

Because of the canals, roads, railways, and inns, the Victorians' Niagara was no longer an isolated wilderness spot. By the time the famous landscapist Frederic Edwin Church painted the Falls in the 1850s, Niagara was visited by an estimated 60,000 people a year and dubbed the "Honeymoon Capital of the World."[10] By the 1870s, working- and middle-class excursionists started to arrive at Niagara on one-day rail passes. Along with the excursionists came the bustling industry of guides, photographers, and souvenir hawkers. Many of the upper-class travellers began to complain that the tourist industry was catering to the "wrong" sort of visitor, who in turn was ruining the image of the place.[11]

During the late 1870s, a public movement to "save" Niagara from the drosky-drivers, the "huskers" (buskers), and the wrong kind of traveller saw the state of New York and the province of Ontario purchase lands and buildings around the Falls in order to "naturalize" the area. The famous American landscape architect Frederick Law Olmstead, dubbed the "Saviour of Niagara Falls," designed secluded woodlands and unobtrusive walkways for the American Reservation. On the Canadian side, Roderick Cameron, working with a different aesthetic value system, set out to beautify the park with picturesque flower beds, arched walkways, benches, and fountains.

After the opening of these international parks in the mid-1880s, the number of visitors increased from approximately 120,000 per annum to over 300,000.[12] Despite the restoration of the area to "nature," the growth of industry and tourism at the turn of the twentieth century, combined with the invention of the automobile and the emergence of the working-class holiday, made Niagara into a "carnival" again for the day-tripping, lower-class sightseer.[13]

One century later, 14 million people visit Niagara annually.[14] Besides being the most popular tourist attraction in North America, the river and waterfalls are scenic backdrops for television shows, motion pictures, documentaries, and fiction.[15] Niagara is also featured as a Web site—a live, ten-second picture of falling water that receives thousands of cyberspace visitors a day.[16] And, amid all these modern images, an IMAX cinema in downtown Niagara Falls, Ontario, features a thrice-daily show, *Niagara: Miracles, Myths and Magic.* In this docudrama, we can watch the actor who plays Louis Hennepin express feelings of fear and awe, and we can witness the filmmakers' concepts of an "untamed" waterfall in the middle of the wilderness.

THERE ARE NUMEROUS ACADEMIC ARTICLES and monographs about Niagara Falls. The topic of how the wilderness was transformed into a tourist mecca is taken up in Elizabeth McKinsey's *Niagara Falls: Icon of the American Sublime* (1985), Jeremy Elwell Adamson's article in his edited collection *Niagara: Two Centuries of Changing Attitudes, 1697–1901* (1985), Rob Shields's *Places on the Margin: Alternative Geographies of Modernity* (1991), Patrick McGreevy's *Imagining Niagara: The Meaning and Making of Niagara Falls* (1994), William R. Irwin's *The New Niagara: Tourism, Technology and the Landscape of Niagara Falls, 1776–1917* (1996), and Karen Dubinsky's *The Second Greatest Disappointment: Honeymooning and Tourism at Niagara Falls* (1999). McKinsey and Adamson, both intent on showing how Niagara was the icon of American nature until tourism caused its "fall" in the 1860s, use numerous writers and painters to support their arguments, but they champion American landscapist Frederic Edwin Church as the grandest interpreter of a sublime Niagara. While many different ideas of enjoyment and marvel underpin descriptions and depictions of Niagara, sublimity became the standard nineteenth-century aesthetic by which to measure the Falls. Theoretical discussions of the evolution of the sublime as an aesthetic of taste usually begin with Longinus, and then jump from the first century to the early eighteenth, where the topic was taken up and elaborated by many authors.

The Greek literary critic known as Longinus is best known for his fragmentary *Peri Hupsous,* written around AD 200 but not published until 1554 (in Basel). In this treatise, Longinus argued that sublimity was always an eminence and excellence in language; that it was established by consensus; and that only a work that aroused universal admiration qualified.[17] Between 1554 and 1652, when *On the Sublime* was first translated into English by John Hall, *Peri Hupsous* had been available in England in at least five different editions.[18] But it was the French poet and critic Nicolas Boileau-Despréaux's 1674 translation, *Traité du Sublime ou du Merveilleux traduit du grec du Longin,* that brought Longinus's writings to the attention of a group of British critics. After John Dennis, Anthony Ashley Cooper (1st Earl of Shaftesbury), and

Joseph Addison read Boileau's translation, they began to develop a theory—often called the "pre-sublime" and focused more on nature than on rhetoric—by which to explain their experiences of the European Alps. In turn, these ideas about how mountains and other natural objects could inspire feelings of horror, joy, astonishment, and amazement were eventually made into a system by Edmund Burke.

John Dennis was the first to pay much attention to the effect that nature (as opposed to Longinus's more rhetorical poetry and prose) had upon the beholder. Dennis travelled to the Alps in 1688 and wrote about the "delightful Horrour" and "terrible Joy" in a journal that was later published as *Miscellanies in Verse and Prose* (London, 1693).[19] While his description paraphrased passages from Longinus, Dennis's main contribution to the aesthetic was his distinction between the sublime and the beautiful.[20] On the other hand, the Earl of Shaftesbury, who made the grand tour two years before Dennis (in 1686), published his observations as *The Moralists* (1709). In it, Shaftesbury, who advocated a kind of nature worship—

> Even the rude Rocks, the mossy Caverns, the irregular unwrought Grotto's and broken Falls of Waters, with all the horrid Graces of the Wilderness itself, as representing Nature more, will be the more engaging, and appear with a Magnificence beyond the formal Mockery of Princely Gardens—[21]

did not so much distinguish between the beautiful and the sublime as argue that the sublime was necessarily a higher, more majestic type of beauty.[22] With Joseph Addison, we begin to see much more of a differentiation between the beautiful and the sublime, and between the Longinian rhetorical and the natural sublime. Addison, who set out on the grand tour in 1699, published his responses to the Alps and other destinations in *The Spectator* (June 21–July 3, 1712). In these essays, he did not confine himself to just two "genres"; rather, he placed the beautiful alongside the great (sublime) and the uncommon.[23] Addison went on to distinguish between beautiful objects as "symmetrical" and sublime ones as "great...too big for the mind to grasp"; further, he drew a comparison between beautiful experiences as "cheerfulness and delight," and sublime/great ones as "astonishment...stillness and amazement." Yet, despite these differences in aesthetics, Addison believed that the properties of beauty and sublimity "can be united in the same object and that, when they are, pleasure is increased."[24]

At this turning point in the history of sublimity and beauty, another, almost separate, paradoxical attitude toward aspects of nature had begun to emerge. This ambivalence in taste, often referred to as the aesthetics of the infinite, is best represented in Thomas Burnet's *The Sacred Theory of the Earth* (Latin edition published in 1681; English translation in 1684), which was characterized as a "quarrel" over mountains that was itself based in "a war of Ancient versus modern" and of "religion versus science."[25] As we shall see, the Hennepin illustrator seems to have been as influenced by this late seventeenth-century aesthetics of the infinite as Hennepin was by aspects of the pre-sublime.

While all of these ideas about nature and sublimity were important, the most influential work on the subject of aesthetics during the eighteenth century was undoubtedly Edmund Burke's *A Philosophical Enquiry into the Origin of Our Ideas of the Sublime and Beautiful* (1757). As the title suggests, Burke inquires into these two qualities and establishes an absolute contrast between the beautiful, which he credits with inspiring feelings of tenderness and affection, and the sublime, which he describes as growing out of an ecstasy of terror: "terror is in all cases, whatsoever, either more openly or latently the ruling principle of the sublime."[26] Interestingly, Burke marks these distinctions by examining felt experience: whereas beauty relaxes, the sublime suspends the soul in some degree of horror—a kind of paralysis associated with primitive feelings of dread, danger, and even death that became a common response in nineteenth-century percipients at Niagara. Burke's *Enquiry* is called a system because in it he creates a list of the attributes (which eventually became so linked to Niagara that they could serve as its *definitio*) by which to measure an aroused sublime passion: obscurity, power, darkness, vacuity, silence, vastness, magnitude, infinity, difficulty, and magnificence. Criticism of Burke has repeatedly insisted that this system itself creates a tension between "empiricism" and "irrationalism"—between a dependence on an individual's sense data as valid and measurable information, and a reliance on the passions as a common, universal indicator of taste.[27]

The Burkean sublime was the most popular aesthetic influence at Niagara. In *Niagara Falls: Icon of the American Sublime,* Elizabeth McKinsey documents the "fall" of sublimity as a fall from Burke's system of taste. McKinsey's sense is that the improvements of the mid-nineteenth century—tourism, industry, and development—removed the danger from the landscape, and thus destroyed the awesome, overwhelming aspects of the experience. While McKinsey does look at the *pre-sublime* responses at Niagara, which are based on the writings of Dennis, Shaftesbury, and Addison, she mostly describes the nineteenth-century records based on Burke's system and claims that this *British sublime* was "actually incarnated at Niagara Falls, the icon of [American] nature."[28] Other, more specialized variations investigated by McKinsey include the *American sublime,* which was developed by Archibald Alison and applied to Niagara by American painters and writers between the 1820s and the 1860s, and late nineteenth-century *post-sublime*—her label for the picturesque and the beautiful—which she calls "less prestigious."[29] Interestingly, for McKinsey this devaluation of taste (the post-sublime) coincides with the "fall" of Niagara, when it was *sentimentalized* and "feminized."[30] Yet, because McKinsey ultimately designates the post-sublime (the picturesque and the beautiful) as a separate "womanly" category that is lesser than the more "manly" Burkean sublime, her treatment is not in keeping with the historical development of aesthetics, especially the picturesque.

In England, an important late eighteenth-century form of landscape art called the picturesque (an anglicization of the French *pittoresque* or the Italian *pittoresco,* meaning "what pleases the eye") created certain manners of viewing that were, from their inception, a practice culturally coded "male."[31] Initially, "picturesque" meant whatever was suitable for painting, with no particular reference to travel, or landscape (or to gender!). Then, Reverend William Gilpin, who relied on picturesque concepts in his sketches and in his writings, published journals of his tours around Britain in the late eighteenth century and established the craze for picturesque tourism. While Gilpin made his first trip along the River Wye in 1770, he did not publish his description of it until 1782. After several more journeys took him to the Lakes (1772) and the Scottish Highlands (1776), Gilpin gave his notion of the picturesque—a type of beauty, not a separate aesthetic category—a more extended theoretical discussion in *Three Essays* (1792). In these essays, he applied a refined code of appraisal and judgment to make the point that a picturesque sight was meant to provide amusement and evoke admiration. But it was the connection between travel and scientific observation which was formalized at this time, that marked a transition in rhetoric at Niagara Falls, especially as regards references to unique geological features and to the type of "manly" traveller deemed capable of exploring them.

After Gilpin, a debate regarding the nature of the picturesque opened up between Uvedale Price and Richard Payne Knight. Price's *Essay on the Picturesque* (1794) basically repeated Burke's explanations that the sublime causes ideas of pain and terror and that beauty relaxes, and then went on to suggest that the picturesque holds "a station between beauty and sublimity."[32] Conversely, in his polemic against Price delivered in the second edition of *The Landscape* (1795), Knight questioned whether the aesthetic is an adaptation and continuation of Burke and proposed that aesthetic experience is only a perception and is independent of objects themselves.[33]

The picturesque has been described as a transitional fashion that led to another aesthetic variant—the Romantic sublime.[34] Other writings that altered and expanded the theories of taste and led to the Romantic sublime include the Prussian metaphysician Immanuel Kant's *Critique of Judgement* (1790), and William Wordsworth's "Lines Composed a Few Miles Above Tintern Abbey, on Revisiting the Banks of the Wye During a Tour" (1798) and *The Prelude* (1805 version). Kant relied on the language of Burke's theory, and adapted Addison's distinctions between beauty and greatness, and Knight's emphasis on perception rather than physical nature, to argue for an experience in which the subject passes through humiliation and awe to a heightened awareness of reason.[35] And Wordsworth's poems brought to an artistic climax many of the moods and themes that had also been expressed since the aesthetics of the infinite. While his Romantic perception included notions of Genesis and geology, the picturesque, and Burke's sensory-based sublime, the real source of Wordsworth's sublime was, like Knight's and Kant's, not found in nature but within the perceiver. But rather than an aesthetic category, with Wordsworth the sublime became a psychological event capable of moral significance; in a sense, he transformed the sublime back to the sacred.[36]

At different times, Niagara seems to be regulated by all of these theories. In this book, I consider the different aesthetics to show how writers or artists worked within the boundaries mapped out by these guiding texts—and within the traditions established in prior documents—to stake out new territories with their own impressions.

Patrick McGreevy's many publications also look at the way in which a body of texts helped to establish certain expectations that encoded Niagara experiences. However, McGreevy does not analyze the importance of aesthetics; instead, his framework is more associative, and he sets up a series of binary opposites (such as utopia vs. dystopia, nature vs. technology) to draw connections between his favourite topics in Niagara literature—love and death—and the various "accumulations"—tourist traps and funeral parlours—built up around the site.

Rob Shields's chapter on Niagara Falls in *Places on the Margin* also examines binary themes (and cultural production). Central to his discussion of marginal places and "site[s] of illicit or disdained social activities" is his focus on Niagara as the "Honeymoon Capital of the

World." But, by arguing that the Falls "acquired a reputation through self-promotion" as a socially constructed heterosexual site that is part of, and alternative to, the dominant culture, Shields gives Niagara an almost human agency.[37] He describes how the place constructs itself "in consciousness," not the various ways in which people have constructed Niagara through descriptions and images.

Karen Dubinsky's *The Second Greatest Disappointment* looks at how the tourist industry made Niagara famous. Dubinsky, a historian of tourism, popular culture, and sexuality, decodes the waterfalls' gendered and sexual imagery to investigate why Niagara has been the mecca for honeymooners in North America. To do this, she examines the private upper-class wedding tour of the nineteenth century and shows how it evolved into the public honeymoon of the twentieth. In her view, entrepreneurs commodified, popularized, and advertised this industry and linked it to Niagara. To analyze honeymooning practices, Dubinsky uses different sources—marriage manuals, popular iconography, and the literature produced by the tourist industry at Niagara—than I do in my study of art and writing—both literary and scientific. Dubinsky also highlights different contexts, such as honeymoon culture, travel theory, and the history of tourism, whereas I look at aesthetics, the rhetoric of empire, Native history, and the social history of technology. Yet, I am indebted to her important contribution to Niagara scholarship, especially her observation that Victorians at the Falls had vastly different views of male and female physicality.[38]

William Irwin, who explores Niagara's cultural significance as an icon of progress and technology, follows a shift from what he calls the natural sublime to a technological sublime, though he does not explain how he uses these terms, nor does he historicize the discourses over the centuries. For my discussion of the technological sublime, I rely on some of Irwin's ideas and on the critical work of David E. Nye, whose *American Technological Sublime* (1994) has added much to my reading of more contemporary commentators at Niagara.

WHILE SCHOLARSHIP CONCERNING Niagara Falls has been dominated by interpretations of what it has meant for generations of Americans (McKinsey, Adamson, McGreevy, Shields, and Irwin), some recent articles and books have examined Niagara as a symbol of pride and national identity for Canada. Patricia Jasen's article "Romanticism, Modernity and the Evolution of Tourism on the Niagara Frontier, 1790–1850" (1991) tracks visitors on the Canadian side and frames their responses as profoundly Romantic. Her subsequent book, *Wild Things: Nature, Culture and Tourism in Ontario,* 1790–1914 (1995), continues to concentrate on the experiences of mid-nineteenth-century British and Canadian tourists to show how the growth of industry and commerce on the Canadian side, combined with a shift in aesthetics, served to reduce the experience at Niagara from sublime to sentimental, from wild to utilitarian.[39] Jasen's premise is similar to that of McKinsey, Adamson, and Irwin; however, she looks to the aesthetic and political context of the emerging colony of Upper Canada to suggest that nineteenth-century writings about Niagara can be associated with Canadian nationalism.

Other books about the considerable role of the Falls in fashioning the "story" of Canada include two popular histories: George Seibel's *Ontario's Niagara Parks: A History* (1991) and Pierre Berton's *Niagara: A History of the Falls* (1992).[40] Berton tends to focus on Niagara's "characters"—the stuntmen, daredevils, and tightrope walkers, the war heroes and heroines. Seibel deals with the characteristics of Niagara's landscape. And whereas both authors are interested in showing how the Canadian side of the Falls was physically altered over the centuries by bridges, hotels, railings, roads, and railways, it is Seibel's chronological presentations of landscape development and reconstruction that have served as bedrock for my research. In addition, Charles Mason Dow's immense, two-volume edited collection, *Anthology and Bibliography of Niagara Falls,* contains an extensive sampling of visual, literary, and scientific representations that have been indispensable to my study.

Other relevant works that analyze the importance of aesthetics to depictions of Canada (and, sometimes, Niagara) in literature and art include Mary Lu MacDonald's "The Natural World in Early Nineteenth Century Canadian Literature" (1986), Susan Joan Wood's *The Land in Canadian Prose,* 1840–1945 (1988), and Susan Glickman's *The Picturesque and the Sublime: A Poetics of the Canadian Landscape* (1998). MacDonald, in her investigation of the connections between the conventions of literature and the ideas and attitudes expressed in early Canadian works, takes issue with Northrop Frye's "cold pastoral" theory, especially the notion that nineteenth-century Canadians perceived themselves as surrounded by a hostile natural world. Wood raises the stakes when she examines nineteenth- and mid-twentieth-century

English- and French-Canadian attitudes toward the land, suggesting that forces such as religious life and economic conditions were as much an influence on attitudes as the tension that Frye saw between human responses to nature's beauty and human terror at nature's otherness.[41] Similarly, Glickman argues against the "mental frameworks" idea. While she documents the evolution of traditional Old World forms and imagery that emphasize the fearful, mysterious, or impersonal qualities of nature, she stresses that Canadian writers have not been rendered incapable of meaningful response to the worlds they inhabit and have consistently transformed their literary inheritances into language that conforms to their experiences of the new land.[42] Glickman's investigations into how nature made early Canadian writers feel, how it looked, and what moral lessons it taught, as well as information she gleaned on the context of production and the critical reception of certain poems, inform my work.

For *The Niagara Companion,* I have chosen to focus on particular painters and writers who have taken what twentieth-century travel critic Michel Butor calls a "double journey"—a kind of "horizontal" progress ("the line of the text") along a predetermined path ("the route of the voyage").[43] Another travel theorist, William W. Stowe, sums up Butor's comment in this way: "the travelling class was a reading class, and travel was seen as a preeminently literary activity."[44] Accordingly, the practitioners examined here follow sets of conventions—and follow in the footsteps of Hennepin, or another writer or painter ("the line of the text")—but eventually they exploit and expand the traditions associated with art history, literary history, or natural/geological history and, through interactions with other kinds of expressions along "the route of the voyage," they create for themselves something unique. Such a treatment, which examines the credentials of individual authors and artists and provides the background conditions out of which each emerged, adds to the field of Niagara studies because it contextualizes both the commentators and their works.

I have divided this book into three chapters, each of which deals with a different medium of construction—fine arts, literary travel writing, and scientific travel writing. The rationale for these chapter divisions comes, in part, from the distinctions made in Edmund Burke's *Enquiry* between "empiricism" and "irrationalism," or a reliance on measurable data versus a dependence on the passions. These two almost logically exclusive positions form the basis of the separation of scientific commentators (chapter 3) from literary respondents (chapter 2). But my main reason for dividing the work into three separate groupings comes from distinctions made by travel theorist Daniel Boorstin, who identifies, in the history of European travel, three different figures (the explorer, the traveller, and the tourist) during three different historical eras (the Renaissance, the bourgeois age and the proletarian "time").[45] I also work with three main figures, but I modify Boorstin's periods and cultural values to suit my undertaking. First, there are the painters on the frontier of North American expansion, converting theories of taste into art and creating what theorist Mary Louise Pratt would call the "domestic subject" in the "contact zone."[46] Next, there are the literary writers at Niagara. Travel was the measuring-device of the great moral truths—identity, nationhood— that governed human behaviour. Finally, there are the scientists documenting the Falls, whose spirit of inquiry valued empirical knowledge over abstract speculation. What makes the scientist different from the painter or the literary writer is the descriptive apparatus of natural history and other discourses around measurements, climatic phenomena, and samplings.

Chapter 1, "Indian Icons and Wilderness Ideals," begins with the first artifact to emerge from a European vision of Niagara—Louis Hennepin's report on the Falls. Hennepin was schooled in theories of seventeenth-century art and swayed by contemporaneous ideas about nature. At the beginning of his description, for example, Hennepin wishes that someone else was there to describe the scene, a longing that is part of John Dennis's pre-sublime desire to be "transported" beyond words. When Hennepin's New World description became the basis for the first picture of Niagara, some of the features included in the illustration, especially the mountains, were meaningful within the context of artistic and scientific traditions of the seventeenth century. The military illustrators, amateur artists, and professional painters who came next drew Niagaras that conformed to the aesthetic conventions and the causal events of their times (such as numerous wars with First Nations tribes). Some of the earliest pictures reveal shared repertoires of devices and conventions associated with Hennepin's vision, but successive versions tend to constitute something independent of, and different from, the original pattern of representation. Cultural-historical content (such as the inclusion or exclusion of Native figures) governs the work and makes Niagara into a wild, a civilized, or a spoiled landscape.

Although the locus of this study is the way in which European aesthetic concepts of nature were individually inflected by writers and artists at Niagara, other discourses coming out of eighteenth- and nineteenth-century Europe found, in the rhetoric of empire, a justification for the conquest of nature and, by extension, of North America's primitive peoples, those "children of nature." These discourses, which alternately idealized and reviled the "Indian," may be seen as part of a larger ambivalence surrounding the aesthetic concepts of nature, and of naturalization. Among the important philosophical works concerning representations of North America's "savage"[47] inhabitants are Jean-Jacques Rousseau's *Essay on the Origin of Languages* (1781) and John Stuart Mill's essay on "Nature" (1873). The particular languages of these French and British philosophers show not only how imperialism created the "other" for European readership, but also how Europe constructed differentiated conceptions of itself in relation to this otherness. These concepts help to provide insights into the ways in which Niagara paintings belonged to the historical process of colonization. The analysis in this chapter looks at different eras in the history of the First Nations peoples and, using this context, studies the way in which artists manipulated the Indian figure to create different identities of the "other" as symbolically attuned to resistance and, eventually, subservience.

Whereas the painters at Niagara after the eighteenth century relied less and less on the Hennepin model, many writers continued to read Hennepin well into the nineteenth century, and at Niagara they judged whether or not the scenery conformed to his view. Addison would call this a reliance on "secondary pleasures"—the stimulus coming from books instead of from the more "primary" imagination. These writers would "uncloud" their views when they shifted into the pleasures of the imagination through the cultural discourses associated with the sublime, the picturesque, and the beautiful. Chapter 2, "Challenges of the Niagara Sublime," looks at the way in which Niagara writings were influenced by these key aesthetic theories of the period.

Chapter 3, "Naturalist Observations and Feats of Physical Endurance," examines amateur scientists who set out to validate or champion new ideas. Because the commentators presented in this chapter drew on different discourses, such as the conventions of natural history, geology, and technology, the individuals making the claims sometimes seem to have advocated a sort of objective analysis. Where the travel writers in chapter 2 would have used rhetorical devices such as hyperbole, pathetic fallacy, irony, and conceits to express an extravagance of feeling, chapter 3's natural scientists tended to devise tests or experiment with equipment to satisfy a more detached spirit of connoisseurship.

Throughout the chapters, the focus is on what Niagara Falls has meant to people, from discovery through the twentieth century. What do people do when they get to Niagara? Where do they stand? How do they physically move around the place? These preoccupations go hand in hand with the different ways in which the landscape has been drawn and described. Another preoccupation: how do women experience Niagara? Some of the most interesting responses came from female travellers, whose social/historical contexts were different from those of their male counterparts. Finally, because of the cultural expectations in the field of travel writing and the imperialist attitudes in the culture of empire, some visitors to the Canadian side of the Falls had a significantly different experience from those on the American bank. Wherever appropriate, I examine those commentators who draw distinctions between the domestic subject (the "colonized" Canadian) and the "imperial" spectator (the "colonizing" European) and look at how cultural difference is invented, or conventional notions are entrenched. I am as interested in tracing the application of general tendencies of thought and cultural attitude to the act of judging Niagara—whether they be stock features and phrases of aesthetics, or stereotypes of empire—as I am in looking at how these writers and artists, who depended on the use of myth, symbol, metaphor, hyperbole, and other rhetorical and painterly procedures, created something unique of themselves, of their writings or paintings, and of Niagara. Taken together, these tropes, mapped through a range of centuries and representations, constitute a kind of repertoire of Niagara discourses.

Indian Icons and Wilderness Ideals

I wish'd an hundred times that somebody had been with us, who could have describ'd the Wonders of this prodigious frightful Fall, so as to give the Reader a just and natural Idea of it, such as might satisfy him, and create in him an Admiration of this Prodigy of Nature as great as it deserves. In the mean time, accept the following Draught, so as it is; in which however I have endeavour'd to give the curious Reader as just an Image of it as I could.

Louis Hennepin, *A New Discovery of
a Vast Country in America* (1697)

I N *A New Discovery*—the first detailed depiction of Niagara—Louis Hennepin wishes that someone had been with him to portray the scene better than he could; then he goes on to attempt description anyway, calling Niagara "prodigious" and "frightful," and talking about how it inspired "Admiration." Contemporaneous seventeenth-century European ideas about nature frame Hennepin's writing, especially John Dennis's "pre-sublime" expressions published in *Miscellanies in Verse and Prose* (London, 1693). Then again, Hennepin's claims of unworthiness associate him with a companion rhetoric to the pre-sublime—the aesthetics of the infinite, which saw observers, astounded yet enthralled by infinite space, unable to comprehend it intellectually, but imaginatively liberated to the wonders, the greatness, anyway.[1] When Hennepin does go on to document all the features of this "prodigious frightful Fall," he exaggerates the number of cascades, their dimensions, and the topography surrounding them to make the scene more frightening, vast, and wonderful. The European printmaker who based *The Falls of Niagara* (1697) on Hennepin's description attempted to convey the author's emotive impression through the expressions and gestures of the human figures and through the presentation of landscape. The features in the illustration, which include three water-falls, two appearing steep and flat and another just a thin cross-stream, and a chain of mountains far off in the distance, also connect the picture to other seventeenth-century scientific and artistic concepts of nature.

Since Hennepin's "new discovery," there have been many thousands of descriptions, and paintings and drawings of Niagara. In this chapter, I begin with the first Hennepin report and the illustration based on it, and then go on to outline the history of Niagara pictures from Hennepin's particular viewing perspective. I chose five landscapes that were composed from where Hennepin claimed to have stood (the upper bank of the eastern side of the river, approximately 200 feet downstream from the American Falls). A comparison of the report of Pehr Kalm (1750) and the art of Henry Fuseli (1776), Robert Hancock (1794), W.R. Callington (1837), and Frederic Edwin Church (1867) to Hennepin's description, to one another's paintings, and to related images that give them context reveals that these respondents retained many of the features of the seminal picture. Of course, a few things change: the terrified Europeans of the original print are replaced by indifferent sightseers in the engraving based on Kalm's work, who are in turn displaced by Indians in Fuseli's and Hancock's views. And, in the pictures of the mid-nineteenth century, very few people are featured. These paintings by Callington and Church coincided with a new valuation of the Indian and of the wilderness—nature was something that the "civilized" got to savour in solitude. In reading these pictures, I will focus on how the Indian became linked to concepts of nature, and how ideas of naturalization belong to the historical process of colonization.

According to theorists David Spurr and Mary Louise Pratt, the notion of nature is for colonial discourse as equivocal as the concept of the Indian. On the one hand, nature is opposed to culture and civilization, but nature, or natural law, is also that which grants dominion over the earth. On the other hand, primitive peoples are often described as living in a state of nature, yet the land is deemed to belong, by natural right, to the more "advanced" peoples who understand its value. The important eighteenth- and early nineteenth-century writings of Swedish botanist and taxonomist Carolus Linnaeus, French philosopher Jean-Jacques Rousseau, Prussian metaphysician Immanuel Kant, British natural historian Charles Darwin, and British philosopher John Stuart Mill which brought the figure of the Indian into the discourse of aesthetics and colonialism, will help to illuminate the role of the indigene in Niagara art.

All things considered, there are three ways to describe Niagara's paradoxical wildness/civility: visually, both through exaggerated or tamed landscapes and through overwhelmed or nonchalant spectators; and verbally, through heightened or measured language. I begin with Hennepin. Since his description of Niagara and the art based upon it serve as both the central conceit of this chapter and the main influence on many of the percipients in this book, I start by tracing, in detail, the historical and intellectual concepts that shaped his verbal artifact, the first to come out of a European vision.

On the Niagara Frontier

IN THE MID-1600S, before Hennepin joined the party whose mission was to explore the two lower Great Lakes and their surrounding tributaries, the Niagara region was inhabited by the Seneca Nation, members of the Confederacy of the Iroquois, or the Five Nations, that included the Oneidas, Mohawks, Cayugas, and Onendagas. Well-defined travel routes had been forged on river and on land. Along the lower Niagara Gorge in particular, a path beside the eastern shore (later known as the American side) enabled the Seneca and other members of the Five Nations to bypass the rapids and the waterfalls to get into the upper gorge and thereby gain access to the rest of the Great Lakes waterway.

Even though the first Europeans in the Great Lakes system spent most of their time exploring the area north and east of Niagara, they still drew the Niagara River, based not on actual sightings but on the oral reports of their Native guides. Hence, the earliest outlines derived from these accounts are characterized by a lack of technical expertise and a great deal of guesswork. These maps, attributed to geographers appointed by the French king, were meant to provide the most up-to-date information about resources and territorial expansions in the New World. A number of seventeenth-century map-makers included information about the locations of garrisons built on the banks of the Niagara River, intimating the strategic importance of the waterway.

Samuel de Champlain, geographer to Henry IV, was the first to make notes about the Niagara River.[2] Champlain's explorations of 1603 did not take him beyond the southern shores of Lake Ontario; nevertheless, he drew outlines of the Niagara River, Lake Erie, and possibly Lake Superior on his map (1612).[3] Also indicated by Champlain were areas where the various Indian tribes known at the time lived— information that was essential to the expansion of French culture into the wilderness. Once Champlain became New France's first head of state, he insisted that all explorations of the interior include missionaries, and he arranged for Récollets to come from France from the beginning of the seventeenth century. (Later in the century, these missionaries became the "official weapons brokers" for the French, distributing guns en route to their Indian converts.[4]) Le Sieur Gendron, one of these French missionaries, heard from his Native guides that the spray from Niagara Falls had healing properties and he included this observation in his mid-seventeenth-century account.[5] Gendron's description was later copied by Jesuits Paul Ragueneau and Francesco Guiseppe Bressani and their versions of the "healing spray" legend were published, along with other reports sent back to France, in the Jesuit *Relations* project (1647–48 and 1653).

More maps were published in Europe at this time. N. Sanson's map (1656) and René Brehan de Galinée's map (1669) placed the waterfalls at various points along the Niagara River, but did not illustrate what they looked like.[6] De Galinée also wrote a description of Niagara (even though he had not been there). A Christian missionary belonging to the Sulpician order, de Galinée had accompanied René-Robert Cavelier, Sieur de La Salle on his first sponsored exploration of Lake Ontario in 1669 and included in his narrative a guide's estimation of the height of the Falls (about 200 feet).[7] A few years before Hennepin went to Niagara, two other cartographic studies printed in Europe included the as-yet-unexplored river and waterfalls: Jacobum Meursium's map (1671) and Louis Joliet's map (1674).[8] By the time that Récollet priest Louis Hennepin accompanied the second La Salle expedition in 1678, he had probably heard details of these reports and may have seen copies of some of the well-known maps.[9]

The La Salle expedition, Hennepin's first assignment in the New World, went up Lake Ontario all the way to the mouth of the Niagara River. There, the French party was met by Senecas, who guided them along the portage routes on the eastern (American) side to the waterfalls. As theorist Mary Louise Pratt remarks about other, typical European-Native encounters, "discovery in this context consisted of a gesture of converting knowledges (Native discourses) into European rational and continental knowledges associated with European forms and relations of power."[10] Since the Hennepin "discovery" involved hiring, then asking, the local inhabitants of the lower Great Lakes region about the features of the land, the explorers proceeded to find out what the indigenes already knew, and then to make that information "real" by bringing it into being through two texts: a description and an illustration.

Louis Hennepin

LITTLE IS KNOWN ABOUT THE EUROPEAN credited with discovering Niagara. Born in the Spanish Netherlands around 1640, Louis Hennepin emigrated to New France in 1675.[11] After he accompanied the second La Salle expedition into the interior, Hennepin stayed in the Niagara area for three years (1678–81). During that time, the French staked out formal claims of possession, erecting a stockade at the mouth of the Niagara River, boosting trade with the local Five Nation tribes, and constructing the first sailing ship (the 60-ton *Griffon*) above the waterfalls. The *Griffon* served the French on further expeditions into the upper Great Lakes and along their tributaries, from whence they searched for inland routes to the Gulf of Mexico and to China. (As the La Salle party was claiming the waterways, the British were seizing the land beyond Lake Superior, in an area referred to as the *pays d'en haut*. In response to these European expansions, the Ojibwa to the west and the Mississauga to the north moved closer. In the late seventeenth century, the area that Hennepin and his party explored was not an unoccupied frontier.[12])

Sometime during his three-year stay on the Niagara frontier, Hennepin wrote a page-long report about the Falls which was later published in *Description of Louisiana, Recently Discovered in the South West of New France, on the authority of the King...* (1683). Afterwards, he expanded this report into a six-page description and published the revised impression in *A New Discovery of a Vast Country in America, Extending Above Four Thousand Miles Between New France and New Mexico; with a Description of the Great Lakes, Cataracts, Rivers, Plants, and Animals...* (1697).[13] The 1697 edition and the 1699 translations based on that version contain an engraving by an anonymous artist.[14]

Hennepin's two written records of Niagara are fascinating because they contradict each other.[15] In the one-page narrative, the Récollet missionary defies previous reports which estimated the height of the waterfalls at 200 feet; instead, he suggests that Niagara has three cascades, all 500 feet high, with two hanging like sheets and the third appearing as a cross-stream. In his revised description fourteen years later, Hennepin makes the three waterfalls 600 feet high. Because his

six-page version became so widely known through numerous translations, through an accompanying illustration, and through three editions, I call it the foundational depiction of the North American
cataracts.

Hennepin's increasingly exaggerated account coincided with an
intense emphasis on the prodigious amount of water coming over the
Falls. He admits to spending half a day considering this issue; yet, in
spite of these lengthy deliberations, his description is characterized
by confusion:

> I could not conceive how it came to pass, that four great Lakes, the
> least of which is 400 Leagues in compass, should empty themselves
> one into another, and then all centre and discharge themselves at
> this Great Fall, and yet not drown a good part of America. (23)

Because maps of the period show a large body of water west of Lake
Superior and east of the present-day Rocky Mountains—the fabled
Sea of the West—Hennepin may have thought that Niagara was connected through the Great Lakes system (the "four great Lakes") to this
legendary water source. He continued to scan the flat horizon for other
clues about Niagara, and the features he describes accord with those
on maps showing passages beyond:

> Our surprise was still greater, when we observ'd there were no
> Mountains within two good Leagues of this Cascade; and yet the
> vast quantity of Water which is discharg'd by these four fresh Seas,
> stops or centers here, and so falls about six hundred Foot down
> into a Gulph, which one cannot look upon without Horror. (24)

As we read of Hennepin's "surprise" and "Horror," it becomes clear that
he stands at a turning point in the history of seventeenth-century aesthetic concepts. Hennepin's expression of awe and unease links him
to John Dennis's "transports … [that] were mingled with Horrour, and
sometimes with despair."[16] The essence of "Horror" for Hennepin seems
to lie in the sheer size of Niagara—its "Gulph" is vast. Further, he is sur-
prised by the fact that there are no perceivable mountains in the distance and therefore no explanation for the prodigious "discharge."
Hennepin's reaction to the "missing" mountains (and the illustrator's
insistence on drawing them in) links the writer (and the artist) to the
contemporaneous "mountain debate" which came on the heels of the

theory of the pre-sublime and ultimately symbolized the beginning of the aesthetics of the infinite.

Before the eighteenth-century writers John Dennis, the Earl of Shaftesbury, and Joseph Addison composed lyrical rhapsodies on the exalted emotions they experienced in the European Alps, seventeenth-century poets had dismissed mountains as distasteful and repulsive. Twentieth-century theorist Marjorie Hope Nicolson argues that the idea that mountains were a blemish on the earth was the "unconscious presupposition" of a classical and Biblical heritage. In tracing the various positions in what she calls "the Lord's controversy," Nicolson outlines how seventeenth-century commentators saw mountains arise as a result of the sin of Cain, and how other distortions of the earth— valleys, for example—were for them a manifestation of the immediate impact of the Fall of Adam and Eve. The basic premise that emerged from these ruminations was that the earth's more "irregular" features were both a warning *and* a rebuke—"a visible reminder of the sin of man and the wrath of God."[17] The "philosophical unease" that stemmed from this reading of nature went against the universe as divinely ordered, perfectly smooth and regular. The task of reconciling these positions fell to English theologian Thomas Burnet. In *The Sacred Theory of the Earth* (1684), an imaginative and romantic cosmogony suggested to him by a voyage across the Alps, Burnet argued that the world became "deformed" as a result of a force that "burst forth from inside and wrecked its surface."[18] In writing about the earth's emergence by natural forces, Burnet bridged "the Lord's controversy" by bringing the aesthetic, theological, and scientific worlds together.

The basic principles of the scientific debate over mountains were formulated by Nicolaus Steno in 1669. According to Nicolson, Steno argued that the earth's surface consists of deposited strata and that the alteration of layers by subterranean forces accounts for superficial irregularities. This account was in conflict with theological theories that the earth had emerged because of a miraculous word ("special creation") or an ancient Deluge ("diluvian catastrophe"). When Burnet attempted an explanation, he picked up Steno's argument, and then developed it by explaining that earthquakes caused the once-smooth earth to collapse upon itself in wild irregularities. Burnet's expressions of exultation over these forces in turn came from a companion vocabulary made available through Boileau's translation of Longinus's rhetorical treatment of the sublime (1674). After Burnet, nature writing changed to reflect a love of variety, diversity, and irregularity.[19]

In his search for the presence of mountains, Hennepin borrowed the language and the images associated with these contemporaneous perceptions of the natural world to describe how Niagara resembled a kind of "Deluge." In addition to the magnitude of the drop and the violence of the flow, there is also the thunderous roar that plays on his emotions:

> Two other great Out-lets, or Falls of Water, which are on the two sides of a small sloping Island, which is in the midst, fall gently and without noise, and so glide away quietly enough: But when this prodigious quantity of Water, of which I speak, comes to fall, there is such a din, and such a noise, that is more deafning than the loudest Thunder. (25)

Hennepin's description of where the cascades are situated and what they sound like—"[t]wo other great Out-lets...on the two sides of a small sloping Island" which are silent, and another "prodigious quantity of Water" which is "deafning"—adds much to the "surprise" and "Horror." So too the perpetual mists, which make the scene even more bewildering:

> The rebounding of these Waters is so great, that a sort of Cloud arises from the Foam of it, which is seen hanging over this Abyss even at Noon-day, when the Sun is at its height...[high] above the tallest Firrs. (Ibid.)

Even though Hennepin might not comprehend the source of Niagara's flow intellectually, the sight of the "Abyss," the prodigious amount of water, the thunderous din, the clouds and foam open his imagination to nature's awe and terror. He sums it up best in an epilogue to one of his revised editions: "When one stands near the Fall, and looks down into this most dreadful Gulph, one is seized with Horror, and the Head turns around, so that one cannot look long or steadfastly upon it."[20] It is true that most travellers of the seventeenth century complained of moments of vertigo—what Nicolson calls "no head for heights"— but the dread and horror that Hennepin expresses were beyond a doubt part of the new language associated with the pre-sublime, especially the work of John Dennis.

Hennepin's extended description of Niagara must have had a great impact on the creator of *The Falls of Niagara,* for he drew mountains and a little stream off to the right-hand side of the broadest water-

Figure 1: Anonymous, *The Falls of Niagara* (from Louis
Hennepin's *A New Discovery,* first English edition, 1697).
Courtesy Toronto Public Library.

fall—a curious feature, as it is not obvious where the water comes
from to supply this most westerly cascade (see figure 1).[21] Some well-
known images of Europe's waterfalls may provide clues as to why the
landscape has jagged peaks (not visible in the picture above), a winding, receding river crowding the horizon, and a cross-stream that seems
to have no point of origin. We have already seen how the mountains
in the description were meaningful within the context of seventeenth-
century writings. Other artistic traditions of this period, particularly
the waterfalls of Gaspard Dughet (a.k.a. Gaspard Poussin) and Claude
Lorrain (a.k.a. Claude Gellée) and the mountainscapes of Cesare Ripa
(a.k.a. Giovanni Campani) and Salvator Rosa, may have influenced
the Hennepin illustrator's composition of Niagara.

The French baroque-era painters Gaspard Dughet and Claude Lorrain are both known for their classical Arcadian images of Italy's Tivoli
and Terni waterfalls, which typically include cascades falling in stages
around a broad expanse of cliffs. While these "tamed" landscapes provide a contrast with Niagara's "Gulph," the Hennepin illustrator may
have been drawing on the tendencies presented by the European cascades in making Niagara look as if it was a steep declivity issuing from
a far-off mountain range. Other popular iconography of this time that

associated waterfalls with wildness includes the Italian writer and illustrator Cesare Ripa's allegorical *Danger*. This drawing shows a young boy on the edge of a rocky waterfall being bitten on the leg by a snake. Published in Ripa's *Iconologia* (1603), it came to represent all that could be associated with dangerous nature.[22] Another painter, etcher, and poet of the Italian baroque era, Salvator Rosa, dubbed "savage Rosa," drew desolate mountainscapes in which grimacing *banditti* (wild men) set upon unfortunate travellers. Eventually, the art of Dughet and Lorrain became associated with the picturesque, and the work of Ripa and Rosa came to be paradigmatic examples of the sublime, influential in promoting what one critic calls "the cult of agreeable terror."[23]

The Niagara engraver seems to have reflected the sentiments so popular in the Ripa and Rosa prints through figures that convey terror. Three of the four European spectators look into the middle-ground area at (from left to right): the tall American Falls; Goat Island, a wedge of rock that Hennepin describes as a "small sloping Island"; the broad Horseshoe Falls; and the thin cross-stream. The picture also validates Hennepin's claim that the waterfalls were huge: their immensity is conveyed through other figures—ten tiny people placed in the lower right-hand corner near the river basin. The effect of painting humans dwarfed by nature adds another element of surprise, yet the placement of these figures is a physical impossibility. According to maps constructed during the first European explorations of Niagara, a footpath on the western side of the river did not exist. These small embellishments (the mountains, the cross-stream, the footpath on the western side) demonstrate that the engraver relied as much on his imagination as on the explorer's description. Yet, it is the way in which one of spectators in the foreground has fallen off the ledge and been seized with "Horror," and the way in which he twists away from the "dreadful Gulph" and holds his hands to his head to block out the thunderous "din," that catch the eye. The other figures have thrown their arms wide as if to dramatize how overwhelmed they feel too. The spectators' gestures and expressions, along with the exaggerated landscape phenomena—two huge waterfalls, an outlet with no visible source, some far-distant mountains—"mirror" Hennepin's experiences of unidentified noises, intense pressures, and feelings of surprise and horror.

Well into the eighteenth century, a number of map-makers included little vignettes of this first view.[24] With these placed in the margins of their widely known maps, the illustrators helped to promote Hennepin's claim about the size and dimensions of the waterfalls,

Figure 2: Sebastian LeClerc, *View of Niagara Falls* (ca. 1700).
Reproduction by permission of The Buffalo & Erie County
Public Library, Buffalo, New York.

the "imaginary" mountains in the distant background, and the thin cross-stream with no visible source. While cartographers reproduced the popular view, artists Sebastian LeClerc, Herman Moll, Metz, and Thomas Davies, and writers Paul Dudley and Pehr Kalm tried to adjust Hennepin's description, mostly through waterfall schemata ranging from two to four cascades.

It is not known if the first artist to adapt the Hennepin view even went to Niagara. In any case, Sebastian LeClerc's *View of Niagara Falls* (ca. 1700) repeats many of the original's features—a winding river, mountains, two curtains of rock and tall fir trees enclosing the cascades (see figure 2). But LeClerc's higher cataracts, more rugged rocky cliffs, and curved westerly Horseshoe Falls seem to function merely as background for his figures: in the upper left-hand corner is the prophet Elijah on a chariot, ascending to heaven. The result is a scene as awesome as Hennepin's. Similarly, the painter Herman Moll created an astonishing picture when he portrayed a community of beavers "improving" the Falls before the arrival of human industry (see figure 3). In the background of his *The Cataract of Niagara* (1715) is an extra *chute* on the eastern side to balance the western cross-stream. On the other hand, Metz's *The Falls of Niagara* (ca. 1750) reproduces the two-waterfall model. In this mid-eighteenth-century picture, the easterly waterfall is broad and squat, and the westerly is long and thin.

Figure 3: Herman Moll, *The Cataract of Niagara* (ca. 1715).
Courtesy Toronto Public Library.

Other features in the Metz picture include spectators who gather on
a western bank in the foreground that is much like Hennepin's vantage point. Since there were no paths on the western side of the river—
the Canadian side—at this time, Metz's picture is probably a mirror
image of Hennepin's (minus the cross-stream). Topographical water-
colourist Thomas Davies created yet another four-waterfall version.
His *Niagara Falls from Below* (ca. 1766) has two thin streams to the
right of each large waterfall (see figure 4). While all of these two- and
four-waterfall variations were in circulation, neither schema was as
popular as Hennepin's three cascades, because they were less widely
disseminated.

The pictorial tradition established by Hennepin served as the starting point for painters, and the narrative description fulfilled the same
function for writers. Paul Dudley's motive in writing about Niagara
was to dispel the first explorer's "exaggerated" view. His "Account of

Figure 4: Thomas Davies, *Niagara Falls from Below* (ca. 1766)
accession number 1954.3. Collection of
The New-York Historical Society.

the Falls of the River Niagara, Taken at Albany, October 10, 1721, from Monsieur Borassaw, a French Native of Canada," a correction to the received view, was published in the Royal Society of London's *Philosophical Transactions* (1722).[25] However, this readjustment was not based on a first-hand impression, because it was gleaned second-hand from an "informant" (Monsieur Borassaw). It is not known if Dudley went to Niagara.[26] According to a textual fragment, Dudley, a member of the legal profession—and presumably a man concerned with gathering facts before making judgments—asked Borassaw for the "true measurements" of the cataracts, which Borassaw gave as twenty-six fathoms, or 156 feet. Dudley's French guide goes on to describe the "prodigious noise," the mists, and the "terrible whirlpools" in the river. While Borassaw's account supplies a new measurement (156 feet, instead of Hennepin's 600 feet), it reproduces familiar effects and features (its "corrected" height notwithstanding). These various versions by LeClerc, Moll, Metz, Davies, and Dudley, which made much of the size and properties of Niagara, were counterpoints to the original pattern of representation; nevertheless, Hennepin's description and its attendant illustration continued to dominate thinking about Niagara for another century.

Pehr Kalm's description, the first after Hennepin's to be founded on an actual (known) sighting of the waterfalls, both accedes to Hennepin's particular construction of the site and proposes a counterclaim. Even though Kalm set out to describe different phenomena at Niagara from those that Hennepin found—he admits to going there to sort out fact from fiction—sections of his description, and features of the view based upon it, borrow from Hennepin's.

Pehr Kalm

A SWEDISH BOTANIST, PEHR KALM studied natural history with Karl von Linné (a.k.a. Carolus Linnaeus) in Uppsala and was sent abroad by the Swedish Academy of Sciences in 1747.[27] Confident of his own abilities to see and evaluate the natural world, Kalm went to Niagara to prove Hennepin, whom he called "the great Liar," wrong.[28] At this time, North America was being claimed by two other European empires; even so, the Swedish scientist travelled across the continent, "observing, recording, measuring, comparing, gathering specimens, writing letters."[29] Kalm sent his description of Niagara in a letter to the American scientist Benjamin Franklin, who then had it published in the *Pennsylvania Gazette* on September 20, 1750. The "Letter" was later reprinted in the British monthly periodical, *The Gentleman's Magazine* (1751), and was also included in the last chapter of John Bartram's popular travel book, *Observations on the Inhabitants,* published the same year in London by Whiston and White. The "Letter" and its reprints were translated into French, German, and Dutch and were accompanied by an illustration done by an anonymous engraver.

Kalm begins his letter to Franklin by describing the voyage to the waterfalls. In the autumn of 1749, he reported to Fort Niagara (the garrison built as a stockade by La Salle), but was told to wait for instructions from Paris before proceeding upriver (53). Travel to Niagara in Kalm's time was more complicated than in Hennepin's, even though the actual journey was easier—a portage trail had been cleared on the west side of the river. Soldiers were posted along the route all the way to the waterfalls. There were many reasons for this. The Niagara River was of great strategic importance to the colonists of the mid-eighteenth century. It was a designated spot for trade with the Six Nations[30] and the point of departure for coureurs de bois travelling upriver into the Great Lakes system. The French had complete possession of the water and land routes around Niagara, but their control was often punctuated by British incursions. As Kalm notes in the letter: "the French there seemed much perplexed at my first coming, imagining I was an English officer, who under pretext of seeing Niagara Falls, came with some other view" (54). As Kalm was not a native of France nor a member of the militia, his mission to the Falls was unusual, so precautions were taken by the French soldiers in case he was an enemy. His excursion was delayed until May 1750. Permission was finally granted, and Kalm was received with equanimity the second time he reported to the French garrison.

Kalm was thoroughly prepared for his first sight of Niagara—indeed, his motivation for going there was to compare his view with the impressions of others:

> I had read formerly almost all the authors that have wrote anything about this Fall; and the last year in Canada, had made so many enquiries about it, that I thought I had a pretty good Idea of it, and now at supper, requested the gentlemen to tell me all they knew and thought worth notice relating to it, which they accordingly did. I observed that in many things they all agreed, in some things they were of different opinions, all of which I took particular notice. (Ibid.)

Kalm was at the waterfalls to check these different details. As he goes on to confess, he intended to gather all the accounts together before adding his own, more "accurate" opinion:

> As I have found by experience in my other travels, very few observe nature's works with accuracy, or report the truth precisely....I cannot now be entirely satisfied without seeing with my own eyes whenever 'tis in my power. (Ibid.)

This desire to amass knowledge and strip away "inaccuracies" was the product of Kalm's eighteenth-century scientific training, which ultimately informed the way in which he applied all the "different opinions" to the scene before him, observed nature's work "with accuracy" and then built a model from the data, or reported "the truth precisely" (ibid.). This way of experiencing nature, different from Hennepin's, allowed the observer to assume that he could objectively view and scientifically evaluate the world.

Even though Kalm wanted to "discover" Niagara for himself, the French commander gave orders that two officers from the garrison, one of whom served as the on-site surveyor, were to guide Kalm up the river to the Falls. The commander also sent along a man named Jonqueire, who "had liv'd ten years by the carrying-place, and knew everything worth notice of the Fall, better than any other person," to "show and tell [Kalm]...what-ever he knew" (54–55). In the end, three officers, three soldiers, and Jonqueire, the guide, paddled Kalm up the Niagara River; when the rapids became too turbulent, they abandoned the canoe and proceeded on foot, along the eastern cliff path, to the edge of the waterfalls.

The botanist's initial description of Niagara's various features, different from Hennepin's, focuses on all the separate topographical details, beginning with the most westerly waterfall:

> To the river (or rather strait) runs here from s.s.e. to n.n.w. and the rocks of the great Fall cross it, not in a right line; but forming almost the figure of a semicircle or horse shoe. (55)

Hennepin, who was unnerved by Niagara's violent flow and thunderous roar, developed his description with metaphor (the man with his head spinning), and the emphasis placed on what the Falls made him feel—"Horror" and "Admiration"—suggests that he worked with John Dennis's description of the "Joy" and "Horrour" of the European Alps. Kalm, on the other hand, who was trained in the Linnaean system of binomial nomenclature, was at Niagara to "observe nature's works with accuracy." His measured reading makes the place seem much less dangerous and wild. Not only does Kalm establish Niagara's exact location with a compass, but he also classifies the river as a "strait," and describes the shape of the most westerly cascade as "a semicircle"—a more exact depiction than Hennepin's "great Out-let." It is also significant that Kalm does not mention the cross-stream, which Hennepin's illustrator placed to the west of the Horseshoe Falls. Kalm goes on to describe the other features, one at a time:

> Above the Fall, in the middle of the river is an island, lying also s.s.e. and n.n.w. or parallel with the sides of the river; its length is about 7 or 8 arpents (an arpent being 180 feet). The lower end of this Island is just at the perpendicular edge of the Fall. (Ibid.)

He uses the same detailed, measured language for Goat Island, but not as much attention is paid to the most easterly American Falls. Instead, Kalm shifts his focus to points upstream and contemplates the flow of water and where it comes from:

> On both sides of this island runs all the water that comes from the lakes of Canada, viz. Lake Superior, lake Mischigan, lake Huron, and lake Erie, which you know are rather small seas than lakes, and have besides a great many large rivers that empty their water in them, of which the greatest part comes down this Niagara Fall. (Ibid.)

Kalm's choice of words to describe the waterway beyond his vision—"all the water," "a great many large rivers"—suggests that he was not as exact about phenomena that he could not see. His depiction of Niagara as connected to the "small seas" is similar to Hennepin's description of Niagara as part of an archipelago. However, the fact that Kalm does not even mention mountains, or the third cross-stream, is further evidence of the difference between his eighteenth-century natural history context and the philosophical and theological approaches, especially the seventeenth-century "mountain debate" that probably influenced Hennepin.

Kalm, the Linnaean disciple, observed and catalogued nature and his letter is typically structured as a scientific report; but having collected all the measurable data, he digresses from the formal tone of the narrative to offer a more personal impression:

> When all this water comes to the very Fall, it throws itself down perpendicular! It is beyond all belief the surprise when you see this! I cannot with words express how amazing it is! You cannot see it without being quite terrified; to behold so vast a quantity of water falling headlong from a surprising height! (56)

In spite of his scientific training, Kalm's sensory experience of Niagara—his surprise, amazement, and terror—is both unquantifiable and immeasurable. His choice of words and the punctuation he employs ("all this water," "beyond all belief the surprise when you see this!," "so vast a quantity of water falling headlong from a surprising height!") are borrowed directly from the first description. Kalm falls back on the qualities accentuated by Hennepin at the expense of more rational ones.

After using Hennepin's description as a trope to codify his surprise and awe, Kalm quickly reaffirms the uniqueness of his own kind of expression by denouncing his "source":

> Father Hennepin supposes it 600 Feet perpendicular; but he has gained little credit in Canada; the name of honour they give him

there, is *un grand Menteur,* or The great Liar; he writes of what he saw in places where he never was. 'Tis true he saw this Fall: but as it is the way of some travellers to magnify every thing, so has he done with regard to the fall of Niagara. (Ibid.)

Even though he has borrowed aspects of the original pattern of expression, the botanist feels the need to strip away his predecessor's reputation and advance his own view. He declares Hennepin's 600-foot waterfalls to be "exaggerated" and, with exacting mathematical instruments (and with the help of his guides), he surveys the crest lines "accurately" and finds the perpendicular drop to be exactly 137 feet (ibid.). After he has recorded his "measured" opinion, Kalm ensures his own accuracy by comparing his data with those collected by the on-site surveyor ("the king's engineer," Morandrier). They both agree the drop is 137 feet.

Kalm continues to correct Hennepin's description of Niagara as if he were checking items off a list. After reading the compass bearings, giving his impression of how the sight of the waterfalls made him feel and measuring their size, he goes on to discuss their sound effects as neither extraordinary nor great: "we could easily hear what each other said, without speaking much louder than common when conversing in other places" (57). Although the botanist did not have an instrument with which to conduct a sound test, he qualifies his assessment by measuring the noise level against that of normal conversation. This became important to other respondents. In chapters 2 and 3, I have selected a number of accounts in which travellers also "measure" the volume of sound. Perhaps Kalm's concession that others might have different reactions actually encouraged people to test their aural impressions at Niagara.

In the same way as Kalm relied on his scientific training to write about Niagara's physical nature (and on Hennepin's account to express his emotive response to nature), the engraving associated with Kalm's report seems based as much on the botanist's description as on the Hennepin-derived view and on the anonymous artist's own idea of "wildness." In *A View of the Famous Cataract of Niagara in North America* (1751), two cascades hang straight as sheets (see figure 5). In size and style, these waterfalls are linked to the picture based on Hennepin's description. So too are the mountains in the background and the large coniferous trees on either side of the cascades.[31] However, there is no cross-stream and the people appear to be very different. Five regal French soldiers and a little dog pose elegantly in the

Figure 5: Anonymous, *A View of the Famous Cataract of Niagara in North America* (from Pehr Kalm's "Letter," *The Gentleman's Magazine*, 1751). Reproduction by permission of The Buffalo & Erie County Public Library, Buffalo, New York.

place where Hennepin's observers stood. Some face each other and some glance at Niagara. None appear to be discombobulated by the view or pained by the noise; instead, they are watching the (roughly drawn) figures on a ladder slung down the face of Goat Island. It is not obvious whether these figures are climbing up or down. To the left of Goat Island, upstream from the America Falls (almost at the point where the island forms a "V"), two men on wooden stilts negotiate the rapids (indicated in the picture by a "b"). Spectators watch their progress from the American bank. Below Table Rock, on the western side of the river, others haul packs down to the carrying place. In the letter, these labourers are identified as belonging to the Six Nations; consequently, this illustration marks the first appearance of Indian figures, who are to have a role in Niagara representations. Kalm visited Niagara at a time when many of the tribes had forged alliances with the French. This political association between the colonized and the colonizing meant that Natives worked for the soldiers, building their roads, paddling their canoes, carrying their packs. What Kalm saw on the portage path below Table Rock on the western shore and a legend he recounts later are the reason why his illustrator drew those figures there:

> I saw above 200 Indians, most of them belonging to the Six Nations, busy in carrying packs of furs, chiefly of deer and bear, over the carrying-place. You would be surpriz'd to see what abundance of these things are brought every day over this place. (55)

Originally concerned only with nature's flora and fauna, Kalm expands the scope of his expedition here to include an elaborate story about the Native people who lived in the vicinity of the Falls. This tale was reportedly told to Kalm by the French soldiers who escorted him to Niagara.

Kalm introduces the legend by talking about the danger of the Falls: how inaccessible it was to the French, how the Indians, not "hindered" by the boiling water and vast height of the cascades, ended up almost drowning in the water. That is how this island adventure came about, he suggests. It was a near-fatal accident. "The history is this," he writes, and then goes on to relate how two drunk Indians fell asleep in a birchbark canoe and drifted downstream. They woke at the sound of the water, and almost at the very brink, they managed to steer toward the Goat Island shore:

At first they were glad; but when they had consider'd every thing, they thought themselves hardly in a better state than if they had gone down the fall, since they had now no other choice, than either to throw themselves down the same, or to perish with hunger. (59)

Even though the Indians were drunk on imported French brandy—their payment for carrying the soldiers' goods—they could still rely on "primitive" instincts. They constructed a ladder out of the bark of a linden tree: "one end of this bark ladder they tied fast to a great tree that grew at the side of the rock above the fall, and let the other end down to the water" (59–60). Once they had climbed down the ladder, though, there was nowhere to go but into the lower basin. However, they were unable to swim across the churning channel to the carrying places below the Canadian and American Falls, so they ascended the ladder to Goat Island again. At this point in the narrative, they simply abandoned themselves to fate.

Kalm's image of the indigene is based on what the French colonists in the mid-eighteenth century imagined Indians to be: brave and primitive, yet also childlike and in need of protection. Critics Mary Louise Pratt and Robert F. Berkhofer would argue that the legend reflects Europe's imperialist agenda, and that this agenda was one of colonial genocide which coincided with contemporaneous writings about the nomenclature of race.

When the word "race" first entered the lexicon of the natural sciences, it referred to the characteristics or common qualities of certain types of people.[32] The first known racial studies emerged in the late sixteenth century with Giordano Bruno's and Jean Bodin's categorizations of human populations according to whether their skin was "duskish," "black," "chestnut," or "farish."[33] This was followed almost one century later by François Bernier's *A New Division of the Earth* (1684), a classificatory system for general appearance, including skin colour, that divided humanity into four groups—Europeans, Far Easterners, Negroes, and Lapps.[34] By the mid-eighteenth century, the growing influence of a certain type of thinking that came back to Europe from the edges of empires in explorers', traders', missionaries', and travellers' reports and drawings led to the presumption that each human grouping exhibited different qualities of behaviour. This appears in Linnaeus's writing as a commingling of physical features with behavioural and psychological traits. *Systema naturae* (1735), Linnaeus's famous matrix of classifications, designated creation as a continuous chain of gradations of resemblance, leading from heavenly creatures down to humans and further on to the animal, plant, and mineral realms. Initially, he grouped human beings with the higher primates under the order "Anthropomorpha," and divided the genus "Homo" into four basic varieties: "Europaeus, Americanus, Asiaticus, and Africanus." In later editions of his work (published in the 1740s), he elaborated on these classifications by adding descriptions of physical features and supposed traits of character. For "Europaeus," Linnaeus wrote, "white, sanguine, muscular; hair long, flowing; eyes blue; gentle, acute, inventive; covers himself with close vestments; governed by laws"; and for "Americanus," "reddish, choleric and erect; hair black, straight, thick; wide nostrils, scanty beard; obstinate, merry, free; paints himself with fine red lines; regulated by customs."[35] These later revisions also added several other types that served as intermediates between apes and humans—the "missing link" as it were.[36] They included "Homo ferus," or wild men, and "Monstrosus," a category that lumped together real humans, such as dwarfs, with fantastical creatures like troglodytes and satyrs.[37]

In Linnaeus's ranking, the aboriginal and autochthonous race *Homosapiens Americanus* (Indians) was always a variety of humanity listed below *Homosapiens Europaeus* ("whites," or, later, *Caucasians*).[38] Similarly, Pehr Kalm's depiction of the reckless, fearless Indians as stranded and likely to "perish from hunger" on Goat Island seems to capture some of these social complexities about where particular races ranked on the Linnaean scale of being. On Goat Island, there were no more ingenious, remarkable escapes: the Indians simply waited for death. But within nine days they were spotted by two of their brethren. Unfortunately, these people could not rescue them either: "[they] saw and pity'd them, but gave them little hopes of help" (60). Finally, their would-be rescuers ran to Fort Niagara and notified the French commander of the situation, which says much about colonialist ideology at this point of contact. During this historical period, alliances with the French colonists came with the assumption of Native submission, and in the legend they are seen begging the advice of the highest-ranking colonial official to solve the problem at hand. In the end, the commander of the fort advocated a solution when he instructed the would-be rescuers to walk across the rapids above the Falls on wooden stilts: "Each had two such poles in his hands, to set against the bottom of the stream, to keep them steady" (ibid.). Kalm highlights how rational and logical the French were when he adds the commander's parting advice: each rescuer should take an extra set of poles over for the stranded Indians to use as a means of conveyance back to the mainland. And, as Kalm makes clear at the end of the legend, others had not been as lucky: "[The French] often found below the Falls pieces of human bodies, perhaps of drunken Indians, that have unhappily come down the Fall" (62). The message of the story seems to be that Indians are ignorant about survival and overly dependent on Europeans. (Interestingly, the French never depict themselves as dependent, even though they rely heavily on Natives for guidance, protection, wisdom, and labour.)

Kalm ends the legend and also his letter by apologizing for not satisfying the curiosity of the reader: "For my part, who am not fond of the Marvellous, I like to see things just as they are, and so to relate them" (56). Similarly, Hennepin apologizes to the reader before launching into his description of the place (see the epigraph to this chapter). In Hennepin's case, he feels he is not competent enough to describe the wonders and terrors of the natural world, and then goes on to do so. In Kalm's case, he asserts that he will not exaggerate to satisfy the reader who has come to expect measurements that astonish and ends up doing just that when he refers to wild feelings (and relies on Hennepin) and when he relates the legend. I call Kalm's two different kinds of expression—the scientific and the marvellous—civilizing and wild discourses.

After the letter and its attendant illustration were published in *The Gentleman's Magazine* and in Bartram's *Observations on the Inhabitants,* other well-known image-makers painted Indians at Niagara. Among these artists, Lieutenant Thomas Davies, the creator of a four-waterfall version of Niagara, arranged his figures into a small social group on the western bank downstream from the Falls (see figure 4). Davies, an officer in the Royal Artillery who trained in topographical drawing and watercolour painting at the Royal Military College at Woolwich, was stationed at Niagara during the French and Indian wars (1754–63). During these battles, the French relied on Native forces to ambush the British, but mid-way through the conflicts more complex alliances developed when the French joined with the British so that a united European army could conquer the North American aboriginal. One of these ambushes between Europeans and Natives took place at Fort Niagara in 1759. In the ensuing skirmishes, bands resumed alliances with their former European enemies. Thomas Davies painted *Niagara Falls from Below* after the 1763 proclamation that permitted British use of the portage at Niagara Falls. The figures in Davies's picture include two British officers, who are outnumbered by four Indians.

But the British do not express fear or astonishment at either the Indians or the waterfalls. This says much about how the colonizers viewed the Native presence after the French and Indian wars.

The style of Davies's picture may have been based on the picturesque compositions of Claude Lorrain. In fine arts, the picturesque was generally expressed through variegated groupings of dissimilar features, colours, shades, and textures, all of which were meant to bring harmony to the scene. Lorrain's landscapes are known for their variations of light and atmosphere, and Davies's Niagara painting reflects this influence in the way in which the sky and waterfalls dissolve into mist and merge together. Other features of the picturesque that may have been borrowed from Lorrain include the clump of trees on the left-hand bank which contrasts with the rocky forest floor in the foreground and the expanse of bright open water in the middle of the picture. Further, Davies's foregrounded Indians are in the same position as the reclining river god in Lorrain's *Landscape with Apollo and the Muses* (ca. 1650s). Lorrain's Arcadian ideals are meant to express a supreme happiness now lost, and Davies may also be suggesting that the contemporaneous arrangement between the colonized Indian and the British imperial nation is both harkening back and failing to recapture an earlier (and imaginary) sense of harmony.

As they had done with their French allies during the 1750s, members of the Six Nations continued to live beside Fort Niagara and to receive gifts from the colonists; in the later decades of the eighteenth century, however, the British were in control.[39] When the American colonies went to war against Britain, the Niagara area became a refuge for all Native allies of the British. Those who emigrated to the fort at the opening to Lake Ontario received guns and ammunition for their loyalty. In a picture created three-quarters of a century after Hennepin and twenty-five years after Kalm, the Anglo-Swiss painter Henry Fuseli records this period at Niagara and includes an armed Indian.

Henry Fuseli

HENRY FUSELI (A.K.A. HEINRICH FUESSLY) was born in Zurich in 1741. He decided to become a painter instead of a priest when his drawings were praised by Sir Joshua Reynolds in 1767. After this encouragement, Fuseli moved to Italy and stayed there for the next nine years, painting, among other works, *View of Niagara Falls* (1776). The image was commissioned for a book written by English travel writer Henry Vernon.[40]

Figure 6: Henry Fuseli, *View of Niagara Falls* (1776). Sigmund Samuel
Canadiana Gallery/Royal Ontario Museum, 955.74.1.

Fuseli's landscape is composed in a different style from that of the
Hennepin and Kalm illustrations: the cliffs are craggier, the trees are
softer, and the clouds have a thicker vapour (see figure 6). Yet, the
faintly drawn third cascade and the shimmer of mountains in the
background imply that Fuseli may have copied the Hennepin illustration. Additionally, the muscular Indian dressed in full regalia who
sits with chin resting in one hand and weapons cradled in the other
suggests that the Fuseli composition is a pastiche, made up from various sources. Elizabeth McKinsey points out the link between the figure in the Fuseli painting and the Indian in Benjamin West's *The Death
of General Wolfe* (1770), but she does not examine the aesthetics that
influenced their individual constructions.[41] Such a study of the Indian
in West's and Fuseli's paintings yields insights into these processes.

The American-born Benjamin West, official painter at the Court of
St. James and President of the British Royal Academy of Arts in London,
dedicated *The Death of General Wolfe*—a painting that chronicled one
of the decisive steps in the formation of the British Empire—to the
king of England. The painting was unveiled in London in the spring of
1771 (five years before Fuseli's) and made into an engraving by William
Woollett in 1776. Fuseli may have seen this painting, or one of the
Woollett engravings; in any case, his Indian is identical to West's war-

rior, who is squatting on his haunches, his chin resting contemplatively in his hand, watching his commander expire at the moment of victory. This battle-weary Indian became an enduring visual image for English audiences because the British won the Battle of Quebec. West's picture, painted twelve years after that war, depicts its subject in contemporary uniform instead of classical dress (as was the custom with military painting at that time). This resistance against Neoclassical styling, along with the muscular, exotic Indian, made West's painting unique.[42]

When Fuseli painted his Niagara Indian in 1776, conflicts between the colonizing nations in North America had resulted in another war. This one involved Britain, with the full support of the Iroquois and Mohawks, fighting the United States (1775–83). Perceived in terms of late eighteenth-century British values, the figure in Fuseli's painting symbolizes all the qualities associated with certain Native tribes at this time—strength, bravery, and loyalty.[43] The early writings of Immanuel Kant would have supported this view too. In his *Observations on the Feeling of the Beautiful and Sublime* (1763), Kant associated the image of the Indian with sublimity: "among all the savages there is no nation that displays so sublime a mental character as those of North America."[44]

But European power in North America was to shift once again, and with this rearrangement came other ways of valuing Natives. After Britain lost the war with the United States, their Native allies were caught in the wake of new antagonisms. International treaties had put North America's Native peoples in no position to bargain: on both sides of the border, they were forced to negotiate land rights in their own territories.[45] By the late 1790s, when the British painter Robert Hancock composed his painting of Niagara, most tribes had been relocated onto crown land. In spite of this, Hancock included Indians at the Falls because the figure of the Indian had symbolic implications.

Robert Hancock

ROBERT HANCOCK, BORN IN 1730 in Badsey, England, became an engraver in 1756, at the Worcester Porcelain Company where he made copperplates for transfer-printing on porcelain. Many of his designs were adapted from the rococo paintings of Antoine Watteau. In the early 1790s, Hancock left the porcelain industry, moved to Bristol, and became an engraver of bookplates and a painter of portraits (of poets

Figure 7: Robert Hancock, *The Waterfall of Niagara in North America*
(1794). Sigmund Samuel Canadiana Gallery/
Royal Ontario Museum, 981.35.1.

and essayists such as Robert Southey, Samuel Taylor Coleridge, William
Wordsworth, and Charles Lamb).[46] Since Hancock's Niagara painting
was commissioned for Charles Theodore Middleton's *Complete System of Geography* around the time he moved from Worcester to Bristol, he had to have used other illustrations as his model (rather than
going to Niagara himself).[47] The topography of *The Waterfall of Niagara in North America* (1794) resembles that of the Kalm engraving,
especially the treatment of light and shade, and the placement of trees
around the waterfalls (see figure 7). But some of the spectators in Hancock's engraving, particularly the man who has fallen, overwhelmed,
to the ground, suggest that Hancock did rely, in part, on the Hennepin-based print. Yet, Hancock has included a dark-skinned, barely
clad man—an Indian—who appears to be leading five Europeans, two
of whom are dressed in black robes. They have bushy white beards,
their feet are bare, and around their waists are belts of beads with
large crosses dangling from the ends. Given the date of this painting,
they might be members of a pacifist sect ("late Loyalists") who are
being escorted to free land on the other side of the river. However,
they are dressed as French Jesuits—the "black robes"—from
two centuries earlier. Hancock's figures probably derive from com-

positions featuring Jesuits, Indians, and other seventeenth-century men. The historical fantasy produced by the British engraver after the War of Independence—an image of Niagara during early contact— nostalgically reinvokes European power at a time when an imperialist nation (Britain) had been forced to withdraw from the southern part of the continent. This is particularly evident when the image-maker stresses the Indian's subservience (and not his warlike nature or his sublimity) by drawing figures at work: below Table Rock they carry packs above their heads, and on the upper bank one guides Europeans to the view.

The Noble Savage

DESPITE THE FACT THAT NATIVE PEOPLE were struggling against re-moval and land loss, the Indian figure remained central to the art of Niagara. Other discourses coming out of Europe may have contributed to the popularity of the Indian in late eighteenth-century Niagara paintings. In an essay that is widely recognized as propounding the first biological theory of race that partially anticipated theories of the evo-lution of species, Immanuel Kant supported the idea of distinct races, but did not differentiate whites as a separate species from non-whites.[48] Indeed, in "Of the Different Human Races" (1775), Kant postulated that there are no different species of humans at all, since such an assumption would, in his thinking, deny the unity from which every-one has originated. However, Kant did believe that blacks, whites, ori-entals, and Indians had managed to transform themselves (or, to use a term coined one century later, had "adapted") to the point where they had permanently different minds and characters. This proto-genetic argument was his concept of race.[49] And, French philosopher Jean-Jacques Rousseau's *Essay on the Origin of Languages* (1781) essen-tially argued that "man" is only good when "in the state of nature," and that this "noble savage" is made unhappy and is corrupted by society. Rousseau is credited with conflating the nature of primitive peoples with ideals of physical nature.[50]

Turning to artistic representations of the Indian at Niagara Falls, one can see the connection between specific paintings and the writings of eighteenth-century philosophers who profiled race. For example, Isaac Weld's *View of the Horseshoe Falls of Niagara* (1799) confirms the European idea that the North American Indian was a "noble sav-age." Weld, a member of the Royal Dublin Society who exhibited at the Royal Hibernian Academy, published a sketch of Niagara in his

Figure 8: Isaac Weld, *View of the Horseshoe Falls of Niagara* (1799).
Reproduction by permission of The Buffalo & Erie County
Public Library, Buffalo, New York.

Travels through the States of North America in 1795, 1796 and 1797
(London, 1799).[51] The view, which shows only the Horseshoe Falls as
a long broad cascade with a dip in the middle and a sliver of land
from Goat Island, contains six Indian figures, arranged in two groups
of three (see figure 8). The most obvious group stands on a low bank,
near the water's edge, about one mile downstream from the waterfalls, and the other cluster appears very close to the Horseshoe Falls.
All of these men are spearfishing. At this time, it would have been
impossible for people to stand that close to the river, as a mill had
been built at the bottom of the Falls. Yet, despite the facts that Native
people were not living in the area and that industry had begun to
impede activities close to the water, Weld depicts Indians spearfishing
in order to suggest that Niagara represents a primordial wilderness.
Edmund Henn paints a similar scene in his *A View of Niagara Falls,
with Indians* (1799). Three figures and a dog gather on the lower bank.
They include a woman carrying a baby in a papoose; she appears to
be walking toward the man with the fishing spear. These images of
Indians fishing were meant to confirm a popular European idea that
Niagara Falls was an exotic wilderness inhabited by people who lived
free in nature (even though at the time of painting all had changed).[52]

The critical charges acquired through these revisions include sublimity and nobility—purchases that have symbolic implications for the Indian figure, the image-maker's relationship to North American expansionism, and the various forms of colonizing authority.

Thomas Cole's 1830 painting of Niagara, in which two Indian figures contemplate a wild, vast landscape, is another example of how the trope had been divested of its "real" history (displacement and genocide) and invested by association (through imperializing rhetoric) with awe, peace, and harmony (see figure 9). The American-born Cole (1801–48) visited Niagara in May 1829, and painted *A Distant View of the Falls of Niagara* from a position a few miles downstream from Hennepin's lookout. Another widely disseminated representation of Niagara of the nineteenth century, Cole's view was engraved by T.S. Woodcock and published in John Howard Hinton's *The History and Topography of the United States* (1831). A reproduction of Cole's painting also appeared as an inset on a map of Canada West, published by J. & F. Tallis of Edinburgh around 1850.[53]

Cole was the founder and leader of the Hudson River School (1835–70), a painting group that adapted European aesthetics and applied them to America's wilderness landscapes. Basing their ideas on Edmund Burke's theories in *A Philosophical Enquiry into the Origin of Our Ideas of the Sublime and Beautiful,* and on the sublime landscapes of England's J.M.W. Turner, Cole and other members of the school developed a technique called "luminism" to depict "sublimity surrounded by beauty."[54] In fine arts, depictions of the sublime generally concentrated on massive features to solicit from their wildness an immensity and extravagance of feeling. On the other hand, the manifestation of the beautiful occurred in features that were small and uniform, and the spectator viewing these landscapes would experience pleasure and delight. The various treatments of the Hudson River School synthesized these positions. The typical scene was painted on a large scale, with panoramic horizons that seemed to radiate beyond the paintings' borders, suggesting unlimited expanse. American rhetoric that permeated this particular ideology included notions of the frontier as a "moving stage" for the drama of progress, order, and control,[55] and the government policy of manifest destiny that became a stimulus for American expansionism.[56] Indeed, as Richard Slotkin argues, the myth of the frontier as an unlimited expanse was connected to the idea that white Americans had superior racial traits, and the doctrine of manifest destiny was an extension of this belief to those "chosen people" who were destined to dominate others.[57] Hence, the Natives on the frontiers who seemed so unwilling to either trans-

Figure 9: Thomas Cole, *A Distant View of the Falls of Niagara* (1831).
From *The History and Topography of the United States,* edited by
John Howard Hinton. The President and Fellows of Harvard College.

form themselves culturally or submit to the depredations of the white
settler, were just further evidence of that race's inferior character.

Thomas Cole's *A Distant View of the Falls of Niagara* reflects some
of these values: the slightly raised perspective blurs the distant vista,
indicating an infinite expanse beyond the waterfalls. His painting
expresses other popular ideas too. The vast array of trees on Goat
Island, on the riverbanks and in the foreground makes Niagara into a
primeval place. Cole has even paid attention to the minute detail of
the foliage to make it look freshened by the passing thundershower.
To add to the sublimity of the scene, he has created tensions in the dark
foreboding clouds admitting a dazzling burst of sunlight, and in the
peaceful Indians in full regalia holding onto their guns. In its representation of the Indian, this painting appeals to the "noble savage"
idea of Kant and Rousseau. This appeal is nostalgic because the Native
of Cole's time had been conquered and removed from the Niagara
area. Hence, the way in which the trope of the Indian has been invested
by Cole with nobility erases this history of colonization, violence, and
exploitation.

From the time of early contact onward, numerous wars had an impact on the Native presence and on landscape development. Each successive colonization brought a new valuation of land, wilderness, and ownership. Another complex of historical influences during the 1830s—the encroachment of commercial and industrial developments and a near-clash between the British and the Americans—saw image-makers presenting Niagara as a wilderness again. As with the earliest picture, the "untamed" element is mirrored by exaggerated landscape features and by the gestures of the spectators. The other figurative element in W.R. Callington's sketch, a burning boat tipping over the edge of the Canadian Falls, symbolizes the danger associated with claiming the land.

W.R. Callington

THE BOSTON-BASED ENGINEER W.R. CALLINGTON was at Niagara during the Upper Canada Rebellion (1837). His sketch *The American Steam Packet* Caroline, *Descending the Great Falls of Niagara after Being Set on Fire by the British, December 29th, 1837, with a Distant View of Navy Island,* which was lithographed by J. Grieve and published by J. Robins in London in 1838, features the Canadian Falls, the American Falls, and a tiny portion of Goat Island (see figure 10). Another char-acteristic encoded by the artist—the rather copious cross-stream—reflects a particular influence. While Callington labours to adjust his Niagara to the sublime, the presence of the third cascade links this particular sketch with the Hennepin-based picture drawn almost a century and a half earlier.

The scene is meant to evoke terror: two men are being precipitated over the brink of the Falls. But these figures are awkwardly drawn, slightly out of proportion. The artist is not quite successful with the presentation of his victims or his landscape. The crudely drawn Goat Island seems stunted by another land mass upriver (Navy Island, which is actually two miles away and not visible from this perspective). Call-ington's sketch of this event relies as much on his imagination as on the "facts," for the historical boat-burning actually took place at night and the ship was a steam-driven, side-wheel paddleboat.[58] Moreover, only one of the men aboard the *Caroline* was killed (the American Amos Durfee), while Callington's sketch shows two people falling to their death.

The entire rebellion consisted of an unsuccessful attempt to take the capital at Toronto; after that failed, the Upper Canadian rebels

Figure 10: W.R. Callington, *The American Steam Packet* Caroline, *Descending the Great Falls of Niagara after Being Set on Fire by the British, December 29th, 1837, with a Distant View of Navy Island* (1837). Royal Ontario Museum, 960X282.52.

retreated to Navy Island just above Niagara Falls, close to their allies in New York state. Newspaper editor and parliamentarian William Lyon Mackenzie and his rebels proclaimed a provisional government on the island. They were joined by a number of American sympathizers, who arrived in the steamer *Caroline*. The British captured the boat on December 29, 1837, and sent the burning ship over the Horseshoe Falls. After this event, many Americans demanded war because their property had been destroyed and a soldier had been killed. But the British tendered an apology and another war was averted.

For an English audience, this drawing served as a symbol of the tension between the rebels and the British. Ultimately, it celebrated a British victory at the expense of the Americans. The uprising, meant to unseat British policy-makers in the new colony, was, for the most part, a failure, because the majority of Upper Canadians clung to British connections (and not American ideals) in order to defend themselves against expansionist tendencies south of the border.

Throughout this chapter, I have stressed the ways in which Niagara was transmuted into the artists' idioms through features such as the size, shape, and number of waterfalls, through the inclusion of mountains, and through the ambience achieved with different techniques. The reactions of spectators and victims also codified the nature of the landscape. The last artist to be considered, Frederic Edwin Church, a second-generation Hudson River painter, managed a new kind of wilderness in his two famous depictions of Niagara. One of his paintings is peopleless and the other includes very civilized onlookers, but with both views Church manages to celebrate the moment when all the terror at Niagara is transformed into peace.

Frederic Edwin Church

FREDERIC EDWIN CHURCH, born in 1826 in Hartford, Connecticut, began art studies at the age of sixteen when he moved to Catskill, New York to work with Thomas Cole. Church may have visited Niagara in August 1851, but his first documented sketching trip occurred in March 1856 when he painted *Niagara from Goat Island, Winter, 1856*.[59] He returned twice more that year, in July and late August; on these separate visits, Church made numerous pencil sketches and oil studies.[60] Once back in his studio, he assembled the pieces culled from many angles to work up a scene of the Canadian side.[61] It took Church less than two months to complete the painting.

Elizabeth McKinsey calls *Niagara Falls* (1857) the culmination of sublime American paintings of the Falls (even though it is a view of the Canadian side!).[62] As popular during Church's time as the Hennepin-based view had been one century earlier, *Niagara Falls* was hung in galleries across the United States and Britain and on the Continent, made into a lithograph, copied into books, and imitated by many artists. Initially shown at a one-picture special exhibition in April 1857 at the commercial gallery of Williams, Stevens and Williams on Broadway in New York, the Niagara painting could be viewed without charge for the first two days: thousands of people crowded in, overflowing the exhibition room.[63] Then, in June 1857, *Niagara Falls* travelled to a London gallery, after which it was chromolithographed by Day & Son, Britain's leading firm of commercial fine art printers.[64] Next, the canvas was shipped to Glasgow, Manchester, and Liverpool, before being returned to New York in September 1858. The Williams, Stevens and Williams gallery bought it for $2,500, plus $2,000 for the copyright.[65] The following year, the painting toured Baltimore, Washington, Richmond, and New Orleans, and less than a decade later, in 1867, it was shown to critical acclaim at the Universal Exposition in Paris. By this time, it was simply known as "the Niagara." In 1876, when Buffalo's

W.W. Corcoran bought it from the New York gallery for $12,500, thousands more viewed it. And, since the gallery was included on the standard Northern Tour, travellers examined the painting before stopping over at Niagara. (As we will see in chapters 2 and 3, a typical person on the Northern Tour arrived at the site anticipating the scenes depicted by image-makers. Artistic renderings represented, for some, the "real" Niagara and, when travellers stood before nature's view, they were often disappointed.)

Church's famous 1857 picture of Niagara was not done from the Hennepin perspective, nor was it imitative of Thomas Cole's *A Distant View of the Falls of Niagara*; rather, it was painted from the Canadian shore, above Table Rock (see figure 11). The most striking aspect of the image is the lack of foreground, giving the viewer the sense of hovering above the river, close to the brink. Church indicates the awesome drop over the edge by painting in streams of water and cloudy mists. Along with the ingenious perspective, he foreshortens the rapids upstream to suggest the infinite expanse of the river. This last panoramic technique was common among members of the Hudson River School, but on the whole Church's painting is not imitative of their compositions, because he abandons their convention of including land in the foreground to focus on two bands of sky and water.[66] In leaving out the land component, he has also left out all the tourists, and the human-built structures that allowed people access to Niagara, such as the railings and lookout platforms. (In the mid-1850s, more than 60,000 people flocked to the Falls each year.)[67] Because Church's view promotes the Falls as wild, natural, and unpeopled, it may, ironically, have encouraged more tourists to travel there.

Like the Hennepin-based drawing before it, Church's Niagara became the image to imitate. Albert Bierstadt painted his *Niagara Falls 1869* from a similar perspective, and Louis Remy Mignot's *Niagara*, also composed in the late 1860s, takes in the Horseshoe Falls too, but this time from the Terrapin Tower—the other side of the curve, directly across from where Church and Bierstadt had stood.[68]

Church visited the waterfalls again in April and August 1858. Near the end of his stay, he chartered the *Maid of the Mist* to take him to the very base of the Horseshoe Falls. *Under Niagara* (1858), a four-foot by six-foot canvas, was completed in one day. In May 1862, it was shipped to London and reproduced as a chromolithograph, after which the painting disappeared.[69] Church's last rendering of the scene, *Niagara Falls, from the American Side* (1867), is his only self-titled "American" view. It was commissioned by the New York art dealer Michael

Knoedler. Church did not revisit the Falls in order to construct this painting; instead, he reviewed a number of sketches and worked up one that had been done "on the eve of his first trip [i.e., in 1851 or 1856]."[70] After being exhibited in New York City, the painting was chromolithographed in London. Two decades later, in 1887, Church's canvas was bought at an auction by John S. Kennedy, a Scottish-born New York businessman, and then donated by the purchaser to the National Gallery of Scotland.[71] Church may have based his *Niagara Falls, from the American Side* on the famous seventeenth-century sketch. The perspective is slightly below the Hennepin vantage point, but off to the right-hand side of the broad Horseshoe is the small residue of the third cascade, a visual reference that aligns this view with the seminal image (see figure 12). Although there was never any geological proof that this third waterfall existed, Church may have painted it in because he was supposed to see three cascades at Niagara. But even if *Niagara Falls, from the American Side* has some similarities to the Hennepin-derived drawing, it is an entirely different painting. The nineteenth-century view shows the American Falls in receding perspective and the Horseshoe, in the distance, as curved and flat. And Church adds rainbows, swirling mists, and colours—gold and blue pigment—to create the effect of peace and tranquility.

As in the first artifact to emerge from a European vision of Niagara, in which the spectators are disoriented by the noise and the view, the figures in the picture attributed to Church react with intense interest. The barely perceptible couple off to the left-hand side are suspended in a "viewing basket" high above the American Falls. These tourists—a bearded man in a dark suit and woman in a bright red dress—lean out to study nature's grandeur.[72] Niagara's wildness is a pleasure to be savoured and enjoyed. This pictorial tradition established by Church influenced Arthur Lumley's *Niagara Seen with Different Eyes* (1873), a cartoon that catalogued late nineteenth-century intentions toward art, nature, tourism, and industry as sublime.

Lumley's drawing, published in *Harper's Weekly* in 1873, encapsulates the spectacle that Church and his contemporaries (such as Mignot, Richardt, Hunt and Inness) blocked out (see figure 13).[73] Even though Church's painting was the model, this is Niagara as human spectacle and sublime wilderness. Yet, because the landscape is filled with people, nature seems relegated to the background. Lumley, a freelance illustrator, composed his Niagara cartoon as a pictorial parody that utilizes satire or humour.[74] The tenor of such a drawing served to sharpen the public view of a contemporary event or trend.[75] Lumley's

Figure 11: Frederic Edwin Church, *Niagara* (1857).
In the Collection of The Corcoran Gallery of Art, Washington, D.C.

Figure 12: Frederic Edwin Church, *Niagara Falls, from the American Side* (1867). The National Gallery of Scotland.

satiric approach to nature is obvious not through caricature, but through gesture and intent: the Indian mother earnestly turns to her child and ignores the Falls; the lovers are so busy with each other that they do not even see Niagara; the geologist backs away from the water to conduct his earth studies; and the businessman stares right at Niagara, dreaming of the river harnessed for power. Slightly below the businessman is a poet. These two figures symbolize the late nineteenth-century dispute between industrialists and preservationists, between those who advocated an unlimited use of Niagara power regardless of the grandeur of the Falls and those who, while believing

Figure 13: Arthur Lumley, *Niagara Seen with Different Eyes* (1873).
From *Harper's Weekly*. The President and Fellows of Harvard College.

in a proper use of this power for economic purposes, still held out for
restrictions to preserve Niagara's beauty.[76] The patriotic figures of
Uncle Sam and John Bull appear in the lower left-hand corner of the
picture too.[77] Although this drawing was done seven years after the
Dominion of Canada came into existence, there are no "icons" of the
new nation, such as Johnny Canuck or Miss Canada.[78] Lumley's record
of mainly nineteenth-century tourists, very much a product of American ideals at the time of its construction, includes an Indian family. The
male in full regalia has laid down his weapons and extends his arms
to Niagara, a gesture whose meaning lies layered in discourses that
both idealize and degrade the non-European.

As Europeans opened up the New World, their explorations gave
rise to new forms of knowledge. Hennepin's seventeenth-century
description left out mention of the exploitation of and violence against
Native peoples resulting from political and religious expansion and

colonial domination. Instead, in the first drawing based on the first discovery narrative, Europe turns the "mirror" back on itself. Similarly, the first depiction of Indians at Niagara, Pehr Kalm's, can be located within the European taxonomic tradition, which identified non-European peoples as "lower" on the scale of humanity. Other themes and metaphors of art during the eighteenth century reflect a tendency to draw them as sublime, or as "noble savages," as expressed in the philosophies of Immanuel Kant and Jean-Jacques Rousseau. Then, the concept shifted again in the mid-nineteenth century due, in part, to the writings of Charles Darwin and John Stuart Mill.

During the early decades of the nineteenth century, the study of the physical differences between the various races developed into an obsessive demarcation of British (and European) people into "physical types" (the science of physiognomy) and "cerebral types" (the science of phrenology). In *An Historical Display of the Effects of Physical and Moral Causes on the Character and Circumstances of Nations* (1816), British schoolmaster John Bigland (1750–1832) argued that cerebral anatomy is a factor in human constitutions, and not climate. This new doctrine of phrenology was taken up by illustrators to explain the differences between Europeans and blacks. The best examples are the Caucasian and Negro drawings of French anatomist George Cuvier (1769–1832), published in *Le règne animal* (1836).[79] The discipline of philology, or historical linguistics, was also established at the beginning of the nineteenth century, and it described the relationship between ancient Asian and European languages. Further, there were various approaches to anthropology that emerged at this time.[80] But, with Charles Darwin's and Alfred Russel Wallace's virtually simultaneous discovery of the chief mechanism of biological evolution, attention was diverted from the scientific ways in which races could be differentiated to natural selection.

Charles Darwin's naturalist studies serve as both a construction of the "other" and a finding of the European "self" in relation to it. His early writings report on the distance between "savage" and "civilized" human beings, especially his 1832 *Diary* of a voyage to Tierra del Fuego (later published as *The Voyage of the Beagle* [1845]), which describes in detail what the Fuegian people wore, their skin colour, language, and forms of government.[81] And in his chapter "On the Races of Man" in *The Descent of Man and Selection in Relation to Sex* (1871), Darwin argues that species are not fixed, but develop according to rules of natural selection. While Darwin's doctrine of natural selection eventually displaced some racial theories (such as the dispute about whether humans were descended from a single source or were "multiple creations"), it gave more credence to others, including the notion of the supremacy of civilized whiteness.[82]

The ideas about savagery and civilization presented by Darwin found a different kind of expression in an essay by philosopher John Stuart Mill. In "Nature" (1873), Mill protests against the view (Kant's and Rousseau's) that the ideal of human conduct is found in conformity to nature. According to Mill, "the ways of nature are to be conquered, not obeyed."[83] By means of conflation or substitution, Mill also suggests that it was the European's duty to civilize those races that had yet to free themselves from nature's power. The illustration by Arthur Lumley can be located within this complex written tradition of Kant, Rousseau, Darwin, and Mill. Yet, it is clear that Lumley's iconic Indians—no longer a threat—are part of the touring masses. This in itself shows how much the image of the Indian at Niagara had changed: they are no longer identified with the forces of nature, or in opposition to cultures, but are part of the spectacle. Finally, with regard to the female characters in the Lumley drawing—those who stand, overwhelmed, on the brink (upper left-hand corner)—it will become obvious that these "sentimental women tourists" operate as a new trope to convey the seminal message. In analyzing the literary respondents—men and women—whose landscapes are replete with Indians and other descriptives that astonish, we will also be searching for writers whose "hysteria" stands in synecdochic relation to the forces of nature within the self.

Challenges of the Niagara Sublime

> Happy were the first discoverers of Niagara, those who could come unawares upon this view and upon that, whose feelings were entirely their own. With what gusto does Father Hennepin describe "this vast and prodigious cadence of water, which falls down after a surprising and astonishing manner, insomuch that the universe does not afford its parallel. 'Tis true Italy and Swedeland boast of some such things, but we may well say that they be sorry patterns when compared with this of which we do now speak."
>
> Margaret Fuller, *Summer on the Lakes in 1843* (1844)

WELL INTO THE NINETEENTH CENTURY, travellers continued to envy the earliest explorer at Niagara. As in the epigraph, Margaret Fuller wished she could arrive at Niagara "unawares," even though she also acknowledged Hennepin's own confession that he compared Niagara to European cascades. And, despite her desire to have feelings "entirely [her] own," Fuller (and her contemporaries) put a lot of emphasis on anticipating the scene: she read Hennepin's account, referred to his view, repeated many of his phrases, and tried to experience Niagara as she thought he had. In chapter 1, we saw how Hennepin's reaction linked him to the pre-sublime. With Margaret Fuller's account, too, we find her response to the waterfalls closely allied with the sublime of her day, which associated experiences in nature with pain and suffering.

The writers included in chapter 2 have all been chosen because they show influence. Since the organizing trope of this book is the first known account of Niagara Falls, all the subsequent writers and artists considered either inflected Hennepin's description/image or shared in a repertoire of convention associated with successive versions of the seminal depiction. At the same time, this study tries to appreciate how three centuries of respondents at Niagara, connected to their own cultural understandings (and to previous commentaries) also managed to create accounts that differed from each other. This study of the writers, therefore, also looks at how they followed sets of conventions associated with the aesthetics of their time (and followed in the footsteps of Hennepin, or another writer influenced by the Hennepin pattern of representation) to show how each percipient eventually widened and altered the traditions associated with literary aesthetics (and with Hennepin) and, through interactions with other kinds of expression, created for themselves something unique.

IN HIS SEARCH FOR THE PRESENCE of mountains, and for the words to express his admiration and horror, Hennepin borrowed the images and language associated with seventeenth-century perceptions of the natural world. Although Longinus's study of the rhetorical sublime—*Peri Hupsous*—had been available in English and on the Continent since the mid-sixteenth century, the natural sublime was not developed until the late decades of the seventeenth century and the early decades of the eighteenth with John Dennis's *Miscellanies in Verse and Prose* (1693), *The Moralists* of Anthony Ashley Cooper (Earl of Shaftesbury) (1709), and Joseph Addison's "Pleasures of the Imagination" (published in *The Spectator,* June 21–July 3, 1712). Dennis's contribution to the aesthetic concerned the causes and effects of the pre-sublime—the "transports," the "Horrours," and the "despair." Hennepin's expressions of exultation come from vocabulary made available through Dennis's writing. While Shaftesbury contributed to the critical theory, he used the term "sublime" infrequently—he preferred "enthusiastic" to describe the grandness of nature, the emotions it evoked, and the style in which those emotions were expressed. And, although the words "sublime" and "sublimity" appear frequently in Addison's essays (always in association with literary values and effects), it was his distinction between the primary and secondary pleasures of the imagination, between looking directly at nature and just reading about it, that may have encouraged travellers to go to Niagara to see the sight for themselves.

Addison's treatment of "greatness" and the psychological effect it has upon the soul shows the impact of nature as overwhelming, but suffering played no part in the pre-sublimes of Dennis, Shaftesbury, and

Addison. The eighteenth-century philosopher who transformed the sublime into this attitude of mind was also the writer most indebted to Longinus. In *A Philosophical Enquiry into the Origin of Our Ideas of the Sublime and Beautiful* (1757), Edmund Burke seems to apply Longinus's ideas about the emotional impact of the sublime as intense, even violent. However, where Longinus's sublimity is human-made and morally uplifting, Burke's is overwhelming, terrifying, and awful—it can be human-made, but it is more likely to stem from phenomena drawn from nature. And, while Burke allies feelings of fear and pain with the aesthetic, he also constructs a perceiving self that is "mastered" by the sublime. The following quotation from Burke is an account of this phenomenological process:

> In this case the mind is so entirely filled with its object, that it cannot entertain any other, nor by consequence reason on that object which employs it. Hence arises the great power of the sublime, that far from being produced by them, it anticipates our reasonings, and hurries us on by an Irresistible force.[1]

Twentieth-century critics Frances Ferguson, Samuel Monk, and Thomas Weiskel analyze this as the moment in Burke when the phenomenology of perception is set against the psychology of perception. While I shall say more in chapter 3 about how Burke sets up this deconstructive gesture, it is essential to note that the claim for his argument relies on a binary opposition between what the critics also call "empiricism" and "irrationalism."[2] Another deconstructive gesture that Burke employs in constructing sublimity sees a distinction between it and its alternative—beauty:

> There is a wide difference between admiration and love....The sublime, which is the cause of the former, always dwells on great objects and terrible; the latter on small ones, and pleasing; we submit to what we admire, but we love what submits to us.[3]

According to Frances Ferguson, the sublime "masters" us and is admired for having the power to do so. On the other hand, the beautiful relaxes and cajoles: it submits to us, and is what we "love" because we are superior to its power.[4] This linking of the sublime with submission/abasement became the modus operandi for many of the writers discussed in this chapter. Also of importance is the way in which Burke's theory of taste represents what Ferguson calls a violation of the social contract, "a kind of opting out of the pressures and dangers of the social because the sublime elevates one's individual relations with [nature]…above one's relationship to other human beings."[5] Thus, we arrive at another basic equation of the aesthetic with elevation/ transcendence. The tensions between these arrangements (submission/abasement, elevation/transcendence) became the contradictory basis for many of the accounts considered in this chapter.

The next development saw late eighteenth-century aestheticians disregard the sublime, and the "passions which concern self-preservation," to focus more on the picturesque and the beautiful, and on the "passions of society."[6] William Gilpin's *Three Essays* (1792), Uvedale Price's *Essay on the Picturesque* (1794), and Richard Payne Knight's *The Landscape: A Didactic Poem in Three Books* (1795) all reworked definitions of the sublime and the beautiful to illustrate rules of picturesque painting. The disagreement between Price and Knight about whether the sublime and the picturesque were categories distinct from each other or from the traditional concept of beauty was complicated, at its height (1798), by Gilpin's use of the dual term "picturesque beauty," and by his definition of the picturesque as "that kind of beauty which would look well in a picture."[7] In this chapter, we look at how different ideas of aesthetic enjoyment were applied through versions of Gilpin's picturesque beauty and Price's sublimity by one of the first recorded women travellers to Niagara—Elizabeth Simcoe (1790s).

Commentators at the waterfalls during the early to mid-nineteeth century revealed influences of the Burkean sublime (and other companion rhetorics) when they associated the experience of viewing the Falls with things painful (Frances Trollope, 1832, and Margaret Fuller, 1844), frustrating (Nathaniel Hawthorne, 1835), and demanding (Anna Jameson, 1838). Yet, even as they were circumscribed by their traditions, their writings extended beyond the pale of sublime convention. Some created unique experiences that were mystic or even liminal (Hawthorne, Caroline Gilman, 1838, and Charles Dickens, 1842), and others imagined different "recoveries" after they had been mastered by the sublime (Fuller and Jameson).

Because the aesthetic as Burke envisioned it was totally bound to the senses, adaptations of sublimity by Immanuel Kant and William Wordsworth de-emphasized the violent sensations and the melodramatic machinery to stress an intellectual component. These developments were called the "educated" and the "Romantic" sublimes. In later nineteenth-century responses to Niagara, we see a sense of aesthetic satisfaction becoming more and more closely allied with the will, and with moral imperatives (Anthony Trollope, 1862, and Henry James, 1871).

In his "Analytic of the Sublime," published in *Critique of Judgement* (1790), Kant argues that the sublime, which causes reverence as well as pain, is "a negative pleasure":

> The feeling of the sublime is, therefore, at once a feeling of displeasure, arising from the inadequacy of the imagination in the aesthetic estimation of magnitude to attain to its estimation by reason, and a simultaneously awakened pleasure, arising from this very judgment of the inadequacy of the greatest faculty of sense being in accord with ideas of reason, in so far as the effort to attain these is for us the law.[8]

For Kant, the subject acknowledges his/her weakness (in "estimation of [the] magnitude") as well as insignificance ("the inadequacy of the imagination"), but this repression of certain aspects of the human spirit becomes a positive experience when a sense of superior self-worth (by "reason") is recuperated in the interest of a higher, moral good ("the law"). Similarly, for Wordsworth the sublime is an event capable of moral significance. What he describes in "Lines Composed a Few Miles Above Tintern Abbey" (1798) and in *The Prelude* (1805 version) involves a reworking of the aesthetic so that both beauty and terror are inevitable parts of the experience. In Wordsworth's sublime, though, there is nothing awesome or fearsome, but only a loss of that Burkean "self-consciousness" and a growing sense of unity with external forms. By virtue of his idea of "spots in time"—memories infused with current perceptions—the scene is informed with a host of recollections, associations, and, ultimately, meanings. The resulting sense of elevation and transport leads to a release from the senses (and the limits of language). While it has been argued that Wordsworth transformed the sublime back to the sacred, he did this through a recognition of the habitual and the familiar as especially remarkable.[9] The Niagara writings that describe a level of consciousness associated with the Kantian and/or Wordsworthian sublimes involve the struggle of reason over irrationality and are preoccupied with the principles of taste (Hawthorne, Anthony Trollope, and James). These last authors also relied on the importance of repeatability—the habitual, the familiar, the "spots in time"—just as earlier responses were based on the original pattern of representation. We turn now to one of the first known female writers at Niagara, who had read her Hennepin but who ended up composing a different view from his, and then we move into the nineteenth century and through the developing aesthetics of the sublime.

Elizabeth Simcoe

THERE ARE NO RECORDED female explorers at Niagara Falls until the late eighteenth century. According to Mary Louise Pratt, the pre-Victorian woman's access to travel outside Europe was very limited, and her ability to publish in the field of travel writing was even more so.[10] As readers, though, women were significant and active participants in the genre. Hence, maps, travel books, and testimonies contributed substantially to Elizabeth Posthuma Gwillim Simcoe's geographical knowledge of North America before she arrived there and long after she took up residence. Simcoe, who had read many of the missionary accounts, including Hennepin's, was fond of drawing maps and sketching landscapes.[11] As wife of John Graves Simcoe, the first Lieutenant-Governor of Upper Canada, she travelled widely in her husband's domain, taking long trips into the interior and around the Niagara frontier. Simcoe met many people on her excursions, and, according to one observer who dined with her, she acted "superior" and held a "traditional" view of the role of women.[12] While she may have presented herself differently as the Lieutenant-Governor's lady, in her *Diary* she describes an unconventional woman who fishes for her supper and sleeps in a tent:

> We came to so miserable a house where we were to lodge tonight within a league of Grenadier Island that we preferred pitching a Tent for ourselves letting the Children sleep in the Boat, & left the House for the Gentlemen. While the Tent was pitching I fished & caught a small Perch. (70)

As a child in England, Elizabeth Simcoe was often unwell, and as a young married woman she was confined for long periods in child-birth. In Upper Canada, she led a different, more active life: it was not unusual for her to sleep outdoors or to go off exploring for days at a time without her husband. (Often, she was escorted by his second-in-command, Captain Thomas Talbot.) But her husband's gout, migraines, and chronic ill-health constantly drew her back from these diversions to the domestic world. And their two children who accompanied them to the New World were frequently sick with the "ague."

Writing was Elizabeth Simcoe's other "wild" diversion from wifely duties. In Upper Canada, she kept two diaries—a brief, "rough" one in which she wrote every day, and another, more "polished" version.[13] The first diary, bound in parchment, consists of references to books she had read, factual reports on daily events, including the particulars of her husband's ailments and activities, and lists of letters written to her friend Mary Anne Burges (an author and naturalist) and to her children's nanny, Mrs. Hunt (in charge of the four eldest daughters left in England). Elizabeth Simcoe also used the rough diary to record her nightmares, the most startling of which describes an attack by American rebels in the woods.[14] (Simcoe's nightmare says much about how this late eighteenth-century British diplomat's wife viewed the enemy. Her husband had fought in the war with the United States and after Britain lost, he was moved north of the border and put in charge of Upper Canada.) The second diary, bound in board, revises these on-the-spot entries and also includes small sketches of buildings, watercolours, and maps composed on paper and on birchbark.[15] This second diary was mailed in sections to Mrs. Hunt. Since Simcoe sent portions of her "polished" work abroad, she wrote with the intention of being read. Even though the audience may have been only herself and the children's nanny, the writing is structured according to conventional literary norms—the traveller is the protagonist; the itinerary is the plot; and the departure and return are the formal beginning and ending.

In both versions of the diary, the writing was not a record of emotionally charged events. For example, from the letters to Mrs. Hunt we know that Simcoe's youngest child, Katherine, died during a trip into the interior.[16] There is no mention of her daughter's death in the *Diary*, though, and no diary entries immediately after the child's burial (from April 18 to May 2, 1794). Her silence is significant. Simcoe's writing, sketching, and other forms of "interior" escape were apparently considered inappropriate during the period of mourning. Instead, writing was a mapping of important political and historical events, a record of travel, and an artful arrangement of the world and the people within it. For example, the following close observation of Native customs, described in the manner of pictures with words such as "ease," "composure," and "smooth," relates how they moved their canoes through the watery landscape:[17]

To see a Birch Canoe managed with that inexpressible ease & composure which is the characteristic of an Indian is the prettiest sight imaginable. A man usually paddles at one end of it & a woman at the other but in smooth water little exertion is wanting & they sit quietly as if to take the air. The Canoe appears to move as if by clock-work. (107)

Simcoe continues her observations on how congruous and balanced, poised and kinetic Native people are by contrasting them with Europeans, who look "awkward & in a bustle" (ibid.). Perceived in terms of her late eighteenth-century cultural values, Simcoe's tropes—which make the Native appear competent and the European unskilled—are based on the idea of the "noble savage" popularized by Jean-Jacques Rousseau's *Essay on the Origin of Languages* (1781). In that work, Rousseau also treats the aboriginal, who is lacking in "white" civilization, in a positive way and as "one" with nature.

In the *Diary,* Niagara is an important geographical location for Elizabeth Simcoe and an important subject: the Niagara sections take up one-half of the entire book—five out of ten chapters. The Simcoes spent their first year in the area (July 1792–July 1793), as well as the next summer (May–September 1794) and half of the following year (June–November 1795). On the first visit, they travelled by stagecoach to the waterfalls. Simcoe's detailed, sensory record of that journey pays close attention to the composition of the sights—"the road is entirely flat," "the fall is…but 170 feet in height," "the River…[is] on a declivity for 3 miles"—and to the qualities of the sounds—the waterfalls "are heard…before Rain when the wind is Easterly" and the river "rushes in the most rapid manner" (76). Yet, Simcoe's account does not convey the stock of emotions and adjectives that Hennepin's contained even though she had read him and was anticipating his Niagara. Instead, her measured language gives exact distances and heights, and she sums up her first impression of Niagara as "a very fine sight." Simcoe's response to the natural world—neither a self-reflection nor a description of human passions—treats its composition and symmetry:

> The falls itself is the grandest sight imaginable from the immense width of waters & the circular form of the grand fall; to the left of which is an Island between it & the Montmorency Fall [the Horseshoe Falls]. A few Rocks separate this from Ft. Schlosser Fall [the American Falls] which passing over a straight ledge of rock has not the beauty of the circular form or its green color, the whole center of the circular fall being of the brightest green & below it is frequently seen a Rainbow. (Ibid.)

This kind of landscape analysis includes the locations of various geological features, their shapes (she mentions the "circular form" of the Horseshoe Falls three times in one passage) and their colours (the contrasting shades of green). In addition to describing these visual characteristics in writing, Simcoe composed a watercolour painting of the scene, which she called *Niagara Falls, Ontario, July 30, 1792* (see figure 14). The picture also appears much different from the Hennepin-based engraving, even though Simcoe had anticipated seeing *his* Niagara. The Hennepin view consists of a tall and a broad cascade, a thin cross-stream, a high foreground with a number of figures on the bank, a meandering river stream, and a mountain chain; Simcoe's includes two stunted waterfalls, one of which is broad and curved, a low, unpeopled foreground (directly across the river from where Hennepin stood), and a shortened horizon. Hennepin may have been the important "secondary pleasure" (to use Addison's terminology), but once on-site Simcoe organized, arranged, and measured the scene through a different frame—the picturesque. Its aesthetic conventions are obvious in the ways in which the vertical lines of the tall trees and their horizontal branches are set against the smooth glassy water at the river's bank, which is in turn contrasted with the dark roughness of the land and with the variegated lines and graduated colours (indicating turbulence) closer to the waterfalls. In her composition of the picturesque, Simcoe appears to have been working with Gilpin's varied and harmonized forms, colours, and lights, drawn from his *Observations on the River Wye* (1782). His following methodological description indicates how he thought nature should look, which in turn is echoed in Simcoe's picture of Niagara:

> Nature is always great in design but unequal in composition. She is an admirable colourist; and can harmonize her tints with infinite variety, and inimitable beauty; but is seldom so correct in composition as to produce an harmonious whole.[18]

After Simcoe had sketched Niagara's likeness, she climbed down the steep bank of the gorge with the aid of an "Indian ladder" made of dead trees. Her record of this descent is different from her picture of the waterfalls, possibly because she experienced danger, which does not belong to the picturesque:

> I descended an exceeding steep hill to get to the table Rock from where the view of the falls is tremendously fine. Men sometimes

Figure 14: Elizabeth Simcoe, *Niagara Falls, Ontario, July 30, 1792*.
(Archives of Ontario, F47-11-1-0-71.10006923).

descend the Rocks below this projecting point, but it is attended
with great danger and perhaps little picturesque advantage. (77)

William Gilpin made it very clear in his vignettes of alpine avalanches
in *Observations…on Several Parts of England* (1786) that it is the idea
of perils which excites, rather than the actuality.[19] Hence, Simcoe's
experience may have come too close to the mark. After this, she tried
to find the proper viewpoint—the "elevated eye," which is another
principle of picturesque beauty suggested by Gilpin.[20] From this perspective she resumed her report:

> The prodigious Spray which arises from the foam at the bottom of
> the fall adds to the grandeur of the scene which is wonderfully
> fine & after the eye becomes more familiar to the objects I think
> the pleasure will be greater in dwelling upon them. After taking
> some refreshment on the table Rock we went 3 miles to the
> Chippewa Fort admiring the Rapids all the way. (Ibid.)

Words such as "prodigious," "grandeur," "wonderfully fine," and "pleasure" are also found in the earliest depiction of Niagara. Nonetheless,

Simcoe's excitement, confined to descriptions of nature, is not an emotional affliction like Hennepin's was, because her impression is not filtered through the pre-sublime.

Detouring from the Portage Road to view a spectacle called the Twelve Mile Pond, a "grand," "vast," "wild," "delightful," and "pleasant" scene, Simcoe witnesses eddies so strong that whole trees are spun around, upright, in the current (94). Hers is the earliest recorded visit by a woman to the feature later known as the Whirlpool:

> Vast Rocks surround this bend of the River & they are covered with Pine & hemlock spruce, some cascades among the Rocks add to the wild appearance. These scenes have afforded me so much delight that I class this day with those in which I remember to have felt the greatest pleasure from fine objects, whether of Art or Nature. (Ibid.)

Her way of classifying nature as one "fine object," among others, that affords much pleasure and delight is characteristic of Gilpin's refined code of appraisal and judgment.

On a final visit to Niagara in 1795, Elizabeth Simcoe went back to the Whirlpool, drawn to the great confusion of hewn timber rotating in the water:

[they] whirl about & probably will continue so till the end of the World for they never appear to go beyond the circle of a certain distance & sometimes are set quite upright by the currents, it is a curious scene. (161)

Standing above this dynamic vortex, she seems discomposed by the logs' "curious" whirling, which is uncharacteristic of the language of picturesque beauty. She has entered something that Gilpin's rhetoric does not account for. The Whirlpool's tortured circling—a symbol of infinity, upheaval, dark suffering—is more akin to the language used by Burke in his *Enquiry*, or even by Uvedale Price in his *Essay on the Picturesque* which at one point repeats Burke's ideas of pain and terror. In any case, the painting of the Whirlpool that Simcoe executed represents an artistic detachment from these intense feelings. *At the Whirlpool Rapids* (1795) combines a roughness of texture (the bumpy cliffs), with an irregularity of outline (the spiky pine trees), with contrasting lights, shades, and masses. Again, this is the picturesque as generally expressed through the work of William Gilpin.

For Elizabeth Simcoe, writing and sketching functioned as diversions from the domestic world. But the place to which she "escaped" was not wild in the same way as Hennepin's Niagara was. Simcoe's work does not evoke the level of emotional terror found in the first artifact to emerge from a European vision, which shows the discoverers turning from the scene and covering their ears, because her language comes from different strains of rhetoric. However, the next record to be considered here does convey a sense of fear, awe, and discomfort. In Frances Trollope's description of Niagara are featured many of the qualities of Burke's sublime, including the violent impact of nature on the faculties which results in the paradoxical sensations of pleasure and pain.

Frances Trollope

FRANCES TROLLOPE, who was already fifty years old when she arrived at Niagara in 1830, was not a typical nineteenth-century tourist: she had come to North America with a number of grandiose schemes meant to restore her family's wealth and social position. Various financial disasters induced by the misfortune or mismanagement of her husband had caused the Trollopes to suffer ruin; reduced to poverty and obliged to support her family, she had packed up two of her daughters and one son and followed the children's French and drawing instructor, Auguste Hervieu, and her friend, Frances Wright, to America.

By the first few decades of the nineteenth century, travel writing had become a very appealing medium of expression for women as well as for men. While being popular, it was also an established, respectable, and relatively undemanding literary genre which offered, among other things, "a ready-made form [and] a surefire subject."[21] Trollope's companion, Frances Wright, had already found success with this genre in her *View of Society and Manners in America* (1821) and may have encouraged Trollope to keep a record of their travel.

Their choice of itinerary appears to have been tailored not to a "tourist" agenda but to relieve Trollope's financial needs. First, they went to Tennessee to inspect a utopian settlement. But the colony in Nashoba presented such primitive accommodation and malarial conditions that they left within ten days. When Frances Trollope wrote down her impressions of Nashoba, she used a series of dots (nine in total) to signify the inadequacy of words to convey her thoughts, a form of punctuation that comes up in her later descriptions of nature: ".........one glance sufficed to convince me that every idea I had formed of the place was as far as possible from the truth."[22] The way in which she anticipates the scene, builds up to it, and then is disappointed by it is a pattern that she followed in her writing about Niagara too. After leaving Nashoba, Trollope and her party went north, to Cincinnati. There, they planned success with a wax exhibition at the Western Museum, featuring a spectacle called the "Invisible Girl" and a number of tableaux from Dante's *Inferno*. The show never opened. Next, they funded a commercial-artistic venture—a live/work studio for writers and painters called the Cincinnati Bazaar (and later dubbed "Trollope's Folly"). Conceived in the style of a Moorish temple, it was begun in 1828 and finished in 1829. But, despite the fact that Auguste Hervieu's portraits and paintings, on exhibition in the Bazaar, were successful, the project was yet another financial disaster.[23]

Trollope's enterprising ventures in the United States may have failed, but all the notes and recollections of her travels, later transformed into a publishable product, brought her immediate success and financial reward. Called *Domestic Manners of the Americans*, the book was underwritten by Auguste Hervieu's talents as a portrait painter and published in London in 1832 (two years after her trip abroad). The penultimate chapter of *Domestic Manners* records her visit to Niagara. Trollope was near the end of her journey and had already formed an uncomplimentary view of Americans, when she took advantage of the proximity of Canada, crossed the Niagara River, and stepped onto "colonial" ground. The passage that follows amounts to a mini-essay on stereotypes that made up Trollope's sense of home, for, as Ian Ousby contends, the English take their sense of England with them "like a precious family heirloom or, worse, like a sort of virginity to be preserved intact from all the dangers that threaten it."[24] Hence, we see that Trollope's image of trees, buildings, and children shaped her experience of her own country as much as her reaction to Canada:

> I was delighted to see British oaks, and British roofs, and British boys and girls. These latter, as if to impress upon us that they were citizens, made bows and courtesies as we passed, and this little touch of long unknown civility produced great effect. "See these dear children, mamma! do they not look English! how I love them!" was the exclamation it produced. (278–79)

This perception had also been expressed by a contemporaneous English traveller in Canada. Captain Basil Hall's *Travels in North America in the Years 1827 and 1828* (published in Edinburgh in 1829) contains an extended dialogue on the British "presence" at Niagara Falls (as well as etchings and sketches made with a camera lucida and designed according to picturesque conventions learned at the Royal Military College at Woolwich). Frances Trollope had purchased Hall's *Travels* in Cincinnati in July 1830, and she may have been relying on his description, still fresh in her mind, when she admired the colonial flora and fauna, and when she anticipated Niagara: "I had heard so much of the surpassing beauty…that I expected to be disappointed and [I expected] to find reality flat after description" (263, 270). A way of seeking truth by comparing the representation with the original, or art with nature, Trollope's record also contains aspects of Addison's aesthetic proposition that the description of a visible object is more delightful than the object itself.[25] Accordingly, at first sight of the waterfalls, Trollope measured her satisfaction by the degree to which it conformed to an imagined ideal: "I saw all I had wished for, hoped for, dreamed of" (279). For her, Niagara appears as a kind of utopia—ideally perfect, like the courteous children. She takes such pleasure in the first view that she refuses to deliver up her immediate impression:

> It is not for me to attempt a description of Niagara; I feel I have no powers for it.…If any man living can describe the scene we looked

upon it is *himself* [a fellow tourist and writer Thomas Hamilton] and I trust he will do it. As for me, I can only say that wonder, terror, and delight completely overwhelmed me. (Ibid., emphasis mine)

Just as the first ecstasies of the scene are overpowering her—"wonder, terror, and delight completely overwhelmed me"—the proximity of "himself"—Thomas Hamilton, an important member of the Blackwood group of writers—silences her.[26] While William Gilpin felt disdain for other travellers pursuing the same pleasures, because he assumed that not all tourists were capable of exalted feelings or refined tastes, his was an implied anxiety.[27] Trollope's submission into silence, however, is an actuality. As such, it seems more in keeping with Burke's dissatisfaction with being "imposed upon" because, for him, the sublime represented a kind of opting out of the social for an "elevation" with the natural.[28] Hence, when Thomas Hamilton tries to share Trollope's "moment," the sense of power that may be involved in her submission (her "mastery" by the sublime) is overshadowed by the way she feels "mastered" by the presence of a male writer.

When she finds herself alone again, she breaks her silence and writes of the intensity of her experience, of the strain on her nerves. The pains of her constraint—strangely pleasurable—make her incapable of describing nature, but very loquacious as regards what she calls the "emotion of the senses":

I wept with a strange mixture of pleasure and of pain, and certainly was, for some time, too violently affected in the physique to be capable of much pleasure; but when this emotion of the senses subsided, and I had recovered some degree of composure, my enjoyment was very great indeed. (279–80)

This pattern of anticipation and hesitation, protests of inexpressibility and of sensory inundation, and eventual recovery—"my enjoyment was very great indeed"—became familiar trappings of sublime writing at Niagara during the first half of the nineteenth century.

Frances Trollope's dilemma, which aroused a pleasurable, coercive empowerment, is a different kind of aesthetic from Elizabeth Simcoe's. Simcoe was apprehensive about scaling the side of the cliff, and her subsequent confrontation with danger did not produce glorification of the fear and terror that may have accompanied that experience. Simcoe's pleasure was largely intellectual too—she was not overwhelmed because the precepts of her aesthetic (Gilpin's picturesque beauty) did not encourage her to dwell on sensory deprivations. For Trollope, on the other hand, fear was a condition of the aesthetic. According to twentieth-century aesthetician Walter John Hipple, this kind of sublimity, based on Burke's philosophy, "excites delight from presenting ideas of pain and danger without actually afflicting [her]."[29] Whether Trollope's terror was real or imagined is not the issue. What is important is that she claims to feel pleasure and pain, which shifts again into "surprise and astonishment" when she talks about the "shadowy mystery" beyond the ken of sensory experience:

> To say that I was not disappointed is but a weak expression to convey the surprise and astonishment which this long dreamed of scene produced. It has to me something beyond its vastness; there a shadowy mystery hangs about it which neither the eye nor even the imagination can penetrate. (280)

Trollope has found a tension in the sublime, a dilemma in her pleasurable, coercive empowerment. The aesthetic prescribes that her emotions should elude language: she is supposed to be awestruck, submissively obedient to the pains that constrain her and not rational enough to have powers to describe her experience. She ends with a kind of benign contempt for this process, calling it "dangerous": "…but I dare not dwell on this, it is a dangerous subject, and any attempt to describe the sensations produced must lead directly to nonsense" (ibid.). There are several ways in which artists and writers identify with Niagara's real or apparent danger. The figures in the Hennepin-based drawing react to the waterfalls with curiosity and fear. Other images evocative of untamed wilderness, including armed Indians and drowning rebels, illustrate how the idea of danger evolved through shifts in aesthetics. These shifts are reflected in the way in which writers discuss Niagara too. Hennepin described the violence of the water, the roaring and thunderous noise, and the perpetual mists as horrifying. Trollope's differently aestheticized version of a similar experience also leaves her "stunned by the ceaseless roar," "trembling from the concussion," and "breathing painfully in the moist atmosphere." Somehow, there is "pleasure" in these dangers:

> Why is it so exquisite a pleasure to stand for hours drenched in spray, stunned by the ceaseless roar, trembling from the concussion that shakes the very rock you cling to, and breathing painfully

FIGURE 15: Anonymous, *Horseshoe Falls at Niagara,*
entrance to the cavern on the English side, 1801
(Archives of Ontario, C281-0-0-0-19.10003079).

in the moist atmosphere that seems to have less of air than water
in it?[30] Yet pleasure it is, and I almost think the greatest I ever
enjoyed. (285)

Burke wrote that pain and danger are accompanied by self-glorification; he also prioritized a number of privations, and Trollope pays heed to these stipulations. Hers include a continuous drenching mist, loud, repetitive sounds, difficulty in keeping a foothold, and difficulty in breathing (to name a few). The greater the risk, the more pain and sublimity:

> We more than once approached the entrance to this appalling cavern, but I never fairly entered it, though two or three of my party did,—I lost my breath entirely; and the pain at my chest was so severe, that not all my curiosity could enable me to endure it. (Ibid.)

To enter the "appalling cavern" behind the Horseshoe Falls, one must walk through the cascade of water. This threshold is called "Behind the Sheet" (see figure 15). Here, Trollope has encountered something for which civilized discourse cannot account. Even though the sensibility of the sublime had made British caverns such as Yordas Cave and the Devil's Arse[31] into popular nineteenth-century sites, her way of talking about the "shadowy mystery," the pleasurable pain, and the impossibility of language to describe the experience is meant to highlight the uniqueness of Niagara's watery abode and of her own response to it. Her hesitation—at the cave's entrance, with her writing—is also meant to indicate this: it is "dangerous" to go on because "nonsense" will result.

Nathaniel Hawthorne suffered Niagara in a similar way, but the idea of producing nonsense and his notions of unworthiness prevented him, at first, from experiencing the "breathless" pleasure. To move beyond these feelings to ones of rapture and self-glorification, he created a different tension in the anticipation/disappointment/constraint pattern. This new way of writing about Niagara allowed him to transcend the "cruder" symptoms of fear and, ideally, appear less excited and febrile and more rational and in control.

Nathaniel Hawthorne

NATHANIEL HAWTHORNE, who begins his account of Niagara by comparing himself to a "pilgrim," anticipates looking at the scene from the window of the stagecoach, yet he keeps letting his eyes and mind wander, "because my treasury of anticipated enjoyments, comprising all the wonders of the world, had nothing else so magnificent, and I was loth to exchange the pleasures of hope for those of memory so soon."[32] He sets up Niagara as a pinnacle of experience by using words and phrases such as "treasury of anticipated enjoyments," "wonders of the world," "so magnificent," and "pleasures of hope." Hawthorne follows the same pattern as Trollope—he puts off arriving at Niagara and delays the actual moment of beholding, and of describing, the view. In fact, he had intended to travel in the summer of 1832, but an outbreak of cholera in Canada altered these plans and he did not set out until September 1832.[33] This delay may have allowed Hawthorne to read Frances Trollope's *Domestic Manners of the Americans,* which was published during the first half of that year.

As the coach drew nearer to the Falls, Hawthorne devotes his attention to the auditory experience and confesses that he is apprehensive of the moment when he cannot delay hearing Niagara: "I began to listen for the roar of the cataract, and trembled with a sensation like dread, as the moment drew nigh, when its voice of ages must roll, for the first time, on my ear" (281). The "sensation like dread" is, of course, a property of the sublime. After responding to Niagara's sound effects, Hawthorne makes a point of denying himself the full view. While his coach companion—a French gentleman—expresses loud admiration, Hawthorne "threw [himself] back and closed [his] eyes" (ibid.). This pattern of anticipation succeeded by denial is associated with attaining the right Burkean sublime attitude.

Upon arrival in Manchester (now called Niagara Falls, New York), he finally bolts from the stagecoach, and then confesses that he is "ashamed" of acting so impulsively:

I am quite ashamed of myself here. Not that I ran, like a madman, to the falls, and plunged into the thickest of the spray—never stopping to breathe, till breathing was impossible; not that I committed this, or any other suitable extravagance. (281–82)

He uses words like "madman" and "suitable extravagance"; he wants to run to the Falls and plunge in the spray, but he actually does quite the opposite. For Hawthorne, irrational behaviour could be imagined, but not put into action. If he refuses to dwell on the physical and emotional experience (unlike Frances Trollope), he will not write her "nonsense." Still at a distance from the Falls (he has not seen Niagara, just heard it), he prolongs the tension, savours his anticipation, and keeps his emotions at bay:

> On the contrary, I alighted with perfect decency and composure, gave my cloak to the black waiter, pointed out my baggage, and inquired, not the nearest way to the cataract, but about the dinner-hour. (282)

Whereas Trollope wrote of pain and terror induced by Niagara's spray, mists, and vapours, Hawthorne's privations come from trying to appear "decent" and "composed." He prepares his dress for dinner, focuses on social details, and continues to deny himself the full sublime experience. Yet, the distance he puts between his mind and his emotions appears to have the opposite effect:

> Within the last fifteen minutes, my mind had grown strangely benumbed, and my spirits apathetic, with a slight depression, not decided enough to be termed sadness. My enthusiasm was in a deathlike slumber. (282)

This catalogue of symptoms—numbness, apathy, and depression—entered Trollope's account after the most anticipated moment, when she stood in front of Niagara with all her senses finely tuned. Hawthorne seems to experience a similar sequence of emotions and he has not even faced the Falls.

Hawthorne continues to put off the inevitable: he dines, smokes a cigar on the piazza, walks to the toll house on Goat Island, signs his name in the guest book, examines the knick-knacks in the museum, and reads a few newspapers. With a souvenir—appropriately, a "pilgrim's staff"—he walks to the southern tip of Goat Island and looks upriver. Still not looking toward the waterfalls, still diverging from the traditional view, Hawthorne follows a trail to the edge of the American cascade. His language becomes unspecific when he finally describes the view. Using words like "broad sheet" of water, "precipice," and "headlong" flow, he seems to fall back on Hennepin's impressions. He takes another path to the corner of the Horseshoe Falls and, trying to find a unique perspective, "took in the whole scene at a glance, and tried to comprehend it in one vast idea" (283). Continuing his wanderings, he goes down the slippery Biddle staircase to the base of Goat Island. Right at the edge of the cataract now, Hawthorne sees a rainbow quiver briefly into being before it is whipped asunder by the wind and then enveloped in spray. "Were my long desires fulfilled? And had I seen Niagara?" (ibid.). The fact that he asks the question indicates that Hawthorne is not experiencing the same Niagara as Frances Trollope did. His is a tamer version of her "wild" scene—even the rainbow, like his spirits, is "dashed." Previously, Hawthorne had confessed that anticipation was better than experience; now he suggests that Niagara does not live up to expectations:

> Oh, that I had never heard of Niagara till I beheld it!...Had its own mysterious voice been the first to warn me of its existence, then, indeed, I might have knelt down and worshipped. But I had come thither, haunted with a vision of foam and fury, and dizzy cliffs, and an ocean tumbling out of the sky—a scene, in short, which Nature had too much good taste and calm simplicity to realize. (284)

He had expected a "vision of foam and fury," but the scene "had too much good taste and calm simplicity" and did not compare to the image he had formed (of a wild, uncivilized Niagara). Hawthorne blames himself for entertaining "false conceptions" and attributes his disappointment to unworthiness: "I climbed the precipice, and threw myself on the earth—feeling that I was unworthy to look at the Great Falls, and careless about beholding them again" (ibid.). As with other writers, contemporaneous conventions help to explain this reaction. The precepts of seventeenth-century pre-sublime aesthetics led Louis Hennepin to feel inadequate to the task of describing the scene. Elizabeth Simcoe was influenced by the principles of Gilpin's picturesque beauty, causing her to frame Niagara differently. She was not overwhelmed by the view in the way that Frances Trollope was, nor did Simcoe talk about the impossibility of using language to describe Niagara (and then go on to use it anyway). The way in which Hawthorne anticipated a "wild" Niagara, felt disappointed, then unworthy, had more to do with Burkean sublime expectations than with his merits as a writer (or as a human being). Hawthorne's intentions as a writer prove this point. In a letter to Franklin Pierce on June 28, 1832, he confesses: "[I will] acquire an (undoubtedly) immense literary reputation, but...I cannot commence writing till I have visited Canada."[34] The journey was to yield a collection of stories, which were to be connected by the narration of the pilgrim alluded to at the onset of his Niagara piece. Although *The Story-Teller,* a two-volume manuscript, was never published in its entirety, some tales were printed in *The Token* and others in *The New England Magazine.* "My Visit to Niagara" (1834), published in the latter journal in February 1835, was attributed to the author of "The Gray Champion."[35] The story also appeared in the first edition of

Twice-Told Tales (1837). The rhetorical pressure to produce something new (if only to sell books, which is why authors like Hawthorne wrote travel narratives) is a common factor in writings about Niagara. Hawthorne makes his account unique by denying "his pilgrim" the full Burkean sublime, a form of resistance that creates a satisfying experience for the reader.

After seeing Niagara, feeling a dread-like sensation, expressing his disappointment, and confessing to his unworthiness, Hawthorne retires to his hotel room. With the windows vibrating to the motion of Niagara, he dreams of "a great tempest...of storm and whirlwind" (285). He wakes, "rejoiced to find that my former awe and enthusiasm were reviving" (ibid.). This second aural impression is another way of getting past the "prescribed" view to some other, supposedly deeper experience. On his last day at Niagara, Hawthorne sits on Table Rock with his feet dangling over the edge: "I felt as if suspended in the open air. Never before had my mind been in such perfect unison with the scene" (285). The effect of the rolling water, rising mist, and turmoil "soothes, while it awes the mind" (286). This is a new kind of sublime. After going through anticipation, denial, disappointment, and self-abasement, he has arrived at a state where mind and feelings are awed, yet calmed.

The moment of serenity is broken by other tourists, however. Hawthorne observes how they "do" Niagara—his reports on their varied impressions are followed by comparisons with his own. The summary of their characters and individual approaches to nature highlights the worthiness of his "pilgrim-like," puritanical reaction. For example, he seems taken aback by an American who "labored earnestly to adjust Niagara to the description [in Captain Basil Hall's book], departing, at last, without one new idea or sensation of his own" (287). This is literary foreshadowing, but it also underscores the uniqueness of his own ideas and sensations (and makes Hawthorne sound as if he were already defending his "immense literary reputation").

At sunset, he descends the path to the lower bank. From this more solitary perspective, the narrator writes about another rainbow:

> The golden sunshine tinged the sheet of the American cascade, and painted on its heaving spray the broken semicircle of a rainbow, Heaven's own beauty crowning earth's sublimity. My steps were slow, and I paused long at every turn of the descent, as one lingers and pauses, who discerns a brighter and brightening excellence in what he must soon behold no more. (288)

Like the first rainbow that was "dashed" by a gust of wind, the second rainbow is "broken," but its crested shape is compared to a heavenly crown. These are words of worship, which show how Hawthorne's language is shifting toward a different literary convention. He ends up "enjoying" Niagara's "rapture":

> The solitude of the old wilderness now reigned over the whole vicinity of the falls. My enjoyment became the more rapturous, because no poet shared it—nor wretch, devoid of poetry, profaned it: but the spot, so famous through the world, was all my own! (Ibid.)

This way of finding the real source of the sublime in solitude and in the self draws on Wordsworth's "Lines Composed a Few Miles above Tintern Abbey." In that poem, Wordsworth's narrator, who is on a solitary tour of the secluded Wye Valley (and the ruins of Tintern Abbey), remarks on the differences between the landscape he walks through and the remembered "picture of the mind." In so doing, he often opposes sight (in the first stanza below) and true vision (in the second passage below):

> These beauteous forms,
> Through a long absence, have not been to me
> As is a landscape to a blind man's eye…
> …
> While with an eye made quiet by the power
> Of harmony, and the deep power of joy,
> We see into the life of things.[36]

Hawthorne's narrator does this too when he talks of being "loth to exchange the pleasures of hope for those of memory so soon" (281), and when he moves from mere sensations to a more spirited concept of Niagara, in which he "discerns a brighter and brightening excellence in what he must soon behold no more" (288). Where Wordsworth senses in nature

> A motion and a spirit, that impels
> All thinking things, all objects of all thought,
> And rolls through all things (lines 100–102),

Hawthorne learns to feel "as if suspended in the open air. Never before had my mind been in such perfect unison with the scene" (285). The

American writer's employment of the Wordsworthian Romantic sublime, therefore, sees nature communicating with "[his] mind" as if to console, uplift, and ennoble.

In their writings, Simcoe is curious but not fearful, Trollope is terrified and overwhelmed, and Hawthorne is complacent and enraptured. All have inflected the topos of their aesthetics and offered up individual descriptions. Following, Caroline Gilman, an American poet who came out of a different language world, managed to combine conventional description, psychological effect, and explicitly religious testimony in her waterfalls rhapsody.

Caroline Gilman

CAROLINE GILMAN'S DESCRIPTION of Niagara, which begins with the narrator framing the view through a hotel window that overlooks the Falls, conveys many of Niagara's sensory delights: its aural effect—"I have listened to their roar"; its visual effect—"I have sprung…to see the white foam glitter"; and its emotional effect—"I have felt a spell on my soul."[37] For Gilman, the impression from afar is indicative of a visionary experience, "as if Deity stood visibly there" (205). This is the language of Dennis's, Shaftesbury's, and Addison's pre-sublime: they too were led to thoughts of infinity by grand nature.[38] But it is also evocative of another rhetoric—transcendentalism. Before travelling to Niagara, Gilman had read Basil Hall and Frances Trollope, but her primary influence was a popular transcendentalist: her writing shares the mysticism associated with fellow American Ralph Waldo Emerson, especially as it is expressed in his tract *Nature*. Emerson's essay, published in 1836 (the same year as Gilman's trip to Niagara), describes an epistemology that claims that humans can intuitively transcend the limits of the senses in order to connect with a higher being. The natural world is one of the "media" through which this communion occurs. Gilman's *The Poetry of Travelling in the United States,* published two years after Emerson's essay, works within his theory.

If Gilman begins her description of Niagara from afar by using the pre-sublime (i.e., conventions for writing about nature in which suffering does not play an important part in the experience), upon first seeing Niagara close up her rhetoric shifts to that of Burke's ideology. As the following passage suggests, she feels "oppression," she trembles and has "fears." Then, with her emotions roused, the discourse becomes more transcendentalist, and she is freed from the pains of her constraint:

> At the first approach to the Falls, from the smooth river to the Rapids I experienced a sensation of oppression, followed by trembling and fears...but as I gazed, my thoughts became dream-like; the far distant and dim future blended together; I felt an indistinct and troubled joy, like the bright chaos beneath me. (205)

Gilman's emphasis thus far on "blending"—her conscious "thoughts" become "dream-like"; the past merges with the future; "oppression" shifts into "joy"; she is elevated above the "bright chaos"—shows that she is moving between pre-sublime, sublime, and transcendental models. In mixing these rhetorics, she attempts to go "beneath" the surface to provide a new set of conventions for registering Niagara. Twentieth-century travel theorist James Buzard would say that Gilman borrows from and extends other modes of perception in order to make contact with an authentic, integrated "whole way of life."[39]

Frances Trollope's early impression of Niagara is one of violence, pain, and terror; Nathaniel Hawthorne feels disappointed and unworthy; but Caroline Gilman experiences something more penetrating—"an indistinct and troubled joy." As Gilman gets closer to the waterfalls, so close that she lies down on Table Rock and actually extends her head over the abyss, that reaction goes "deeper": "It was an hour of deep and mighty feelings—none but moral struggles can rival them in my soul" (206). Gilman's experience of nature is not pleasant or soothing: she compares her feelings with moral struggles. Then, after she goes back to her hotel, the roar of the waters continues to agitate her. The sound draws her to the window again—"the white foam looks like a troubled spirit in the darkness" (ibid.). As with Hawthorne, the aural impression takes her beyond the prescribed view. Gilman attributes her subsequent vision and her heightened feelings to God: "I cannot soothe down my heart—it is kindled by deep workings of the Invisible" (ibid.). Her shifting verb tenses, from the past (earlier in the passage) to the present, stress the immediacy of this vision.

Another day devoted to tourist activities prompts Gilman to complain about the ruination of parts of Niagara by development. But she offers advice on the construction of a large hotel and hopes for better walkways around the cataracts (207). This is typical of commentators who condemn the industry that has been built up to serve them: in Gilman's case, the facilities that block out nature are not convenient enough or do not meet her needs. The ever-diligent Gilman ends her touristy day with another moral struggle on the bridge over the brink. She lies down on the Terrapin ramp and extends her head over the

Horseshoe Falls again. It has a different effect the second time—she submits to the sensory experience, is overwhelmed by it, and is then calmed: "I ceased to pray or even to think. I gave myself up to the overpowering greatness of the scene, and my soul was still" (208). By surrendering, as it were, she manages to get beyond the self and connect to the Deity once more:

> I thought of *soul*, and this mighty Fall seemed as a drop compared to the cataract of mind, which has been rushing from the bosom of the Eternal, from age to age, through every channel of human nature, now covered with mists, now glittering in sunshine, now softened by moonlight, now leaping in darkness and uncertainty, and I trust in God, destined to flow in many a happy river around his throne. (Ibid.)

Gilman's transcendentalist rhetoric is designed to penetrate a "mystery," whereas Trollope's particular sublime inflection could only hint at one. The next percipient to be considered also wrote of a dreamy vision at Niagara, but instead of feeling overwhelmed by her sensory impression, unworthy of nature's awe, or uplifted by the presence of God, Anna Jameson rejected sublime conventions and translated her pain and loss into something humorous.

Anna Jameson

ANNA JAMESON'S FIRST DESCRIPTION of Canada suggests that the Irish-born writer was severely depressed: plucked from the European literary scene, forced to play the role of wife of the Attorney General, she lashes out at Toronto, an "ill-built," "ugly," and "vulgar" town that reflects her "mean and melancholy" state of mind.[40] Bemoaning her heartfelt response, for she did not experience what one is supposed to feel ("they say it is a pretty place … I did not expect much" [16]), she ends up describing the town (and her emotions) as frozen, tasteless, and gloomy. Then, she has an outburst and avows herself the mocker: "I am like an uprooted tree, dying at the core, yet with a strange unreasonable power at times of mocking at my own most miserable weakness" (ibid.). This is not the same pattern of anticipation, disappointment, and denial found in Trollope and Hawthorne. Here, nature does not elude language; nor is Jameson awestruck by her experience. The twentieth-century literary critic Lorraine York calls this kind of writing "sublime desolation," which she defines as "a struggle with the two major topoi of the sublime tradition: the 'expanse' and 'singularity.'" And, in York's opinion, the tension between the "sublime" and the "desolation" occurs when Jameson attempts to isolate European motifs in the Canadian landscape.[41]

While the circumstances of Anna Jameson's trip abroad may have had something to do with her desolate state of mind, it also appears that her published work up to this point had been about the futility of happiness. More than a decade before travelling to North America, Anna Jameson had found success with her *Diary of an Ennuyée* (1826). In it, she created a self-conscious fictitious narrator who travelled the Continent and then died of "heart sickness" in her twenty-sixth year, leaving the manuscript unfinished. In that work, too, the writer's subjective disintegration is projected onto the outer scene, so that the scene itself becomes the locus of confusion and disintegration.

By the time Jameson came to North America in 1836, the problem was not so much heart sickness as marital strife. She was legally married to Robert Sympson Jameson, the newly appointed Attorney General of Upper Canada, yet she was in Canada to arrange a formal separation.[42] Her lifestyle would *not* have been entirely acceptable to conventional readers of the nineteenth century. This in itself put the writer in a precarious situation. While she wanted to write a frank and truthful narrative of her own experiences, she also needed to write a saleable account, one that informed the audience about "women's issues" without damaging her husband's public reputation, or her own.[43] Jameson expertly deals with these controversial topics by mixing genres: she infuses confessional commentary about her trip with strongly "feminist" passages about the nineteenth-century "New Woman." Twentieth-century feminist critic Mary Mason describes this approach as a form of autobiographical knowledge-making that acknowledges societal constraints. Yet, Jameson's self-definition is created through identification with another (both the typical New Woman and the friend to whom she is writing) and Mason therefore calls this ploy "double vision."[44] Further, twentieth-century travel theorist Sara Mills calls a similar special awareness of the relationship between the writer, her addressee, and her readers "textual doubling":

> Not only do women travel writers have to produce knowledge that will be interesting enough to sell books in the home country, so that their books are structured around unusual events and activities that are not related within male travel accounts (i.e., I am the first woman to...) but they are also producing knowledge about themselves that will be used to judge them as individuals.[45]

With its many levels of discourse, Jameson's highly personal account reveals her fragile core, while a counter narrative voice, a vocalization of society's constraints, judges that unconventional self for the traditional reader.

Winter Studies and Summer Rambles in Canada, published in London in 1838, is composed almost entirely of letters (their dates spanning the period between December 20, 1836 and May 1, 1838) and philosophical meditations addressed to an absent friend, Ottilie von Goethe. These records were edited into the form of a travel narrative and prepared for publication after Jameson's return from North America. Another twentieth-century literary critic, Bina Friewald, calls the process of letter writing and self-reflection done explicitly for publication "an attempt to restore the presence [of the beloved] through the act of communication."[46] In the end, though, Jameson restores not only her relationship with her friend, but also her own sense of "self": the book charts the progress of her sad, self-imposed exile and her happy return to Ottilie von Goethe.[47]

Jameson's initial reaction to Toronto is echoed later in her first impression of Niagara. She took two trips to the Falls (during the winter and the summer): they function as pivotal experiences, because the initial journey induces an intense anxiety and the second cures her emotional depression. During Jameson's first escorted trip on January 29, 1837 (shortly after the failed Upper Canada Rebellion), she records a conventional sublime impression—an emotional split between disappointment and exultation. Like Elizabeth Simcoe, Frances Trollope, Nathaniel Hawthorne and Caroline Gilman, as she approaches the view, she anticipates it through various impressions: "Well! I have seen these Cataracts of Niagara, which have thundered in my mind's ear ever since I can remember—which have been my childhood's thought, my youth's desire, since first my imagination was awakened to wonder and to wish" (57). Having already read Alexander Henry's descriptions of Niagara,[48] Jameson seems self-conscious about her own reaction, and she makes this anxiety obvious through curious punctuation that forces the reader to use long breaths for each of the long sentences:

> I have beheld them, and shall I whisper it to you?—but, O tell it not among the Philistines!—I wish I had not! I wish they were still a thing to live for:—the reality has displaced from my mind an illusion far more magnificent than itself—I have no words for my utter disappointment: yet I have not the prescription to

suppose that all I have heard and read of Niagara is false or exaggerated—that every expression of astonishment, enthusiasm, rapture, is affectation or hyperbole. No! it must be my own fault. (Ibid.)

The words "magnificent," "astonishment," and "rapture" and the notion that the "illusion," meant to represent the real world, is a far more "magnificent" image in itself, are familiar trappings of the Burkean sublime. This vocabulary, in turn, has accompanying emotional machinery: disappointment and disillusionment. Jameson writes, "O, I could beat myself! and now there is no help!—the first moment, the first impression is over—is lost" (ibid.). Overwhelmed by a sense of loss and emotional stagnation—"something is gone that can no longer be restored"—she is at pains to present her feelings but is also interested in analyzing her responses. What she accomplishes is an odd list of comparisons: "I am no longer Anna—I am metamorphosed—I am translated—I am an ass's head, a clod, a wooden spoon, a fat weed growing on Lethe's bank, a stock, a stone, a petrifaction" (ibid.). This metonymical chain of associations contains ideas from the Wordsworthian sublime (the metamorphosed/translated "I am no longer Anna" notion) and images directly from Shakespeare: the "fat weed" on "Lethe wharf" is in *Hamlet* (I, v, 32); the "ass's head" appears often in *Midsummer Night's Dream*; and "my heart is turn'd to stone" comes from *Othello* (IV, i, 180). Yet, the way in which the metonymy works (Anna becomes an ass's head, clod, spoon, weed, etc.) suggests that this highly stylized parodic vocabulary is meant to deride the conventions even as it imitates them. And, while the writer's frequent outbursts— "O tell it not among the Philistines!" and "O, I could beat myself!"— are often followed by mental obsessions—"I am metamorphosed—I am translated"—she does not let herself become emotionally overwhelmed (like Trollope) or abandon herself to the contemplation of nature (like Hawthorne and Gilman). Instead, through her parodic wit, Jameson translates pain and loss into something humorous ("an ass's head," "a clod," "a wooden spoon," "a fat weed," etc.).

A number of twentieth-century literary critics have seized upon Jameson's key phrase "I am translated" to argue that she is participating in what they call a "feminine aesthetic." For Mary Mason, Bina Friewald, Rachel Blau DuPlessis, and Thomas Gerry, the feminine aesthetic, marked by an inclusiveness—like Mason's "double vision" or Mills's "textual doubling"—is also characterized by a search for self-translation. Accordingly, the practitioner of this aesthetic is on a quest for "another nature" (a "self-translation"), and she achieves this through communion with a real landscape, which she eventually "transcends." During this event, the writer transforms her own—and her reader's—received notions. Using this lens, it would follow, then, that Jameson's hyperbolic speech means that she was thinking in terms of this kind of translation.[49]

The feminine aesthetic is different from the two kinds of expression used by Pehr Kalm (see chapter 1). Kalm's scientific and "marvellous" discourses—based on the Linnaean taxonomic system, on Hennepin, and on an Indian legend—were separate rhetorics used to codify two almost logically exclusive commentaries on landscape features and on accentuated feelings. (Interestingly, Edmund Burke's *Enquiry* makes a similar distinction between "empirical" and "irrational" perceptions, something I will return to in the next chapter.) Jameson's "double vision" or "textual doubling" is not like the two kinds of writing found in Kalm (or in Burke) because hers contains a notion of inclusivity. The feminine aesthetic, then, composed of both "voices" and "texts," does not fall back on one type of description at the expense of another (as Kalm's did) but rather pushes the conventions to their limits—twists them (through parody), turns them (through hyperbole), and forces a "translation."

Jameson's fascination with her own mental state is the subject of much of the second half of her book, too. But the "summer rambles" constitute both a climatic contrast and a change in role or identity. According to twentieth-century travel theorist William Stowe, part of the allure of travel, and writing while travelling, is that authors can shape their experiences, hone their writing skills, and get published, but they also use travel "as a way to shed the familiar constraints of their culture and place, to act out experimental roles, and try out tentative personalities, measure themselves against foreign customs and values, and seek aesthetic or spiritual experience."[50] Hence, Jameson, like Elizabeth Simcoe, decided to cast duty aside to explore the Canadian frontier. As wife of the Attorney General, Jameson was given special treatment—with a social position similar to that of the Lieutenant-Governor's lady, she roamed at will. Unlike Simcoe, Jameson travelled in the wilderness without a male escort, carrying a "small stiletto or poignard" for self-defence.[51] For Simcoe and Jameson, the theme of "wildness" was explicitly connected with their use of travel writing to escape from the conventions of domestic wifeliness. In the woods and at Niagara, both writers experienced something beyond "civilized" protocol.

Not surprisingly, Niagara was the first stop on Jameson's journey into the wild interior. This second impression of the Falls, characterized by a longing to share the sight with her absent friend, seems more contrived than the first description, because it sounds like other accounts:

> I wished more than ever for those I love most!—for some one who would share all this rapture of admiration and delight without the necessity of speaking—for, after all, what are words? They express nothing, reveal nothing, avail nothing. So it all sinks back into my own heart, there to be kept quiet. (203)

Following the more conventional formula of the Burkean sublime, she resolves *not* to describe Niagara; she falls into silence and then, a few lines later, offers up a scene of "dreamy repose":

> the Falls looked magnificently mysterious, part glancing silver light, and part dark shadow, mingled with fleecy folds of spray, over which floated a soft, sleepy gleam; and in the midst of this tremendous velocity of motion and eternity of sound, there was deep, deep repose, as in a dream. It impressed me for the time like something supernatural—a vision, not a reality. (Ibid.)

The idea of disappointment and mockery succeeded by satisfaction, and the connected notion of finally displacing the "real" Niagara with an ideal—signified by the words "magnificently mysterious," "shadow," "dream," "supernatural," and "vision"—would mark the moment when, to use Lorraine York's terminology, the sublime overshadows the desolation.[52]

Jameson's description draws its compelling power not so much from the events that constitute the objective narrative as from the narrator's insistence on its unreal, dreamlike quality. This disorientation and, earlier, her self-deprecating irony are ways to reorient experience and embody something authentic. Charles Dickens also saw in Niagara enchanting visions. His response can be explained in terms of aesthetics and in terms of his association of ideas: he writes of an attraction to the visible Falls, and he contemplates the quiet, invisible power manifest in the river. I trace his preoccupation with phenomenon and noumenon to his observations of Niagara's features and his dreams of Niagara's "spirit" as they are recorded in his writing.

Charles Dickens

CHARLES DICKENS APPROACHED the waterfalls from upriver, on the American side, the same way that Nathaniel Hawthorne had arrived nine years earlier. While it is not known if he had read Hawthorne, Dickens did prepare for his visit by reviewing the work of at least three authors: Basil Hall (at Niagara in 1827; published his account in *Travels in North America in the Years 1827 and 1828* in 1829); Frances Trollope (at Niagara in 1830; published her account of the visit in *Domestic Manners of the Americans* in 1832); and Harriet Martineau (at Niagara in 1834 and 1836; published her account of the visits in *Retrospect of Western Travel* in 1838).[53] (Dickens may also have read Charles Lyell's *Principles of Geology* [1830],[54] part of which discusses the age and makeup of the rocks in the Niagara river system.) Like the previous literary commentators, Dickens anticipates the sound first: "Whenever the train halts, I listen for the roar; and am constantly straining my eyes in the direction where I know the Falls must be."[55] When the train stops, he identifies, through the rain and mist, "two great white clouds rising up slowly and majestically from the depth of the earth" (137–38). Prepared for the sublime experience—Dickens refers to the aural and the visual as "strains"—he jumps from the train and feels "the ground tremble underneath [his] feet" (138). Frantic to see Niagara, he rushes down a steep and slippery path to the foot of the American Falls, below where Hennepin claimed to have stood. Up close, nothing is discernible: "I could see an immense torrent of water tearing headlong down from some great height, but had no idea of shape, or situation, or anything but vague immensity" (ibid.). Burke's sublime can be vast and immense, have uncertain boundaries, sound loud, and look dazzling, and it can cause the viewer pain or fear. Dickens's way of experiencing the Falls is based on these principles of sublimity.

Next, Dickens gets on the *Maid of the Mist*. Halfway across the river, in front of the two cataracts, he still cannot see the whole "picture": "I began to feel what it was: but I was in a manner stunned, and unable to comprehend the vastness of the scene" (ibid.). From the vantage point of Table Rock, looking across the broad Horseshoe "in its full might and majesty" (ibid.), he finally achieves a sublime view.

For the remainder of the trip—nine days, from April 26 to May 4, 1841—Dickens remained on the Canadian side of the river. He might have felt more at home in Canada and more reluctant to stray to the "other side" again because of certain grievances. Like Frances Trollope's visit to the United States, his was fraught with bad feeling.[56]

While the primary reason for his trip abroad was the promotion of a new book, *Barnaby Rudge,* Dickens was also there to sort out the question of copyright. He was having difficulties with America's newspaper "pirates," which were reprinting his works, including the *Pickwick Papers* (1837), *Oliver Twist* (1839), *Nicholas Nickleby* (1839), and *The Old Curiosity Shop* (1840), without compensating him.[57] At his first public event in North America—a dinner given by the Young Men of Boston—Dickens spoke on the copyright problem. The journalists who reported on the evening's event lampooned him as a self-interested mercenary who objected to the practice because "he was not a gentleman but merely the 'son of a Haberdasher.'"[58] For the duration of his visit to the United States, Dickens was hounded by journalists: he was interviewed aboard boats and trains, in restaurants, and on the street. For the most part, he appears both flattered and disturbed by all the attention, as when he overhears his nickname mentioned in a conversation between other passengers on the train to Niagara: "I suppose that Boz will be writing a book bye and bye, and putting all our names in it!" (137).

Dickens's way of dealing with this kind of humiliation at the hands of journalists and the public was to make fun of Americans. He jotted down witty, satiric material throughout his trip, which he later wrote up as *American Notes for General Circulation,* a book published in London in two volumes on October 19, 1842. In his *American Notes,* he judges the conduct of Americans by English rules and standards, employing a facetious tone to describe how old men spit and wear their hats indoors, how old women pick their teeth with hatpins. Other broadly comic sections parody "the folk" who stare into the train windows or mock the landlord who parades him around the main street of small-town America. And, in response to what he calls a "disgusting circumstance" on the American side of Niagara, when he came across several albums of tourist responses to the waterfalls (perhaps the guest book that Nathaniel Hawthorne signed!), Dickens denounces American poetry as "the vilest and filthiest ribaldry" (137).

On "Enchanted [Canadian] Ground," Dickens felt calmer because the view was more "elevating," and because fewer crowds tended to gather and the spectators were not watching *him.* All this inattention allowed Dickens to register sentiments associated with the Wordsworthian Romantic sublime:

> Then, when I felt how near to my Creator I was standing, the first effect, and the enduring one—instant and lasting—of the tremen-

dous spectacle, was Peace. Peace of Mind: Tranquillity: Calm recollections of the Dead: Great thoughts of Eternal Rest and Happiness:
nothing of Gloom or Terror. (138)

In his description, Dickens expresses a mysticism that goes beyond
Romantic thoughts of peace, tranquility, and wonder and into a quasi-
religious moment, with thoughts of the "Creator," the "Dead," and
"Eternal Rest." While Dickens shares with Caroline Gilman a deep-
seated ideological belief in the spiritual essence of Niagara, his writing
does not promote her transcendentalist view (nor does he continue to
pontificate about God's design as manifest in the waters). Instead, he
shifts his focus away from the spirit of creation and toward the spirits
of the dead, his metaphor for memory:

> What voices spoke from out the thundering water; what faces,
> faded from the earth, looked out upon me from its gleaming
> depths; what Heavenly promise glistened in those angels' tears,
> the drops of many hues, that showered around, and twined
> themselves about the gorgeous arches which the changing rain-
> bows made! (Ibid.)

Dickens was fascinated by memory and by death. During the first portion of his American tour, he recorded a dream that he had had of his
recently deceased sister-in-law, Mary Hogarth. In the dream she is
dead, yet she appears to be looking down upon him, similar to the
way in which faces "looked out upon [him]" from the depths of Niagara.[59] Elsewhere in his writing, too, he uses the same language for
Mary Hogarth, who haunts his nighttime visions, as he does for Niagara. In *American Notes,* Dickens suggests that Niagara is stamped
upon his heart and will remain there until his pulse "ceases to beat, for-
ever" (ibid.). And, one year later in a letter to Mrs. George Hogarth, he
echoes this description by claiming that Mary Hogarth is as essential
to his being "as the beating of my heart."[60] While nothing in his prose
specifies whose faces he saw at Niagara, Mary Hogarth's spirit may be
the one fading from the earth, looking out upon the writer. Dickens
ends his association of death, resurrection, ghosts, and memory with
a rumination on Niagara's ceaseless voice and eternal flow:

> But always does the mighty stream appear to die as it comes own,
> and always from its unfathomable grave arises that tremendous
> ghost of spray and mist which is never laid: which has haunted this
> place with the same dread solemnity since Darkness brooded on

the deep, and that first flood before the Deluge—Light—came rushing on Creation at the word of God. (139)

His emphasis on the words "die," "grave," "ghost," and "haunted" makes Niagara into a spectral place of creation and light. Like Trollope's "shadowy mystery," or Gilman's "troubled spirit in the darkness," or Jameson's "dark shadow," Dickens's "ghost of spray" is a further example of how individual experiences at Niagara are raised to visionary heights through aestheticized language. The twentieth-century travel theorist David Spurr would call this kind of writing "colonial melodrama." On the basis of Dickens's motives for being in North America—to keep his books from being "pirated"—and his earlier emphasis on the vulgarity of Americans, Spurr would argue that the writer saw himself as surrounded by the "unreal" or the "insubstantial" and to diminish the anxiety of such an experience he placed his response to Niagara within an existing imperialist discourse.[61] Margaret Fuller's fantasy of an Indian and of Niagara itself as a sort of untamed wilderness is yet another way of dealing with "colonizing" anxieties, physical danger, and physical fear that both accedes to the popular stereotype and highlights her unique reaction.

Margaret Fuller

NIAGARA WAS MARGARET FULLER'S first destination on her "great migration" west. It is also the first landscape described in *Summer on the Lakes in 1843* (1844), her record of that trip to the American frontier.[62] At this starting point, Fuller invites the reader to share the "footnotes…on the pages of my life."[63] This is the voice of a travelling companion rather than that of a guide. Elsewhere in her book, she plays with other conventions of travel writing to "speak" in a number of voices, male and female, real and fictional, intellectual and sensory, analytic and appreciative. Travel theorist William Stowe calls this "polyvocal writing," a way of expressing the disparate aspects of her consciousness, "the conventionally female sensitivity, say, or the conventionally male political enthusiasm."[64] In tracing Fuller's polyvocality, I will look at how this device is another production of the feminine aesthetic.

Fuller begins her description of Niagara by confessing that she is satiated by the scene already and will have little to say about the spectacle because she has been at the waterfalls for eight days and wants to leave. In the next paragraph, she offers a brief explanation: "So great a sight soon satisfied, making us content with itself, and with what is less than itself. Our desires, once realized, haunt us again less readily" (3). Elements of the Burkean pattern can be found in this testimonial, including the feeling of disappointment that Niagara does not match its images and the characteristic refusal to describe the scene. But, unlike others who use a similar sublime formula, Fuller is not overwhelmed by the sight of Niagara, nor does she blame herself for being unworthy; rather, she is "satisfied" and "content" that the anticipated images of Niagara will not "haunt" her viewing experiences. However, when Fuller goes on to describe the various sublime properties "beyond" the visual—such as the sounds of the wind and the constant motion—her writing suggests that she is overpowered:

> My nerves, too much braced up by such an atmosphere, do not well bear the continual stress of sight and sound. For here there is no escape from the weight of a perpetual creation; all other forms and motions come and go, the tide rises and recedes, the wind, at its mightiest, moves in gales and gusts, but here an incessant, indefatigable motion. (3–4)

As with Louis Hennepin, Frances Trollope, Nathaniel Hawthorne, and Caroline Gilman, the sound and the motion ("the continual stress," "no escape," and "incessant, indefatigable motion") seem to paralyze Fuller. The dilemma in her constraint is that these sensations also empower her: "Awake or asleep, there is no escape, still this rushing round you and through you. It is in this way I have most felt the grandeur—somewhat eternal, if not infinite" (4). Fuller's impression has shared elements with Gilman's transcendental vision of Niagara as a manifestation of the divine. But Fuller does not call Niagara infinite and she does not identify the "eternal" with God. Instead, nature's endless, changing, "perpetual" motion is refracted back into the *self* ("rushing round you and through you").

In Fuller's writing, Niagara serves as a kind of portal—a point of entry for her great migration and a gateway into her self. This concept is also made obvious when she calls the Niagara chapter "a magnificent prologue to the, as yet, unknown drama"—a drama that was, of course, known, since she worked up her notes in a library at home. Still, the title and the fragmentary, meandering style of writing give *Summer on the Lakes* the feel of a journey toward self-discovery. Nearly one-third of the book is taken up with ruminations on her summer reading. She interrupts these little book reviews with an autobiographical romance and with poems and letters from her friends.[65] What appears to be a series of digressions includes summaries of the views of her literary predecessors at Niagara, such as Nathaniel Hawthorne and Anna Jameson. Hence, her "double journey" along the line of the text follows Hawthorne's *Twice-Told Tales,* a collection that she had reviewed for *The Dial* and that contained his "My Visit to Niagara," and part of the route of her voyage follows Jameson's path from Niagara into the interior.[66] Other interesting digressions in Fuller's travelogue involve readings of how the biases of "white" culture pervade texts about Natives, interspersed with excerpts from philanthropic books by Henry Schoolcraft and George Catlin. These writers stressed how the aboriginal was a victim rather than a wild and dangerous "foe" (the conventional American view of the 1840s).[67] Mary Louise Pratt calls this way of writing against the prevalent imperializing rhetoric an "anti-conquest narrative." In this form of representation, the Native person is seen as doomed and destined to that fate, but, because European dominance goes absolutely uncontested, this "anti-conquest" perspective is still part of the rhetoric of colonization and appropriation.[68] The following interpretation of Fuller's narrative undertakes such an "anti-conquest" reading and involves looking at the methods of self-representation for examples of partial collaboration with and displacement of the idioms of the conqueror.

After Fuller has described how the waterfalls' grandeur affected her, she backtracks in her narrative to the first sighting, to her impression before she was "seized" by Niagara's motions, rhythms, and vibrations. She does this to explain why, initially, she felt a sense of satiation:

> When I first came I felt nothing but a quiet satisfaction. I found that drawings, the panorama, &c. had given me a clear notion of the position and proportions of all objects here; I knew where to look for everything, and everything looked as I thought it would. (4)

Fuller's backtracking creates suspense in a similar way to Hawthorne's delaying of the moment when he looks on Niagara. She writes of previously seen "drawings" and the "panorama"; she judges the scene for "position and proportions." This is a more picturesque analysis, and Niagara affords her a certain "quiet satisfaction." Then, as if she is experimenting with frames, the proportions of the landscape increase and she uses a different "voice" to bring in another aesthetic: "Daily these proportions widened and towered more and more upon my sight, and I got, at last, a proper foreground for these sublime distances. Before coming away, I think I really saw the full wonder of the scene" (ibid.). Her "wonder" and the way in which she extends the scene into a sort of infinity are features of sublimity. This is an example of the polyvocality that Stowe attributes to Fuller: her different "voices" or frames or modes of appreciation represent various aspects of the experience.

As we have seen from Trollope, Hawthorne, and Jameson, this more emotional aesthetic model (Burke's sublime) also encourages fear. Fuller enters into this state when she writes of an "undefined dread, such as I never knew before, such as may be felt when death is about to usher us into a new existence" (5). For Dickens, the spirits of the dead in Niagara's waters are those of people he knew. For Fuller, death is her own concern. That may be part of her dread. Her narrator is so overwhelmed by this fear (of death) that she cannot hear anything over the sound of the Falls. But she senses someone else haunting the landscape, too. In the perpetual tumbling of the waters, she senses "that no other sound, however near, could be heard" (ibid.). This so unnerves her that she starts, and looks behind for a "foe" (ibid.). Fuller identifies the mood in nature—violent and forceful—with an enemy. Half a century earlier, Elizabeth Simcoe recorded in her *Diary* a description of her "foe"—an American rebel in the woods of Upper Canada. Like Simcoe, Fuller also succumbs to prejudice and stereotyping, even though she had set out to write an impassioned plea on behalf of the Indian:

> I realized the identity of that mood of nature in which these waters were poured down with such absorbing force, with that in which the Indian was shaped on the same soil. For continually upon my mind came, unsought and unwelcome, images, such as never haunted it before, of naked savages stealing behind me with uplifted tomahawks; again and again this illusion recurred, and even after I had thought it over, and tried to shake it off, I could not help starting and looking behind me. (Ibid.)

For Fuller, the sublime is not nature, emotion, or God—it is a naked savage, with tomahawk raised.[69] Indians figured in chapter 1 too. Artists drew their brave and tragic struggles, their battle-weary contemplations, their subservience, and their nobility. Fuller's Indian, part of this complex visual and written tradition, particularly draws on Immanuel Kant's late eighteenth-century association of that figure with the sublime.[70] But Fuller had been influenced by a contemporary American rhetoric too, a popular fantasy available in captivity narratives that told of the Indian attacking (and scalping and abducting) the white woman. According to Mary Louise Pratt, this type of story (the captivity narrative) constituted a safe context in which to narrate the terrorism of the contact zone, because the tale was told by a survivor who had returned, reaffirming the European colonial social order.[71] Another reading of this image of an attacking naked "savage" comes from twentieth-century literary critic Christina Zwarg. Zwarg's theory is that Fuller's Indian was based on a particular painting—the famous rendering of *The Death of Jane McCrea* (1804) by John Vanderlyn. This painting depicts a woman kneeling with upraised arms while two male Indians, both wielding tomahawks, attack her. One of the assailants pulls on her hair, about to scalp her.[72] Even though Fuller had read her Schoolcraft and Catlin, even though she had set out to follow in their footsteps to document the Native's tragic disappearance, one of her self-discoveries at Niagara was this unbidden image of "naked savages stealing behind [her] with uplifted tomahawks." Fuller is obviously uncomfortable with this fantasy. One of her motives in writing was to make an impassioned plea for America's Native people, yet she adopts the same rhetoric that she set out to resist. Part of the way in which the "anti-conquest" narrative works is through polyvocality: Fuller collaborates with the idiom of the conqueror and then, through a kind of subversion, uses another "voice" (the captivity narrative) to suggest something the philanthropists (Schoolcraft and Catlin) did not account for (dread of death, fear of attack). In this way, Fuller experiences vicarious violence through the trope of the Indian who turns on her. This collaboration with dual narratives, only to subvert them, is partially a response to Burke's aesthetic (and to the male philanthropists). Because Burke's phenomenological process involves a perceiving self that is "mastered" by the sublime, some respondents (like Fuller and Jameson) feel discomfort with that submission/abasement. Their way of opting out of the tension is not to switch to another kind of discourse (as some of the male scientists do in chapter 3) but to "translate" their emotional paralysis into a kind of parody (Jameson), or to turn the danger, vicariously, against the self (Fuller). This too is part of the feminine aesthetic.

Following her heightened confession, Fuller moves back into picturesque description of the landscape when she discusses the effect of light and shade from various vantages, including Table Rock, the rapids, the sulphur spring, Goat Island, and the Whirlpool. She describes the latter feature with more emotionally charged words and associates it with "untold mysteries" and with "fear":

the slight circles that mark the hidden vortex seem to whisper mysteries the thundering voice above could not proclaim—a meaning as untold as ever. It is fearful to know, as you look, that whatever has been swallowed by the cataract, is likely to rise suddenly to light here, whether up-rooted tree, or body of man or bird. (6)

Once again, with her aural and visual sensibilities engaged, Fuller evokes a sublime image: her "hidden" phenomenon of motion and noise is like the foe silently stalking, and her fear of seeing some awful apparition rising from the Whirlpool reminds us of Dickens's "ghost of spray." But the difference between Fuller's Indian and his ghost is that hers comes unbidden because it is a fantasy that she dreads.

After this, Fuller comments on how other tourists react to Niagara, and in her description her unique commentary is evident. One man spits in the water—his way of "best appropriating it to his own use" (ibid.). Other people express dissatisfaction with the buildings, and Fuller dismisses their complaints, saying "the spectacle [Niagara] is capable to swallow up all such objects" (7). She is disgusted by tourists and their forms of entertainment—another anecdote of an eagle chained up for the amusement of others illustrates this point (8–9). But she does not disapprove of the structures that had been erected to serve the tourists' needs. Near the close of the chapter, Fuller's discourse shifts again, when she returns to nature, which she associates with God: "then arose in my breast a genuine admiration, and a humble adoration of the Being who was the first architect of this and of all" (12). She has used a number of aesthetics—the picturesque, the sublime, and now the transcendental sublime. As she moves from one vantage point to another, from one model to another, her fear and terror, encountered vicariously, are transformed, through the precepts of art, into "admiration" and "adoration."

Fuller ends her description of Niagara with the passage quoted at the beginning of this chapter. Writing in the "voice" of Louis Hennepin, she confesses her desire to have stumbled upon the scene and celebrated untamed nature: "Happy were the first discoverers of Niagara, those who could come unawares upon this view and upon that, whose feelings were entirely their own" (7). There are a number of interesting fantasies embedded in this epigraphic quotation, the most obvious being the idea that the discoverer of Niagara was "happy" about being the first one there; on the contrary, we have seen that Hennepin felt inadequate to the task of describing the scene and wished that he had been accompanied by someone more capable of doing so. Fuller also seems to have wanted to arrive at Niagara "unawares" with feelings "entirely [her] own," yet she too was circumscribed by the cultural frames from which she wrote/thought. Her fantasy of an attacking Indian shows how tendencies in Western thought framed her response; nevertheless, her terror and dread—experienced all on her own—paint a unique portrait of a fantastically savage, dangerous world.

AS TIME PASSED, it seemed increasingly difficult to make Niagara "wild" because writers were preoccupied with how tourism had "sullied" nature. The year that Margaret Fuller was at Niagara, approximately 25,000 other tourists visited too. Over the next two decades, that number doubled. By the time that Anthony Trollope arrived, Niagara was hosting approximately 50,000 visitors each summer, and a whole industry had been built up to serve the needs of all these people. Because of this, Trollope did not find a wilderness place; nevertheless, through his writing, he found a way to admire, adore, and civilize Niagara.

Anthony Trollope

WHEN ANTHONY TROLLOPE launches into his description of the waterfalls in *North America* (1862), he immediately proclaims, "I know no other one thing so beautiful, so glorious, and so powerful [as Niagara]."[73] This is a different view from the one expressed a few years previously in his *The West Indies and the Spanish Main* (1859). In that book, he dismisses Niagara as "a waste of waters."[74] Trollope found great success with his West Indies travelogue, which went into a sixth edition, and which had been published in the United States by the time he travelled to North America. Before he embarked on this second journey abroad, he was able to arrange a contract with his London publishers, Chapman and Hall.[75]

The youngest of Frances Trollope's seven children, Anthony Trollope did not accompany his mother on her journey to the United States in 1827. As we have seen, she found a great deal in the modes and manners of Americans that was distasteful to her. While Frances Trollope's *Domestic Manners of the Americans* was a best-seller in both

England and America, by the time that her son visited North America she had become a "folk character" in American museums and carnivals, where she was presented, in crude effigy, as a "trollop."[76] Of course the family finances had been rescued by her famous book, yet his mother's legacy left Anthony Trollope "marked." As twentieth-century literary critic Catherine Hall writes, Trollope had a deeply unconventional view of women (like his mother) who ventured out of their "sphere." In his view, they should not engage in public life, nor attempt to comment on economic and political affairs.[77] Hence, in the preface to *North America,* he judges his mother's travelogue "essentially a woman's book," and his own a "social and political commentary."[78]

Unlike his mother, who spent forty-two months abroad (the late 1820s to 1830), Anthony Trollope stayed nine months in North America (September 1861 to May 1862). His journey was well timed, though: the United States was engaged in the Civil War, and the historical moment provided him with a "hot" topic to fill two long volumes. His writing responds to the currents in national life: he defends the Union and its right to fight for democracy.[79] He also addresses the question of whether England should take sides in the conflict, eventually deciding that it should not. He asks his readers to think about the American North and South as a hypothetical domestic couple, Mr. and Mrs. Jones, and the Civil War as a family altercation.[80] As Trollope travels north by rail from Boston, he widens his writerly focus and devotes a few chapters to the idea of American annexation of Canada, confessing that he does not support such a move if it is accompanied by strife. In Ottawa, he waxes poetic on another family struggle—the Empire and the colony—and argues that Canada needs its own king. By the time he arrives in Toronto, he has changed opinions again: Canada needs to remain British and dependent because the English want to do well by the colony. Instead of "leaving the parent's apron-string," Trollope writes, "Canadians should learn to function under a constitutional monarchy" (53). Unlike his comments on the war in America (essentially a "war of the sexes"), the bias of colonialist culture pervades Trollope's solutions to Canada's political situation; he likens the process of imperialism to reproduction and implies that the colony—a child of "mother" England—should learn to behave. Such a vision, with all its assumptions about the inferiority of Canadians, was part of the fabric of Victorian England.

In the mid-nineteenth century, the conventional view was that society moves through a series of stages of development and that particular societies are "higher" or "lower" on the scale. This way of thinking about the highly civilized and the less civilized approximated the values set forth by Carolus Linnaeus's classification of the races in *Systema Naturae* (1735). Hence, when Frances Trollope declared that Americans lacked etiquette, or Charles Dickens wrote in a disparaging way about American "folk," they were comparing the "other" to their most "civilized" English selves. It is interesting that, at one point in his narrative, Anthony Trollope also dubs America "a savage country"[81]—a judgment not unlike his mother's and Dickens's. This went against his intention of writing a complimentary book about the United States—a debt he "owed to Americans" that had been "incurred by his mother."[82] Clearly, it is this slippage into a kind of imperial condescension that makes all these judgments about North American cultures so interesting.

We have heard from William Stowe that one of the reasons why travel writing was such an attractive genre in the nineteenth century was that it provided authors with a stage, as it were, on which to act out their desires for authority and importance. Leading their readers over well-trodden ground, they enacted a kind of drama in which they created for themselves appealing, powerful, and prestigious personas.[83] Frances Trollope wrote in order to claim a social and professional position (and to make money), and her son, Anthony, wrote to justify his "superior" (imperial) values and to demonstrate his taste and intelligence. Therefore, it is not surprising that he spends some time describing how "outlooks" at Niagara Falls are not just geographical or visual concerns, but "ethical" positions. Since his book is about political obligations (which side Britain should take in America's Civil War, what Britain owes to Canada), he advises sightseeing according to nationality: Americans should cross the border to Canada and vice versa (96). His instructions about how to "do" Niagara continue for the duration of the chapter. Frequently, he addresses the reader as "you": "Go down to the end of that wooden bridge, seat yourself on the rail, and there sit till all the outer world is lost to you" (98–99). Margaret Fuller employs the pronoun "you" to forge an intimate connection with the reader, but Anthony Trollope's usage is more imperative than hers, making him sound like a tour guide rather than a companion. What he evokes in this didactic conversation is not a "head-spinning" adventure like Hennepin's or his mother's. Instead of writing about how dangerous the landscape is, he talks about more "civilized" aspects of the Niagara experience—the tourists and tourist structures—and advises the reader to block them out: "If you have that power of eye-control which is so necessary to the full enjoyment of scenery you will see nothing but the water" (99). Travel theorist James Buzard would call this form of "eye-control" the "romantic gaze," which operates much like Mary Louise Pratt's "imperial eye." According to Buzard,

> practitioners of the "romantic gaze" required the crowd they scorned and shunned, for they built their travellers' identities in opposition to the crowd. There is a dialectical relationship between the elaboration of "crowd" and "tourist," on the one hand, and the anti-tourist's privileging of "solitude," which is less a valuing of private experience than it is a rhetorical act of role-distancing in need of its audience, real or imaginary.[84]

This is also in keeping with notions of sublimity, especially Kant's educated sublime which attributes "displeasure" to one's inadequacy or inability to cope, rationally, with an irrational experience. Trollope continues with his description of Niagara:

> You will certainly hear nothing else; and the sound, I beg you to remember, is not an ear-cracking, agonizing crash and clang of noises; but is melodious, and soft withal, though as loud as thunder. (99)

The other aesthetic echoed here is the Wordsworthian Romantic sublime. William Wordsworth also describes an admixture of sensations when he writes about Bartholomew Fair in Book VII of *The Prelude*. The spectacle of London in 1804 that Wordsworth composed could be the scene Trollope evokes at Niagara in the 1860s:

> ...What a shock
> For eyes and ears! What anarchy and din,
> Barbarian and infernal—a phantasma,
> Monstrous in colour, motion, shape, sight, sound![85]

For Wordsworth, the Fair is an allegory of universal alienation—"the great tide of human life...Living amid the same perpetual whirl/Of trivial objects" (lines 657 and 725–26)—curable only by aesthetic insight. Wordsworth's particular inflection of sublimity brings "Composure, and ennobling Harmony" (line 771). Hence, when Anthony Trollope goes on to determine how "you" should experience the aural qualities of Niagara, he describes something similar to Wordsworth's Fair, and then goes on to suggest a transcendence:

It fills your ears, and as it were envelops them, but at the same time you can speak to your neighbour without an effort. But at this place, and in these moments, the less of speaking I should say the better. (99–100)

That Niagara can be "melodious" and "loud as thunder," soft and all-enveloping is somewhat contradictory, though somehow true to the experience offered by Wordsworth. Trollope's reverie on the effects and sensory constraints may be a response to his mother's description of being "too violently affected in the physique to be capable of much pleasure." It is also paradoxical that his is not a solitary experience (and that this does not undermine him, as the presence of another did his mother). The more clear-sighted Anthony Trollope actually moves beyond the immediacy of the aural experience to engage in conversation with this "neighbour." What he shares with his companion, and with the reader, is a continuation of the instructive, step-by-step account of how to react. As such, it is an active, almost muscular engagement of the spirit. According to Trollope, the sublime should surpass emotions, senses, and rationalizations: "To realize Niagara you must sit there till you see nothing else, and think of nothing else. At length you will be at one with the tumbling river before you" (99). Trollope's out-of-body, out-of-mind experience—past physical constraints and beyond feelings of disappointment—is a kind of rebirth, like Caroline Gilman's:

You will fall as the bright waters fall, rushing down into your new world with no hesitation and with no dismay; and you will rise again as the spray rises bright, beautiful, and pure. Then you will flow away in your course to the uncompassed, distant, and eternal ocean. (99–100)

After he has brought himself and the reader to this heightened state, Trollope presents a catalogue of tourist facilities again and adds a warning to visitors not to go up the Terrapin Tower, which "reminds one of those well-arranged scenes of romance" and looks like a "gingerbread house" (100), or down the incline railway: "I have always been ashamed to trust to other legs than my own, but I have observed that Americans are always dragged up" (ibid.). The "civilizing" structures (and the other tourists) are somehow inappropriate to a person of his demeanour:

At such a place as Niagara, tasteless buildings, run up in wrong places with a view to money making, are perhaps necessary evils...

they give more pleasure than pain, seeing that they tend to the enjoyment of the multitude. (101)

More pleasure than pain—that was his mother's lasting impression too. Instead of foregrounding physical danger and physical fear, though, he focuses on the "tasteless buildings" and the devotion to "money-making," and translates capitalism's sin into a democratic tolerance of "the enjoyment of the multitude." This, too, is in keeping with the Kantian notion of sublimity operating to moral ends.

One of the ways in which the first discoverer of Niagara is connected to nineteenth-century travel writers is through the theme of deficiency. For Hennepin, the inadequacy lay in himself: he could not hope to describe Niagara. During the 1830s, it was the scene that did not measure up. Writers such as Frances Trollope, Nathaniel Hawthorne, and Anna Jameson were disappointed by Niagara *and* they found fault with themselves because they had expected much more. Then, there was another shift around the middle of the nineteenth century when travellers recorded unpleasant observations of the expanding industries at Niagara. Anna Jameson was shocked to see that "the Americans have disfigured their share of the rapids with mills and manufactories, and horrid red brick houses, and other unacceptable unseasonable sights and signs of sordid industry."[86] Margaret Fuller and Anthony Trollope joined the chorus and blamed the tourist industry for aesthetic insensitivity. As travel theorist Ian Ousby argues, the history of tourism shows that such dismissiveness often fuels rather than quenches popularity: people still flock to sights labelled disappointing if only to show that they are sophisticated enough to agree when they get there.[87] The ties to Kant's educated sublime, which argues that it is displeasing to be unable to cope, make this the new inadequacy. After Trollope's comments, the amenities increasingly available at Niagara became the subject of repeated ambivalent comment. The last of our literary authors, Henry James, perpetuated the belief that, over time, the landscape went from a wilderness to a "sordid" tourist mecca; however, in spite of this, he still found a civilized sort of beauty at Niagara.

Henry James

HENRY JAMES BEGINS his description of the trip to Niagara by writing about how bored he is on the passage through Lake Ontario. The journey is dull for him because the water is not "raging and swelling," nature's hues are too uniform, and his spirits are not uplifted. He concludes that this episode of vacuity is "a kind of calculated preparation for the uproar of Niagara—a pause or hush on the threshold of a great impression."[88] This is a familiar pattern of response: he anticipates the sound ("a pause or hush") and builds up the scene for the "great impression." As he travels further upstream, he becomes more self-conscious about language and uses the pronoun "you" to share his confidences and emotions: "As you proceed, the river begins to tell its tale—at first in broken syllables of foam and flurry, and then, as it were, in rushing, flashing sentences and passionate ejaculations" (365). James sees the river as articulation, expression—an early indication that he will not suffer the breathless inundations that elude language. His writing has an intimate feel, like Margaret Fuller's, but it is also evocative of Kant's educated sublime, especially his figures of speech for the river as "tale," "syllables," "sentences and…ejaculations" and, on the next page, as "vomitorium" (366)—an opening in an ancient Roman amphitheatre. By describing Niagara in such a way (as "vomitorium"), James binds the elements of sublimity and geology together with an original conceit that sees the convulsive, chaotic force of water rush the "articulation" along a narrow gorge right into the "theatre" of dramatic representation.

Having set the stage, James continues to draw on different analogues to transcend the stock, conventional experience. He postpones describing the actual waterfalls; instead, he lingers on the built structures around them: "the horribly vulgar shops and booths and catchpenny artifices which have pushed and elbowed to within the very spray of the Falls" (366). This moralizing attitude has James dwelling on "sordid" conditions instead of on Niagara's sublimity:

> A side-glimpse of the Falls, however, calls out your philosophy;
> you reflect that this may be regarded as one of those sordid fore-
> grounds which Turner liked to use, and which may be effective as
> a foil; you hurry to where the roar grows louder. (367)

Artifice sets off the natural by contrast and, in the process, a shared "philosophy" develops between James and the ideal reader (who would hate to see such tasteless displays). Margaret Fuller was unperturbed by the buildings—they did not ruin Niagara for her. Fuller's impression, scripted by the discourse of Burke's sublime, implied that nature was too immense and grand to be swallowed by something built by humans. On the other hand, for Anthony Trollope the buildings at

Niagara "cluttered" the landscape and provided his narrator with a personal mission to strike a haughty pose and show himself off as more sophisticated than the "common" tourist. Likewise for Henry James. William Stowe calls the speaker in James's travel sketches a connoisseur of landscape and architecture and an expert creator and packager of aesthetic experience, who invites his readers to distinguish themselves by following closely in his footsteps. The object of his quest is a perfect aesthetic moment, to be translated into charming, descriptive prose.[89]

James may have been intent on helping his audience find aesthetic satisfaction, but in the process he engages in a number of "philosophies" (his word), namely, the theories of good taste and nationalism. Both of these ideologies may have been based on the historical writings of Francis Parkman. In his work, Parkman promoted the philosophy of "supersophistication" about nature and nationality. James, who had reviewed Parkman's *The Jesuits in North America in the Seventeenth Century* (1867) for *The Nation* a few years before venturing to Niagara, was probably influenced by this Boston-based popular historian.[90] In Parkman's epic history, New France is seen as both an "untainted" outpost of European civilization in North America and, contradictorily, as despotic, corrupt, and Catholic. The book also promotes a belief in the authority of Americans over all the inhabitants of the continent, and the notion of Canada as a northward extension of the United States—two concepts that stand in stark contrast to Frances Trollope's, Charles Dickens's, and Anthony Trollope's approval of the British colonial system. (James had also commented on the work of Dickens and Anthony Trollope in *The Nation*.[91]) In any case, James's itinerary reversed the "footsteps" of Parkman's westward-moving missionaries. James's evaluation of his sojourn in Canada appeared in *The Nation* as two essays, "Niagara Falls" and "Quebec City," both of which were published in 1871. When the two compositions were collected together in *Portraits of Places* (1883), their order was reversed, making it seem as if he travelled to Quebec City first and then Niagara last.

Henry James's notions about the history of Canada also reflect many of the same attitudes as Parkman's. A good example of this occurs in James's piece on Quebec City, when he writes about a Canada that is destined to be absorbed by the United States:

I suppose no patriotic American can look at all these things, however idly, without reflecting on the ultimate possibility of their becoming absorbed into his own huge state. Whenever, sooner or later, the change is wrought, the sentimental tourist will keenly feel that a long stride has been taken, roughshod, from the past to the present. The largest appetite in modern civilisation will have swallowed the largest morsel.[92]

His tone is characterized by regret mainly because French Canada's old-world charm appeals to him and he is distressed that America, which he calls "the largest appetite in modern civilisation," will destroy it. The philosophy of "supersophistication" continues to fuel his complaint about touristy Niagara, making him wonder whether it is an unrighteous ideal,

> that with the slow progress of taste and possible or impossible growth of some larger comprehension of beauty and fitness, the public conscience may not tend to confer upon such sovereign phases of nature something of the inviolability and privacy which we are slow to bestow, indeed, upon fame, but which we do not grudge at least to art. (367)

Nathaniel Hawthorne was concerned with "good taste" too. He had expected to be overwhelmed by a wild, untamed Niagara, but the scene he encountered was not as artful as the one anticipated. Conversely, Henry James brings up the idea of taste not to talk about his disappointment and unworthiness, but to describe how his sense of gratification differs from the standard experience. This feeling of satisfaction raises him above the usual crowd:

> The common feeling...I believe, is one of disappointment at Niagara's want of height; the whole thing appears to many people somewhat smaller than its frame. My own sense, I confess, was absolutely gratified from the first; and indeed, I was not struck with anything being tall or short, but with everything being perfect. (368)

The philosophy that James shares with his reader is that the sublime is too common a view. Perhaps James is just a snob. In any case, he uses this moralizing aestheticism not to suggest how the view affects him but, like Elizabeth Simcoe, to describe (how he has the right response to) Niagara's dimensions.

Following this, tourism intrudes into his narration again in the form of hackmen, photographers, and vendors. Similar to Anthony

Trollope, James advises the reader to ignore them and find release "by the fury of your indifference, and stand there gazing your fill at the most beautiful object in the world" (370). And, like Elizabeth Simcoe, James applies the precepts of his aesthetic to analyze that "object." His painterly eye (he studied fine arts with William Morris Hunt, Boston's leading portraitist) breaks the landform into graceful lines: "the incomparable loveliness of the immense line of the shelf and its lateral abutments" (ibid.). The colour of the waters pleases him too, especially the "vividly cool and pure" greens (ibid.). Once more, he appreciates the dimensions of the scene: "The genius who invented it was certainly the first author of the idea that order, proportion and symmetry are the conditions of perfect beauty" (372). After James has offered his opinion of Niagara's "perfect beauty," he switches from the second-person "you" to the third-person "they" and talks about what the so-called common viewer would focus on instead: "They see below them that nameless pause of the arrested current, and the high-tossed drift of sound and spray which rises up lamenting, like the ghosts of their brothers who have been dashed to pieces" (374). This is James's way of satirizing his fellow writers such as Caroline Gilman, Charles Dickens, Margaret Fuller, and Anthony Trollope who had experienced Niagara as haunted by spirits. He goes on to imagine a desperate struggle in the river and describes it as a humorous psychodrama: "They shriek and they sob, they clasp their white hands and toss their long hair; they cling and clutch and wrestle, and, above all, they appear to *bite*" (374, emphasis his). Other writers give form to their Niagara experiences by describing how the spirit of the waters is transformed through the transcendental sublime into God (Caroline Gilman), or how the faces in the water are transformed through Romantic rhetoric into a symbol of memory (Charles Dickens), or how the sound of the waterfalls is transformed through "anti-conquest" discourse into an Indian (Margaret Fuller). James goes back to the vomitorium idea to describe the Whirlpool, and he threads in the analogy of the "ghostly" swimmer when he imagines the swirling waters in terms of bodily distress, as "panting," "smothered," "pressed," and "groping":

[The Whirlpool] breaks into no small rage; the offending cliffs receive no drop of spray; for the flood moves in a body and wastes no vulgar side-spurts; but you see it shaken to its innermost bowels and panting hugely, as if smothered in its excessive volume. Pressed back upon its centre, the current creates a sort of pivot, from which it eddies, groping for exit in vast slow circles, delicately and irregularly outlined in foam. (376)

This is a new kind of Niagara writing. As when he compared the river with the shapes of the classical world (a vomitorium), his description of the Whirlpool's architecture becomes a bodily struggle, and its "agony" is translated into another Greek drama (an agon). In a final rhetorical gesture, he imbues Niagara with nobility too. His metaphor of a classical scene of contest transforms the New World into a civilized, Old-World place:

> The Canada shore, shaggy and gaudy with late September foliage, closes about it like the rising shelves of an amphitheatre, and deepens by contrast the strong blue-green of the stream. This slow-revolving surface—it seems in places perfectly still—resembles nothing so much as some ancient palace-pavement, cracked and scratched by the butts of legionary spears and the gold-stiffened hem of the garments of kings. (Ibid.)

Previously, writers resist, reject, transform, parody, and downplay conventions even as they stick to the basic patterns. James's rhetoric, on the other hand, turns the place first into language, then into history—also Romantic gestures, and a satisfying (reading) experience.

ONE OF THE COMMON THEMES in this chapter is how writers responded to the pressure for "original" descriptions. Part of their challenge was to find ways of portraying Niagara that would sell. Because travel writing was essentially a money-making venture, they wanted to satisfy the reader's curiosity and expectation and offer some new twist, while retaining the sense of beauty or sublimity or civility in one way or another. Even though Elizabeth Simcoe did not write explicitly for publication, her account is "artful." She celebrates Niagara as picturesquely beautiful, and her aesthetic enjoyment seems both straightforwardly accessible and untainted. Simcoe's record acts as a foil for the next century's respondents. Frances Trollope's paradoxical experience of Niagara as an emotional affliction that ends in pleasure is part of the pattern of response based on Burke's principles of the sublime. With this theory of taste, the emphasis is on the experience of the observer rather than that which is observed. Trollope's distress begins with anticipating the scene, building up to it, refusing to describe it, and finally being inundated by it. This final tribulation is manifest as a sort of paralysis that she felt below Table Rock, when she stands in mute rapture—an experience that is far from liberating. Her Romantic recovery at the end, when pain becomes pleasure, is accompanied by a benign contempt for the danger of the process. She complains that the descriptives prescribed by the aesthetic lead to "nonsense"—a peculiar response that marks hers as unique.

The pattern of anticipation, disappointment, constraint, and recovery demonstrated by Trollope is found in the next writers considered too. One way in which each writer prepared for the trip was to read the accounts of others: their task in describing Niagara was to create an individual voice out of the common experience. Nathaniel Hawthorne does this by setting up a different tension in the build up. His tortured, prolonged denial—he actually dreads the moment when he cannot delay seeing/hearing/experiencing Niagara—draws attention to how worthy his "pilgrim" is. The sound of Niagara affects him differently from the sight of it, leading to an experience beyond words. (This may be what Trollope meant when she says that it is dangerous to go on in that vein because "nonsense" will result.) Not surprisingly, Niagara does not live up to Hawthorne's expectations: he blames himself for falsely conceiving of a wild ideal, confesses his unworthiness, and then spends a few hours in solitude below Table Rock, where he attains the right attitude and the full sublime experience. For Caroline Gilman, transcendence also comes through aesthetics. She is grounded in the senses (Burke's sublime); then, allowing herself to become emotionally overwhelmed, she is freed from the pains of her constraint and receives spiritual truths by connecting to the Deity at the Falls (Emerson's transcendentalism). Gilman compares these feelings with moral struggles—her way of individually inflecting the topoi of her rhetorics.

Making fun of the "breathless" tradition is Anna Jameson's way of creating a unique writing experience. She is satisfied when the "real" Niagara can be replaced by a vision; she feels unworthy, and calls herself, among other things, a "fat weed"; she talks about the impossibility of using language and then goes on to use it anyway. Her sublime episodes, her way of deriding civilized language (and protocol) and her parodic recovery all make this "double vision" or "textual doubling" a very gratifying read. Dickens meets the challenge of portraying Niagara by offering yet another twist in the pattern: he achieves the full sublime experience by stepping back, by putting a distance between himself, his anxieties, and the waterfalls. What he sees at Niagara are faces from the past—spirits of the dead. Since, at a certain remove, these faces fade from view, his aesthetic experience at the Falls represents a sublimated exploration of perspective and of memory.

Recovering the Romantic has therefore included being paralyzed by sensory inundations, and then equating the fear with transcendence and the pain with pleasure, with emotions, with God, and with the dead. Margaret Fuller relies on popular American iconography, but her description of paralysis as associated with wildness and conceived as a direct threat from an "imaginary" Indian is unique. She is embarrassed by the unbidden image of the naked savage because her fantasy is contrary to the various philanthropic accounts that inform her text. The dialectic she sets up both juxtaposes and conflates the philanthropist's urge to desire and idealize Indians, and the conqueror's need to despise and dispossess them. The "double" discourse or polyvocality that results from this tension allows her to sound various "voices" and maintain a disparate set of conventions. The trope of the hysterical woman threatened by presences real or imagined twists conventions from familiar meanings to meanings by association, substitution, and displacement. Those writings, such as Trollope's, Jameson's, and Fuller's, that are marked by an inclusiveness, where one voice contradicts the other but is not given priority over it, are part of the feminine aesthetic.

The apprehension that Niagara was no longer wild begins with Anthony Trollope—he disapproves of the way in which Niagara is "sullied" by tourism and advises the reader to block out the structures that ruin the view. As such, an appreciation of the aesthetic experience becomes a form of "eye-control." (This was also an element of Dickens's response two decades earlier. But Dickens advises widening the view to see the whole picture, and Trollope narrows the frame.) Whereas Dickens, who relies on Burke, is principally concerned with the psychology of aesthetic perception, Trollope, who borrows from Kant, seeks to determine standards whereby Niagara can be judged, and from there he goes on to explore the relationship between the moral life and aesthetic sensibility. Both Dickens and Anthony Trollope are also focused on the Empire, but Trollope is more interested in spreading colonial knowledge about Britain's relationship to Canada in readable and accessible ways. The familial imagery he employs naturalizes the power relations between the "mother country" and its offshoot and represents them as benevolent and domestic.

Finally, Henry James wants to appear to have a unique response when he declares that the dimensions of Niagara are perfect, when he puts himself above the rest by satirizing other writers, and when he turns the landscape first into a kind of language and then into a psychological personification. This is another common theme—Niagara as a connection to "internal" experiences beyond words and beyond the limits of civilized discourse. Nathaniel Hawthorne, Caroline Gilman, and Margaret Fuller focus on how Niagara's sound affects them differently from the sight of it; Anthony Trollope and Henry James focus on tourism and then move past it to some other deeper experience; Frances Trollope and Anna Jameson talk about the impossibility of expressing their feelings in language (the "nonsense," the depression) and then go on to describe their sensations anyway; Margaret Fuller uses the rhetoric she set out to resist. All these descriptions of paradoxical sensations and situations, and the way in which commentators adapt, transform, refuse, delay, or parody their rhetorics, make for transcendent experiences.

Travel writers at Niagara used the genre as a "meeting place" for various points of view, emotional exegeses, and literary styles. At their best, these writers combined all these voices and modes of discourse to shift out of the conventional way of seeing or speaking about Niagara, and into a "higher" speech and level of experience. A different tradition of response was created by the next group of commentators. These scientific writers tended to mix naturalist observation with a mode of self-representation that denied the anxiety (and fear and dread) that so paralyzed many of the literary respondents. One of the themes that emerges in the next chapter of scientific descriptions is a mastery over (as opposed to an indulgence in) sensory inundations through various tests and quests. Whereas the trope of danger for the literary commentators was associated with emotions, the Indian, and other haunting spirits, for the science writer it was instruments, a ladder, and the hysterical (female) tourist.

3

Naturalist Observations and Feats of Physical Endurance

> You may remember, to what a great distance Hennepin says the noise of this great Fall may be heard. All the gentlemen who were with me, agreed, that the farthest one can hear it, is 15 leagues.... When I was there, it did not make an extraordinary great noise: just by the Fall, we could easily hear what each other said, without speaking much louder than common when conversing in other places. I do not know how others have found so great a noise here, perhaps it was at certain times.
>
> Pehr Kalm, "Letter" (1750)

EHR KALM'S "LETTER" is in many ways a counterpoint to the original pattern of representation, yet both his and Hennepin's reports (and their attendant illustrations) dominated thinking about Niagara for centuries. As outlined in chapter 1, Kalm, who had read "almost all the authors that have wrote anything about this Fall," felt compelled to sort out fact from fiction.[1] To do that, he promised objectively to "observe nature's works with accuracy" and scientifically to "report the truth precisely" (54). This way of experiencing nature was different from Hennepin's, because Kalm offered an even broader authority for himself by testifying not only to nature's "workings" but to "truth."

Kalm's Linnaean gaze and record-keeping apparatus elaborately documented and classified Niagara's various features: he used a compass to establish the exact location of the waterfalls and another instrument to measure the correct height of the drop. While the account was written as a letter to a fellow scientist, Benjamin Franklin, Kalm's report also included a digression on Indians—a thoroughly compelling story of hardship and danger, not to himself but to *them*. Kalm's way of writing about the Indians' peril and his principles of conduct were part of the scientific method. This method, characterized by a desire to collate and explain, can be detected not only in the content of the botanist's report but also in his rhetoric: in the element of detachment (Kalm uses the pronoun "you" in an indefinite manner, assuming a general human reaction, as Hennepin did with his pronoun "one"), in the narrative tone and manner of observation, in the ways in which emotions and anxiety are repressed or deflected, and in the characterization or treatment of other people on-site.

In this chapter, I look at writers who, like Kalm, mixed objective or naturalist observation, scientific knowledge or testing, and a mode of self-representation I call the "quest-test." As with the previous chapters, I focus on how commentators on Niagara were both connected to each other through the centuries and connected to their own worlds and understandings. Hence, the writers considered here viewed and responded to the Falls on the basis of changing scientific assumptions about what they were seeing, and how to express it. Those who worked within this different tradition of response used language that tended to be specific (not overwhelmed, like the "breathless" descriptions associated with Frances Trollope); they often focused on the features that made Niagara a "wild" place rather than on feelings; and they tended to experiment with instruments, to verify facts by direct observation, or to study the effects of Niagara on characters other than themselves (as Pehr Kalm did with Indians). Finally, as I have suggested elsewhere, the writers in this tradition were as likely to refer to the discourses of natural history or geology as to aesthetic theories. While these scientific narratives of Niagara have received some important attention, few critics analyze the hybridized rhetoric that is common to this writing. Seventeenth- and eighteenth-century theories about how the earth works are an important resource for depicting these acculturating encounters with the waterfalls. But the way in which these ideas about the history of the earth arose from contemporary theories of taste has not been documented.

In chapter 1, we examined "the Lord's controversy," which saw mountains go from being considered "blemishes" to being thought sublime. Early eighteenth-century natural historians based their ideas of terrestrial processes on this controversy too. Those who favoured the Mosaic "chronology" held that, at creation, the earth was smooth and perfect, and only with Adam's fall was it changed by the Flood, after which mountains, escarpments, riverbeds, and waterfalls were formed simultaneously. As the Mosaic purpose was to reconcile the Deluge recorded in the biblical account of creation with the discoveries of geological science, it generally demonstrated the agreement of those findings with scriptural revelation. But a debate emerged in the eighteenth century among scripturalists. Some believed that the earth, still changing through the processes of "erosion" (wearing down to the bare rock) and "recession" (wearing back from a point of origin), was stripping away the evil and ugly and working back to a vision of perfection. Others held that the earth, in laying bare its foundations, was destroying itself. During the so-called "Heroic Age of Geology" (1790–1820), two groups of theorists debated recession and erosion. The Neptunists, who remained faithful to the Mosaic chronology, believed that the earth was "born" fully formed; the Vulcanists, on the other hand, argued that it was still evolving.[2]

Abraham Gottlob Werner, a Saxon mining inspector, founded the Neptunist school in the Hartz Mountains area of Germany. Neptunism, which was popular during the last decade of the eighteenth century, resembled the scriptural account of creation found in the Old Testament in that it gave credence to the primacy of water in the formation of the earth. This school postulated that the world began as a watery substance of particles, which crystallized into a solid form. After being submersed for almost 6,000 years, the earth was formed as precipitates from the primeval sea; winds dried the exposed crust, and the transported layers accounted for varying degrees of surface erosion.

The early Vulcanist model, developed by the late eighteenth-century French scholars N. Desmarest and Elie de Beaumont, took up Thomas Burnet's 1684 argument about subterranean forces and promoted the primacy of heat, as opposed to water, in the formation of the earth's crust. According to the Vulcanist revision, the earth, composed of silts, shells, and "matter" congealed into a solid mass and was heated by an expansive force, which elevated it above the sea. As the land resisted the water, this upward pressure accounted for irregularities on the earth's surface, such as the Great Lakes system and the Niagara gorge. Vulcanists also postulated that further volcanic activity had something to do with the change from salt to fresh water.

The twentieth-century geologist Charles Gillispie points to Vulcanism as the most important theory to develop in the earth sciences,[3] and to James Hutton and Charles Lyell as the school's two "prophets." A Scottish medical doctor, Hutton published his *Theory of the Earth* in 1788. According to one of the ideas in Hutton's book, the geological time scale was drastically lengthened from the biblically allotted 5,700 years to 450 million years. This new chronology clashed with scriptural accounts, and Hutton was widely criticized for its atheistic implications. British geologist Charles Lyell's contribution to the Vulcanist school was his division of the model into a series of catastrophic stages in *Principles of Geology* (1830). Lyell called this panorama of transformation "Uniformitism." This theory eventually reorganized the whole system of geology, and further challenged the accepted place of Biblical history within it. With Uniformitism, Lyell postulated that, during the earth's many different epochs, the ceaseless action of water and wind, elevation and depression sustained countless generations of organisms that were created and then destroyed. Thus, each age was preserved as a residue within the layers of the land mass. The varying nature of the fossilized relics held captive in the solid body of the earth was Lyell's key to the cataclysms that divided each moment of terrestrial history.

Although none of these scientists had been to Niagara before they formulated their ideas (Lyell finally went in 1841), their concepts were applied, and contested, by a number of writers at the waterfalls. In this chapter, I trace the variations of these alternative constructions of the earth as "ruined" or as evolving landscape from the early seventeenth century through the twentieth. As we shall see, these successive theories about the history of the earth connected the scientific approach with aesthetics. Natural historians, compelled to measure and document, conducted active, almost muscular investigations of Niagara's various features. Their accounts of Niagara's rate of "denudation" engage with physical, "manly" feats of artistic judgment.

The two movements that dominated taste in the later decades of the eighteenth century and early decades of the nineteenth—the sublime and the picturesque—have both been culturally coded "male." Edmund Burke's *A Philosophical Enquiry into the Origin of Our Ideas of the Sublime and Beautiful* (1757) makes a clear distinction between beauty and sublimity along gender lines. Burke defines the beautiful as something that flatters the viewer into compliance, whereas the sublime has the power to overwhelm or "master" the spectator. Further, beauty carries with it an idea of weakness and imperfection which Burke associates directly with women:

> Women are very sensible of this; for which reason, they learn to lisp, to totter in their walk, to counterfeit weakness, and even sickness. In all this, they are guided by nature. Beauty in distress is much the most affecting beauty. Blushing has no little power; and

modesty in general, which is a tacit allowance of imperfection, is itself considered as an amiable quality, and certainly heightens every other that is so.[4]

This association of one aesthetic with the physical concomitants of "sickness" (and with women) may account for the nineteenth century's obsession with Niagara's state of "decay." In any case, Burke sees sublime *acts* as the antidote to the dissolution produced by the beautiful (and by women): "The best remedy for all these evils is exercise or labour; and labour is a surmounting of difficulties and exertion of the contracting power of the muscles."[5] This counteraction, which divides the sublime from the beautiful—the men from the women—forms the basis of what Frances Ferguson calls Burke's "neat binarism."[6] Other binates constructed by Burke see the sublime broken down into irrational versus volitional origins; sublime delight arising only when danger and pain do not "press too nearly"[7]; and the habitual and familiar as especially remarkable until repeated exposure annihilates the effect: "It is our ignorance of things that causes all our admiration, and chiefly excites our passions. Knowledge and acquaintance make the most striking causes affect but little."[8] Because Burke's aesthetic is conceived of as both transcendent and muscular, uplifting and practical, his account of the experience is always paradoxical.

In his early essay *Observations on the Feeling of the Beautiful and Sublime* (1763), Immanuel Kant also declares that theories of taste are based on both judgments and emotions. Accordingly, Kant believes that men have an innate appreciation of the sublime, whereas women are more disposed to the beautiful: "The fair sex has just as much understanding as the male, but it is a beautiful understanding, whereas ours [the males] should be a deep understanding, an expression that signifies identity with the sublime."[9] While in his later writings, such as *Critique of Judgement* (1790), Kant held that the sublime was a universal emotion, accessible to all, this early "coding" of the aesthetic as male appears in some of the Niagara accounts considered here.

Lastly, William Gilpin's challenges and discoveries in *Observations...on Several Parts of England* (1786) and his way of experimenting with noise levels afford more awe than the natural scenery or the emotional response. When commentators practised this "male" art of "doing" Niagara, they often felt it was their distinct obligation to make dangerous journeys down rickety ladders, over slippery rocks, to the cavern beneath the waterfalls—"Behind the Sheet"—that some female travellers in chapter 2 refused to penetrate. As Niagara went from an arena for exploration in the natural historian's discourse of the eighteenth century to a place for scientific observation in the geologist's narrative of the nineteenth century, the scientists who visited the Falls often relied on contemporaneous aesthetics when writing up their responses.

To evaluate the claims of eight writers from the late 1790s to the early part of the twentieth century, I have divided the chapter into three main sections. The first section covers the writers from the late eighteenth and early nineteenth centuries who used natural history discourses. Among these were Pierre Pouchot (1755–60) and Isaac Weld (1799), who applied current geological theory to speculate about why the walls of the gorge were crumbling and why the Falls were "slipping backwards." Weld is also important because he initiated a preoccupation with making sightseeing activities into a test of strength. Just as the literary writers kept trying for originality by parodying, rejecting, or downplaying sublime convention, the scientific authors tended to "one-up" each other to retain a sense of uniqueness. Timothy Bigelow (1805) and Christian Schultz (1807) were two commentators who took up Weld's challenge. Their epic series of trials and encounters with the unpredictable shows how they made the Niagara tourist experience into a "manly" adventure. Bigelow and Schultz applied aspects of the scientific method too. Bigelow's evaluation of geological transformations that had changed the landscape mixed naturalist observation, testing, and a mode of self-representation that denied anxiety. And Schultz managed his uneasiness by experimenting with the volume and mass of water.

The scientific percipients also relied on technological innovations to "revise" each other. This is another theme that emerges in the responses of scientific writers at Niagara during the 1820s and 1830s. Basil Hall (1829), who goes one step further than Kalm when he analyzes the distances and variations of Niagara's noise, found scientific meaning in the auditory experiment. Hall's other way of using science, and of recovering his sense of mastery, occurred when he took a barometer "Behind the Sheet." For him, the mystery of that place was not about emotions or nature, but about technology. Thomas Hamilton (1833) was interested in the noise too. By firing a shotgun and by comparing the noise of the explosion with Niagara's "thunder," he found another way of inflecting Gilpin's picturesque and of quelling his fear.

The second section examines a writer from the 1830s—an exceptional British woman who took up the largely male aesthetic of mixing observations about Niagara's features with current geological assumptions. Harriet Martineau (1838) worked against the Frances Trollope type of response by objectifying the experience through science and through the "quest-test" mode of self-representation. Martineau also used another female spectator to undermine the "breathless" tradition.

Niagara discourse changes in the last section as we begin to move into the twentieth century. The axiom that the waterfall was obliterating itself through the processes of erosion and recession and through too much tourist "wear and tear" reached its apogee when the scientists recognized the importance of preserving it. Although for much of the eighteenth and nineteenth centuries the sublimity of Niagara mastered the spectator, different power relations emerged near the turn of the twentieth century when engineers gained sway over nature's awesome force. Even though the ideology of engineering had its foundation in science, which called for the conquest of nature, it also derived support from nineteenth-century philosophies about nature and from an interrelated aesthetic that described the awe and wonder—often tinged with an element of terror—of human-built structures and new technologies.

John Stuart Mill's "Nature" (1873), an assessment of the physical world as imperfect, was crucial not only to imperialist missions but also to scientific studies, because it claims that humans are morally weak if they fail to control nature. According to twentieth-century imperial theorist David Spurr, Mill argues that human progress is "the history of the great triumphs of man over nature—the building of bridges, the draining of deep marshes, the dragging to light of the minerals that nature had buried deep in the earth."[10] This ideology framed the nineteenth- and twentieth-century engineers' understanding of how to change Niagara's landscape over time. For the latter part of this chapter, I have selected a number of narratives that record the triumph of "man" over nature and that show the shift in aesthetic appreciation toward a new technological sublimity. The term "technological sublime" was coined to define this shift. While the idea of the technological sublime is contemporary, not historical, in *American Technological Sublime* (1994) David E. Nye claims that, as a trope, this type of sublimity, one of many interrelated aesthetics, had been deployed since the 1820s. Further, Nye claims that this shaping of the sublime to fit the technological situation was done only by Americans.[11] I disagree with his contention and suggest that this adaptation of sublimity was undertaken at Niagara Falls by British, Canadian, and American commentators and was not specific to one nation or nationality.

In the narratives considered in this last section, discussions about the uses and misuses of technology predominate, especially in the debates about whether Niagara is a natural area or a site for hydraulic development. After the "reclamation" projects of the 1880s, landscaped layouts seemed to settle the matter in favour of the natural. But the hydroelectric plants that came from another period of technological aspiration—the 1890s—inspired awe not for the waterfalls but for the generators and powerhouses built around them. H.G. Wells (1906), who both adopted and subverted the technological sublime, praises and fears "the machine" and other human innovations similarly to the way in which literary commentators were both titillated and terrified of emotions, fantasies, or Niagara itself. The following descriptions, which take us through the natural historians' series of feats and experiments, and through the geologists' attempts to make themselves "masters of the rocks," conclude with the landscape that Wells encountered—redesigned by engineers to control nature and people's experiences of it.

The Quest-Test

NIAGARA BECAME A FEATURED testing site for the earliest (1750s) discussions about recession, which was both a popular model of how the earth worked and an attempt to account for origins and actions. The first known writer to apply these ideas to the landscape at Niagara was Captain Pierre Pouchot. His 1755–60 *Memoir* of the war in North America between the French and British, first published in Switzerland in 1781, was translated into English in the 1790s. Pouchot, a geographer and cartographer, was the last official representative of the French dominion stationed on the American side of the Niagara River.[12] For the most part, his *Memoir* is a sensationalist narrative that dwells incessantly on bloated animal corpses shooting over the Falls and on Native people engulfed (canoe and all) by the rapidly moving river.[13] But the tenor of the narrative changes in the final paragraphs of the *Memoir*. When Pouchot describes how the river's banks have recessed high above the gorge, his language moves away from the anecdotal to the scientific:

> Around the falls we observe the banks eighty feet high, which
> indicate plainly that the channel which the river has formed, was

formerly almost on a level with Lake Erie. The falls of Niagara ought to have then been much higher than at present, and the bed of rock which exists, has been worn little by little to bring it to its present form.[14]

Pouchot's next observation—that "the chain of hills" far below the waterfalls may have worn back from "the old shore of Lake Ontario"—describes Niagara's recession from the Escarpment to its current place, many miles upriver.

Another first-hand account written less than a decade after Pouchot's adopted the current idea of recession too. Published in the *Antigua Gazette,* New York, in 1768 and written by an author known as A.B., this letter may have been based on Pouchot's theory of the retreating waterfall.[15] In any case, the concepts from Pouchot's *Memoir* and the letter by A.B. must have been widely disseminated, since accounts published subsequently frequently mentioned the possibility that Niagara's river system had altered over time and was still changing. A British soldier, Captain Enys, stationed on the Niagara frontier in 1787, wrote a lengthy journal account of his approach to the Falls, which included current opinions. Some of the guides at Niagara told Enys that the cataracts had been seven miles downstream. A medical doctor, Robert McCauslin, who lived near the Falls for nine years, delivered a paper to the American Philosophical Society (1789) in which he disputed the current idea that recession was occurring very quickly. William Maclay wrote a journal account in 1790 which used the testimonies of local inhabitants and guides to compute the rate of recession and the age of the earth: "Now, if 20 feet = 30 years = 7 miles, or 36,960 feet; answer, 55,440 years" (published in New York by D. Appleton and Co. in 1890).[16] Other respondents at Niagara repeated these ideas and helped to make them well known. For example, Enys's 1787 account was published in Frank Severance's *Old Trails on the Niagara Frontier* (1899), and William Priest's letter of 1796, which tells of Maclay's method of calculation, was published as *Travels in the United States of North America* (1802).[17] For natural historians interested in measuring rates of recession, Niagara was a "geological chronometer"—the irregular surfaces in the gorge and the possible origins of the waterfalls helped them to compute the age of the earth. All of these theories—published or not—may have influenced Isaac Weld's impression of Niagara. His account of scientific observation is juxtaposed with aesthetic commentary, which in turn is followed by instructions on the basics of "doing" Niagara.

Isaac Weld went to Niagara partly to draw and paint it. He begins his *Travels through the States of North America…during the years 1795, 1796, and 1797* (1799) by describing the scene eighteen miles downstream from the Falls. The way in which he frames this landscape suggests that Weld came from a different tradition from that of the travel writers considered in chapter 2:

> From the sudden change of the face of the country…and the equally sudden change in the river with respect to its breadth, depth, and current, conjectures have been formed, that the great falls of the river must originally have been situated at the spot where the waters are so abruptly contracted between the hills.[18]

Weld's comment about the origins of the waterfalls and his next observation about terrestrial processes that were still altering Niagara's topography suggest that eighteenth-century geological conjectures and the narratives of A.B., Pouchot, et al. informed his perspective: "it is a fact well ascertained, that the falls have receded very considerably since they were first visited by Europeans, and that they are still receding every year" (97–98). Because Weld was a visual artist, he was most likely aware of other cultural rhetorics too. A painterly interest in aesthetics is suggested by his use of the Burkean sublime pattern to describe how he anticipated the sight of Niagara's mists: "every step that we advanced toward them, our expectations rose to a higher pitch; our eyes were continually on the look out for the column of white mist which hovers over them" (98). Then he builds up to the roar: "and an hundred times, I believe, did we stop our carriage in hopes of hearing their thundering sound" (ibid.). Characteristically, he was disappointed.

Weld begins with the scientific method (when he comments on Niagara's origins and on the changing landscape), only to switch to an aesthetic model (when he anticipates seeing and hearing Niagara). His writing continues to alternate between rhetorics. After he sums up the view as "truly sublime" (99), he begins another discussion about the basics of "doing" Niagara by describing his experience on "Mrs. Simcoe's Ladder." Long after Elizabeth Simcoe had visited Niagara Falls (1792–95), and long after her family had left Upper Canada, the story of her descent down the two conjoined "Indian ladders" became popular. Made out of notched trees and placed on the bank a few miles downstream from Table Rock, the ladders may have been in use before Simcoe arrived on the scene; in any case, she is the first to mention climbing down them.[19] Even though Mrs. Simcoe's *Diary* was never published in her lifetime, other writers after her mention her feat. Perhaps because of her social position as wife of the first Lieutenant-Governor of Upper Canada, the Indian ladders were named in her honour. Whatever the case, the ladders were important to this early landscape not only because they made the place accessible and a territory to be conquered, but also because Elizabeth Simcoe referred to them as *Indian* ladders. Mary Louise Pratt would call this "contact" with the absent indigene. What the ladders historicize is an encounter not with Natives but with the "traces" they have left on the landscape.[20] This is particularly significant because Simcoe's husband was responsible for the removal of First Nations peoples to reservations.

Isaac Weld was the first after Simcoe to mention his descent down these ladders, which now represented traces left on the landscape by the policy-maker's wife. According to Weld, "Mrs. Simcoe's Ladder" made the journey less terrifying:

> [We] proceeded to...Mrs. Simcoe's Ladder, the ladders having been originally placed there for the accommodation of the lady of the late governor. This route is much more frequented than the other [the steep path below Table Rock]; the ladders, properly so called, are strong, and firmly placed, and none of them, owing to the frequent breaks in the cliff, are required to be of such a great length but what even a lady might pass up or down them without fear of danger. (104)

Weld's reference to "the frequent breaks in the cliff" is a reminder of his previous assessment of processes such as erosion and denudation, which altered the cliff face downstream from the Falls. Yet, according to this passage, the ladder facilitated safe, easy access past these terrestrial eruptions, just as it was intended to do. His description seems to encourage parity between travellers too, but this impression is contradicted near the end of the paragraph. The following addendum seems confusing, as it suggests that the ladder stops at a certain point and that the journey to the base of the Falls (sans ladder) is not an easy one:

> To descend over the rugged rocks, however, the whole way down to the bottom of the cliff, is certainly no trifling undertaking, and few ladies, I believe, could be found of sufficient strength of body to encounter the fatigue of such an expedition. (Ibid.)

This passage contains a caution for the woman traveller and a direct reference in words like "sufficient strength of body" to the Burkean and Kantian coding of the sublime as male. Interestingly, Weld himself does not admit to the collection of fatiguing ailments—sensory deprivation, feelings of giddiness, and a kind of paralysis that leads to protests of inexpressibility—experienced by the literary commentators (both women and men).

While Edmund Burke contends that sublime delight arises only through danger and pain, he is careful to insist that one must enjoy these feelings from a position of safety. Nevertheless, Weld's description of the ladder unleashed a masculine spirit of adventure; others tried to outdo him and prove their own worth by going farther than the lowest rungs over the rugged rocks and down to the very bottom. Weld also began a tradition in which naturalist observation was linked to climbing or other feats of physical endurance. The challenge was taken up by Timothy Bigelow. In his *Journal of a Tour to Niagara Falls in the Year 1805* (1876), Bigelow reverses the order of scientific information followed by anecdote by first offering his own practical advice on what to expect. Then, his rhetoric switches from impressions of the difficult terrain below the waterfalls to considerations of the rock strata before he goes on to add another feat to the itinerary.

Timothy Bigelow begins by describing how the very sight of the ladder almost frightened *others* away. He calls it "perilous" and provides an account about gentlemen who "forego their curiosity rather than attempt it."[21] He then goes on to present all the dangers before actually starting his descent. The details about how the ladder leans down the cliff and how it is only secured to the brambles growing from the top by "pieces of old iron hoops" set the scene and draw the reader in. So too does his use of the pronoun "you":

> After you have descended a few feet, you perceive that the bank
> from whence you stepped on the ladder projects, and that you
> seem to be suspended in the air. From the foot of the ladder, the
> approach to the foot of the falls is rendered extremely difficult by
> the immense and irregular masses of rock which have fallen from
> the side, and a guide is necessary to conduct you. (133)

The guide at the bottom of the ladder adds an element of humanity, of domestication, to this wild and dangerous place. The implied function of this person also means that the traveller's movements are being regulated according to the guide's course of action.

Like Pouchot and Weld, Bigelow does not dramatize his internal processes because he is writing from a tradition that mixes objective observation with scientific knowledge. His shift from descriptive to analytic language shows that he is geologically trained:

> The rock which constitutes the bank is disposed in strata, the upper and principal of which are limestone, others are of slate, no freestone or granite. Many other mineral substances are to be observed in it; and streams of pure sulphur ooze from crevices of the rock in several places, and leave a yellow concretion on the wall from thence to the bottom. (Ibid.)

This cross-section, or stratigraphy, is a conventional nineteenth-century geological "reading" of a river landscape. The bank appears as a column that starts at the bottom of the river and proceeds in "strata" through to the top layer of sediment. Bigelow's observations on the "ooze" and "concretion" on the wall are references to early Vulcanist ideas about each period in the earth's history being preserved as a residue within the layers of the land mass. (One-quarter of a century later, the eminent British geologist Charles Lyell outlined this process in great detail in his *Principles of Geology*.)

Like Isaac Weld, Bigelow switches from the descriptive to the scientific and back again. The "quest-test" mode of self-representation begins after he has reached the lowest rungs of the ladder. At the entrance to the cavern behind the waterfalls, Bigelow draws his reader's attention to the crumbling landscape, which he says "would scarcely support [me]" (ibid.). As he stands on this unsafe ledge, the wind behind the column of water "deprives [him] of breath by its violence," and the tempest of spray dashes mist in his eyes (ibid.). Yet, in spite of the fact that he is blinded and stumbling, Bigelow reports seeing live eels squirming through the curtain of water, his way of adding to the danger of going "Behind the Sheet."

Twentieth-century travel critic Ian Ousby claims that the late seventeenth-century cult of nature—a sensibility of the sublime—developed not only on European mountain peaks but also in British caverns. These subterranean marvels seemed the best places for testing complex geological formations—the earth's "deformities"—which could appear ugly or frightening. Even so, the veneration of caves and grottoes was not advocated until Shaftesbury wrote his version of the sublime in *The Moralists* (1709).[22] And, almost one century later, at the time of Bigelow's visit to Niagara (1805), going all the way "Behind the

Sheet" had not yet become a regular part of the itinerary. When describing Niagara's cavern, Bigelow does not dwell on violence, pain, or fear, but tends to bypass the problems of sensory paralysis and inexpressibility. He does admit that, "from these considerations, it will readily be believed that not many adventurers have proceeded further, and none much further, than we did" (134). Few of the scientific writers using this male aesthetic expressed self-glorification for "going further," even though they tried to outdo each other in the "ladder tournament."

Another male chronicler who tried the ladder and entered the cavern acts out his manhood in bravado and writes an account that amuses and instructs. Christian Schultz, who visited Niagara in 1807, wrote up his description as a lengthy "Letter" of response. In a postscript to his epistle, Schultz asserts that Thomas Ash's *Travels in America,* which describes part of the same route that Schultz himself travelled, "is found to abound in mistakes, misrepresentations and fictions."[23] Like Kalm, Schultz went to Niagara and described what he saw there with the intention of setting the record straight. Despite the forceful tone of the postscript, though, Schultz begins with a humorous account of "Mrs. Simcoe's Ladder":

> You will perhaps excuse my timidity, when you are informed that this ladder, which is eighty feet in length, is placed in a perpendicular direction over sharp and cragged rocks; and its being spliced and bound together in several places with grape vines, did not tend to lessen the ill opinion I had already conceived respecting its sufficiency. (137)

Like Kalm and Bigelow, Schultz addresses the reader in the second person, but his is a more personal usage. So is the way in which he constructs his "timid" persona: through it, he strikes a tone of innocence and vulnerability. This becomes obvious in Schultz's itinerary and choice of subject matter. He dwells on the suspenseful experience of mounting the ladder (the guide has already disappeared, and this heightens the atmosphere) and creates a self-deprecating anti-hero who does not dare anyone to do anything:

> I was at length under the necessity of descending alone, and had already gone about half the way, when I found the poor ladder, by some accident or other, had lost four of its rounds; this circumstance, added to its constant tremulous motion, did not render my situation a whit more pleasing; so making one more effort to

reach the yet distant step, and finding it impossible, without slid-
ing down the side of the ladder, and recollecting at the same
moment that I could not slide up again, I determined to ascend.
(137–38)

Kant, too, attempts to distinguish between the sublime effects of
height and depth, the former engaging a sense of "wonder" and the latter "the sensation of shuddering."[24] Yet, Schultz's account of his unac-
companied descent does more than just link Niagara to a European
theory of taste; the author is also undermining his authority as con-
querer of the wilderness. Mary Louise Pratt would call this kind of
rhetoric "anti-conquest." As Pratt observes, writers of "anti-conquest
narratives" tend to elaborate a rationalizing, extractive, dissociative
understanding of the world.[25] And, as with the method of self-representation of Margaret Fuller, with the "anti-conquest" strategy Schultz
seeks to secure his own innocence in the same moment as he asserts
European hegemony. The comically exaggerated description turns into
a moralizing narrative when Schultz declares that the facilities are just
not suitable for anyone, especially "ladies":

> I am much surprised that a place so celebrated as the Falls of Nia-
> gara, and which is visited by so many travellers, amongst whom
> are no inconsiderable number of ladies, should not yet have
> induced some enterprising person to erect a convenient house on
> this side of the river for their accommodation, as likewise a proper
> stairs for descending to the bottom of the falls. (143)

His focus on words such as "convenient" and "proper" suggests that the
facilities are inappropriate for "ladies" and even for men of a certain
social standing. Encoded in Schultz's struggle on the ladder as well is
his almost obsessive forward-moving task of painting the Falls as wild,
"underdeveloped," and in need of taming or improvement. His concern
is with controlling the "traffic"—(i.e., the type of tourist), not blocking
tourism out. (It would take another half-century for the tourist transformation to occur. After that, the common response was to complain
about how ruined Niagara was.)

Despite his initial timidity, Schultz manages to descend the ladder
and slip "Behind the Sheet." Once inside the cavern, he has difficulty
breathing the compressed air. What Schultz describes is a respiratory
attack that makes him "giddy": he feels "something like a blow in [his]
face" and he loses his hat in the sudden blast of wind. Instead of flee-

ing from the cave or collapsing from discomfort, Schultz conducts an experiment to test the force of the water flow:

> I took up a stone weighing one or two pounds and threw it with all my strength between the sheet of falling water and the rocks; it fell about forty feet from where I stood, as if it had there met something to oppose its farther progress. I repeated the experiment above a dozen times, and always found the same results. (139)

Stone-throwing, the first of many experiments inside the cavern, was one of the ways in which "manly" commentators regained their sense of mastery. Instead of Romantic recuperations through which the more aesthetic writers recovered language, these authors triumphed over timidity, surprise, or fear by trials of strength and experimentation. With each came different quests, new concerns, and, finally, more advanced technology.

The cavern that others (Isaac Weld and Timothy Bigelow) found too intimidating was a place of scientific discovery for the travel writer and "quest-tester" Basil Hall. He began his experimentation as Pehr Kalm did, by gathering all the accounts together before adding his own hypothesis. The retired Scottish naval captain visited the Falls early in July 1827 and published his description in *Travels in North America in the Years 1827 and 1828* in Scotland in 1829. Frances Trollope, who had read Basil Hall's *Travels*, wrote of being silenced before Niagara: she wept and vowed not to describe the sensations produced because this would lead to "nonsense." The sound of Niagara affected Trollope to such an extent that she found the scene disorienting and incomprehensible; Hall, on the other hand, achieves the distance necessary for interpretation through technological analogy and is able to analyze variations of sound: "In hunting for similes to describe what we heard...we were quite agreed that the sound of the Falls most nearly resembles that of a grist mill, of large dimensions."[26] And Hall may be "answering" Kalm's report (quoted at the beginning of this chapter) when he goes on to describe the farthest locale from which the Falls might be heard:

> There is precisely the same incessant, rumbling, deep, monotonous sound, accompanied by the tremour which is observable in a building where many pairs of millstones are at work. This tremu-

lous effect extends to the distance of several hundred yards from the river; but is most conspicuous on Goat Island, which stands in the centre between the two Falls. (164–65)

Although Hall compares the auditory experience of nature to industry, he then goes on to complain that the scenic effect of Niagara has been "rendered still less attractive" by the erection of mills, manufactories, and tourist facilities (165). He makes sense of the noise by likening Niagara to a machine, yet he cannot find aesthetic meaning in the human-built structures around the Falls, implying, once again, that Niagara's visual and aural pleasures are "recovered" differently.

Basil Hall must have felt it was his distinct obligation to visit the cavern behind the Horseshoe Falls, since he records three trips there and reports on his motives for visiting with such frequency:

first on the 3rd of July, out of mere curiosity; again on the 9th, to try some experiments with the barometer; and lastly, on the 10th, in company with a friend, purely on account of the excitement which I found such a strange combination of circumstances produce. (166)

In his *Travels*, all the separate journeys "Behind the Sheet" collapse into one "story," the wording of which shifts from an impressionistic description of emotional states (curiosity and excitement) to a scientific case study of the tests conducted with a barometer. Before Hall carries out his series of experiments, he sets the scene through a description of the inside of the cave, including information about the light, wind, and noise:

There was a tolerably good, green sort of light within this singular cavern; but the wind blew us first in one direction then in another with such alarming violence, that I thought at first we should be fairly carried off our feet, and jerked into the roaring caldron beneath. This tempest, however, was not nearly so great an inconvenience as the unceasing deluges of water driven against us. (167)

His language—"alarming violence," "tempest," "unceasing deluges"—makes Niagara into a dangerous place. It seems a test of strength just to stand upright in the cavern. Hall's next observations demonstrate his sense of familiarity with scientific concepts, evident in his phraseology, in words like "condensed" and "rarified," and in the fact that he finds it entertaining to listen to the conflicting arguments (ibid.).

Other respondents had complained of aches, pains and respiratory difficulties when they journeyed "Behind the Sheet." Hall's sense of amusement, and his scientific instrument—a barometer—are meant to dispel and/or quantify these discomforts. The barometer, basically a mercury tube, was invented in 1643 by Evangelista Torricelli to record the difference in air pressure at various altitudes. Before Hall conducts the test, he surmises that the atmosphere inside the cave has too much water (humidity) and not much air (168). Rather than perpetuate the myth about how unsafe the air is, then, he wants to analyze it. Again and again. His description is repeated a number of times, making the application of technology and the story about it into a ritual:

> The controversy respecting the elasticity of the air behind the Fall, was soon settled. I carried with me a barometer made expressly with a view to this experiment. It was of the most delicate kind, and furnished with two contrivances absolutely indispensable to the accuracy of experiments made under such circumstances. (169)

In still another passage, Hall notes that the barometer supplies him with other data too: where the mercury stands "even" at two locations outside the cave, it measures 29.68 inches, and from inside the cave the mercury reads 70 degrees Fahrenheit and "vibrates in the tube about four hundredths of an inch"—an indication that the pressure "Behind the Sheet" is much higher (170).

Despite his scientific stance, Hall's exposure to high humidity and constant vibrations exacts a toll. His emphasis on the physical and intellectual discomfiture is reminiscent of the more aesthetic responses of his contemporaries:

> Though I was only half an hour behind the Fall, I came out much exhausted, partly with the bodily exertion of maintaining a secure footing while exposed to such buffeting and drenching, and partly, I should suppose, from the interest belonging to this scene, which certainly exceeds any thing I ever witnessed before. (Ibid.)

Because Hall admits that "the interest" exceeds any "bodily exertion," he is experiencing apparent rather than genuine danger. Further proof of the influence of the Burkean sublime comes with the next confession—that it is "ridiculous" to try to describe Niagara:

All parts of Niagara, indeed, are on a scale which baffles every attempt of the imagination to paint, and it were ridiculous, therefore, to think of describing it. The ordinary materials of description, I mean analogy, and direct comparison with things which are more accessible, fail entirely in the case of that amazing cataract, which is altogether unique. (171)

Frances Trollope, who refused to describe the Falls, ended up talking about the "shadowy mystery" of the place. She actually gained control over her emotions through the act of refusal and eventually came back to writing. Similarly, Basil Hall is unwilling to attempt representation: "The ordinary materials of description...fail entirely" because Niagara is unique, and he can find no other parallel case. Despite the fact that Hall rejects analogy, he ends up using it (again). (His first analogy compared Niagara's noise to that of a mill.) In the following lines, Hall blends scientific rationale with aesthetics not only in his vision, but also in the language used: "I...left this lower world for the upper sky...I was traversing the Heavens in company of Sir Isaac Newton" (172). According to Marjorie Hope Nicolson, Shaftesbury described a similar cosmic experience in *The Moralists* (1709):

Thus having oft sallied forth into the wide expanse, when I return again within myself, struck with the sense of this so narrow being and of the fulness of that immense one, I dare no more behold the amazing depths nor sound the abyss of Deity.[27]

Further, Hall's reference to Sir Isaac Newton[28] connects his writing to an early work by Joseph Addison. In one of his pieces for *The Spectator*, Addison launched into a treatise on modern scientific philosophy, and sublimity, to defend Newton: "Here we have not only new heavens opened to us, but we look down on our earth and behold with astonishment the reptile mountains of living atoms."[29] While Shaftesbury found God in the cosmic universe, Hall's and Addison's soaring souls linked up with Newton.

Hall had the strength of scientific knowledge underpinning his work, yet he managed to combine a range of concerns. The scientist-aestheticist-metaphysician who tried to regard Niagara objectively seemed to have found in modern technology a barometer (as it were) for his anxiety. Such was the case when he tested the barometric pressure not through his emotions, but with a scientific instrument. Other writers also measured specific aspects of the Niagara phenomenon. Captain Thomas Hamilton, who was at the Falls at precisely the same time as Frances Trollope, did not weep or give in to emotion as Trollope did. Instead, he created loud, sudden noises to "sound out" Niagara's aural effects.

Hamilton was a Scots army officer who had postings in Nova Scotia and New Brunswick.[30] His fifteen-page impression of the cataracts, published in the second and final volume of his *Men and Manners in America* (Edinburgh, 1833), compares Niagara's "thunder" to a normal conversation: "the noise of the cataract is, certainly, far less than might be expected. Even at its very brink, conversation may be carried on without any considerable elevation of the voice."[31] Hamilton's writings about Niagara, far from being sublime in attitude—there is no anticipation or buildup or denial; he is not overwhelmed—constitute another experiment in inductive thinking about nature. Like Basil Hall, Hamilton is rational enough to describe the variations in sound, but, unlike Hall, he analyzes the "noise" as organic and makes a point of stressing how it is not to be compared with machinery or anything human-built:

> The sound is that of thunder in its greatest intensity, deep, unbroken, and unchanging. There is no hissing nor splashing; nothing which breaks sharply on the ear; nothing which comes in any degree into collision with the sounds of earth or air. Nothing extrinsic can either add to, or diminish its volume. It mingles with no other voice, and it absorbs none. It would be heard amid the roaring of a volcano, and yet does not drown the chirping of a sparrow. (526)

Hamilton's analogies seem paradoxical—he says the noise is as intense as that of thunder, yet it does not overpower a volcano's roar or a sparrow's chirp. However, when he proceeds to argue that the sound is generated in the "conducting" cavern "Behind the Sheet," the meaning of his fanciful imaginings becomes a little clearer. What he tries to argue is that, because the unparalleled noise "directed" outward has a tonality all its own, Niagara will not drown out any other sound. Hamilton confesses to being so enthralled by this "thunder" that he "employed a man to fire a musket below, while [he] stood on Table-rock. The report was certainly audible, but scarcely louder than that of a pop-gun" (ibid.). Hamilton's way of mastering the dilemma of Niagara's noise is to create his own powerful, sudden explosions to see how artificial noises compete.

Apparently, the fashion for testing the effect of pistols in caves and at waterfalls began more than half a century earlier, in England in the 1770s. William Gilpin recorded this form of entertainment at the Devil's Arse cavern in Derbyshire in his *Observations...on Several Parts of England*.[32] Ian Ousby maintains that spectators discharged guns for sublime effect; however, he goes on to suggest that this human-made equivalent of thunder clearly showed how nature "began its descent to the thrills of the fairground."[33]

Many of the writers considered in this chapter expressed admiration for Niagara (Pehr Kalm, Isaac Weld, and Thomas Hamilton), and even some excitement (Timothy Bigelow, Christian Schultz, and Basil Hall), but compared to the sentiments of the commentators presented in the last chapter, theirs were impersonal. Instead, the emphasis in scientific writing was on observing and experimenting. Kalm's way of moving beyond the feelings of terror was to measure the crests and assess the noise. Weld put himself to the test on "Mrs. Simcoe's Ladder" and, in a fitful moment, cautioned women not to make the same journey. Bigelow overcame his fear of the ladder—and his fear of unsteady surfaces and squirming eels—to analyze Niagara's different rock strata. Schultz, in all his timidity, mastered the ladder and then threw a rock at the curtain of water in order to determine the force of Niagara's flow. The act of describing Niagara through similes allowed Hall to distance his thoughts from his feelings: he compared the sound to a human-built machine and the sight to a metaphysical vision. Hall brought a scientific instrument into the cavern to measure the air and the resultant findings seemed to account, in part, for his discomfiture. For him, the customary hyperbole of the sublime joined with the hyperbole of new technology. And Hamilton extended the reports of Hall (and Kalm) when he tested Niagara's noise by comparing its thunder to that of a gun. The writings of the next respondent to be considered add to these testimonials. Working against the "breathless" type of response to Niagara, Harriet Martineau upheld the scientist's need to rationalize and to suppress grandiose emotions, and in the process, showed how others lost control.

Harriet Martineau

HARRIET MARTINEAU WAS ALREADY a well-known writer, having achieved early fame with her *Illustrations of Political Economy* (1832), when she visited Niagara. She travelled there twice: for approximately one week in October 1834 and for only three days in June 1836. The records of her impressions are both included in the same chapter of *Retrospect of Western Travel* (1838). In each account, she uses different language and focuses on different events.

On her first visit to Niagara, Martineau stated that it was not her intention to describe what she saw so much as what she did. She offers an account of her movements, on foot, aboard a ferry, and in a stage-coach. Along the way, she reports on the poor conditions of the roads and bridges, but does not complain about the discomforts (as others did). All seems to be taken with good humour, until she states, cate-gorically, that she does not feel "at home" in Canada: "We saw nothing to flatter our national complacency."[34] Here, Martineau sets herself apart from the other British investigators of culture in Canada—Basil Hall, Frances Trollope, Charles Dickens, and Anthony Trollope. This is the first indication that her account is different.

Harriet Martineau made her living by her pen. She had begun pub-lishing after her family suffered financial difficulties with the death of her father. (She could not become a governess—the most common profession for a Victorian spinster—because of a hearing impairment.[35]) She had accepted a commission from Saunders and Otley to publish accounts of her North American travels. Her notes actually became the basis of two publications: *Society in America* (1837), a systematic examination of creeds and cultures; and *Retrospect of Western Travel* (1838), a more impressionistic mix of philosophical and scientific stud-ies, descriptive passages, and hearsay. Part of her writing project was to find a way to comment on a wide range of nineteenth-century intel-lectual pursuits, including political economy, mesmerism, phrenology, Darwinism, and geology, and also to express more "womanly" thoughts. Hence, when she first describes how Niagara looks, the words she uses—such as "majestic oozing" and "volume of the floods"—are explic-itly anchored in the informational scientific mode, but when she describes how Niagara makes her feel, Burke's model of the sublime influences her writing.

In framing her understanding of the landscape, Martineau relies on Neptunist ideas about the primacy of water in the formation of the earth: "The most striking appearance was the slowness with which the shaded green waters rolled over the brink. This majestic oozing gives a true idea of the volume of the floods." (153). While this way of think-ing was more popular during the last decade of the eighteenth century, Martineau's description of Niagara as a flood may have been based on Abraham Gottlob Werner's writings, or on previous approaches that applied Mosaic theory to Niagara's history.[36] Martineau may have read other "scientific" accounts of Niagara too. She mentions the thunderous sound coming from "Behind the Sheet"—a reference, perhaps, to Basil Hall or Thomas Hamilton:

> It is surprising what secrets of the thunder cavern were disclosed to me during a few days of still watching,—disclosed by a puff of wind clearing the spray for an instant, or by the lightest touch of a sunbeam. The sound of the waters is lulling, even on the very brink. (156)

Frances Trollope was paralyzed by her auditory experience; Martineau, on the other hand, is "lulled." (Martineau's hearing difficulties did not limit her aural experience because she used an ear trumpet to "measure" the sound. In her case, technology increased the possibility of control over the environment.) After Martineau has delivered this personal impression—the mode of representation common to the aesthetic respondents—she shares it with members of her party and they have "an outpouring" (ibid.). This is similar to the way in which Anna Jameson "shared" her writing with an absent correspondent, but Martineau's "dialogue" does not move her into a more emotional state, nor does it suggest that talking about Niagara in heightened language made the scene more exciting. Martineau then sets this against the reactions of others around her. An English gentleman "found fault with every body and every thing... it was not surprising that the cataract itself failed to meet his approbation," and an American lady, so preoccupied with where she would "land" for the night, "forgot all about the Falls in her domestic anxieties" (157). Martineau appears amazed at their attitudes: their seemingly inappropriate reactions make her impressions "right." Hawthorne also moved from his own perception to those of the tourists around him, to highlight the uniqueness, the singularity, of his account. Martineau's motive is different, though. Her account seems more didactic than his. The information she shares is as much about how to organize an efficient itinerary as it is about a study of people, places, and cultural ideas. And her tone is ironic, as when she quotes an Irishman on the subject of Americans: "the gentleman [amused me] with some sentiments which were wholly new to me; for instance, he feared that the independence of the Americans made them feel themselves independent of God" (158). Since Martineau was concerned with writing a popular narrative, she incorporates current topics (such as American independence, from an Irish perspective!) but her diction and the fact that she presents these radical views through others undercut the seriousness of her message. Again, when she goes on to discuss a new geological theory, she presents it through someone else. This is a safer bet: if readers do not agree with her ideas, or if the information is false, Martineau will not be judged. This narrative device and her ironic tone are just two ways of writing in the "anti-conquest" mode in order to challenge the scientific tradition.

At the time of Martineau's visit, Charles Lyell's *Principles of Geology* had been published. Although Lyell had not yet been to Niagara, he wrote about the cataract in the first volume of his popular study.[37] Lyell's main argument in that particular volume concerned the rate of the earth's recession. A number of his points were based on local estimates from Niagara (such as Basil Hall's).[38] Martineau, who was familiar with Hall, may have read Lyell's recession argument, or she may have seen the British geologist Robert Bakewell's *Bird's-Eye View, Niagara Gorge and Surrounding Country* (1829)—a popular picture of recession at Niagara. Bakewell's illustration was first published in a science journal, and it also appeared in all three volumes of Lyell's *Principles of Geology*.[39] In any case, it seems that Martineau knew about the terms used by Lyell, and illustrated by Bakewell. Her incorporation of phrases like "worn its way back," "narrowing of its channel," "counteracting agencies," and "inundation" creates the sense that the writer is a scientifically astute observer of the processes that Lyell and Bakewell outlined. Interestingly, Martineau puts all the details in a footnote, because she wants to keep the theoretical discourse in her narrative but also wants to show that this is inserted knowledge:

> It is familiar to all that the cataract of Niagara is supposed to have worn its way back from the point of the narrowing of its channel (the spot where we now sat), and that there is an anticipation of its continuing to retire the remaining twelve miles to Lake Erie. Unless counteracting agencies should meantime have been at work, the inundation of the level country which must then take place will be almost boundless. The period is, however, too remote for calculation. (161 fn.)

According to Martineau, these ideas (about recession) were "familiar" to every visitor; however, my survey of women's literature about Niagara Falls from the nineteenth century reveals that few wrote about geological processes in such detail.[40] Because this geological information appears in a footnote in Martineau's text, it is defined as a separate kind of discourse. As such, it is like Pehr Kalm's digressions from the formal tone, but in reverse: for him it is the personal impression and for her it is the scientific narrative that are given a different priority. This exceptional British woman who takes up the (largely male) geological discourse does so by allowing other male tourists to speak on the subject.

The more scientific writers, like Martineau, created an alternative tradition. There is the act of observing and the sense of objectification, as when Martineau watches other tourists, quotes them, and derides their impressions (which make hers seem sagacious). This may be her way of engaging with the Kantian sublime, which sees percipients contemplating the dangers of nature and then managing a superior attitude by virtue of superior reason. And when she feels observed, she does not suffer a sense of inferiority (as Frances Trollope did), because as a "reasoning" individual she ends up mastering that "irrational" attitude. This occurs on her second visit to Niagara, during an excursion "Behind the Sheet." For Martineau, the adventure begins with the "extraordinary costume" she has to don (see figure 16):

> We ascended to the guide's house, and surveyed the extraordinary costume in which we were to make the expedition. Stout socks and shoes (but I would recommend ladies to go shod as usual), thick cotton garments reaching to the feet; green oilskin jackets and hats;—in this mountaineer sort of costume is the adventure to be gone through. (164)

Words like "expedition," "mountaineer sort of costume," and "adventure" suggest that she is ready to laugh at her own expense. For Christian Schultz, humour was a way of creating a distance from his anxiety about climbing down "Mrs. Simcoe's Ladder." Martineau's jaunty tone may also be playing down her unease about the costume and the rituals that appear to go with it. This becomes more obvious when the guide, a "stout negro," takes her hand and she immediately becomes obsessed by her outfit.[41] As others deflected their fear and terror onto the ladder (Timothy Bigelow and Christian Schultz) or, later, the Indian figure (Margaret Fuller), Martineau displaces hers onto her hat:

> I presently found the method of keeping myself at my ease. It was to hold down the brim of my hat, so as to protect my eyes from the dashing water, and to keep my mouth shut. With these pre-

Figure 16: Anonymous, *Oilskins to Go Behind the Sheet*.
(From *Frank Leslie's Illustrated Newspaper,* Oct. 25, 1879.)
Niagara Parks Commission.

cautions, I could breathe and see freely in the midst of a tumult which would otherwise be enough to extinguish one's being. (165)

Her focus on manners and on clothing (what twentieth-century feminist critic Catherine Hall calls "feminised sites"[42]) seems like a comic refusal to allow any grandiose or terrified emotions about the guide or the "tumult" through which he conducts her. Even when the strings unravel and the bonnet is spirited away, her fear is not described but the flight of the hat is, along with the guide's heroic efforts to rescue it:

> In returning, my hat blew off, in spite of all my efforts to hold it on. The guide put his upon my head, and that was carried away in like manner. I ought to have been instructed to tie it well on, for mere holding will not do in a hurricane. It is a proof that we were well lighted in our cavern, that we all saw the outline of a hat which was jammed between two stones some way beneath us. The guide made for this, looking just as if he were coolly walking down into destruction; for the volumes of spray curled thickly up, as if eager to swallow him. He grasped the hat, but found it too much beaten to pieces to be of any use. (166–67)

Just as when she had witnessed seasickness in others on the voyage out—she had lashed herself to the ship's binnacle to watch the varied effects of an Atlantic storm on her fellow passengers (29)— Martineau is at her best when she stands back to report on what she hears and sees. The situation with the black guide (and with the ocean journey) may have been compromising, but Martineau is not upset; rather, her rhetoric implies that she is in control and rational.[43] Later, she does admit that the gusts of wind and the air pressure were physically painful: "I felt some pain in my chest for a few hours, but was not otherwise injured by the expedition" (167). With this confession, the author is able to make the reader aware that she has had a physically demanding experience. But she was never overwhelmed—that would have been too weak. She makes this sentiment obvious through analogues. She sees a bird perish in the water—it got "bewildered," it "dove" into the spray by the Falls, it "flew directly into the sheet," and then was "swallowed up" (169). Interestingly, Martineau went directly "Behind the Sheet" too, but she had enough wits about her to emerge and tell the tale. And, despite the irony, it is a didactic one: her writing upholds the need for rationality over passion. The tragic tale of the bird is meant to be a warning, then, about what happens if you get too bewildered. Another example of inappropriate reactions to Niagara follows on the next page: "Today, I saw a lady who was sitting on the bank,—as safe a seat as an arm-chair by the fireside—convulsively turn away from the scene, and clasp the ground" (170). This passage makes the reader aware that Martineau, who has also put herself at risk, did not lose control—she shows how others do that. Further, she also makes it clear that she had the composure to look directly into the heart of nature, whereas another woman needs to turn away "convulsively" (as the figures in the Hennepin-based picture of Niagara are shown to do).

One year later, Martineau summed up her lasting impression of Niagara when she wrote in *Society in America* about a woman who questioned her overall experience: "'Did you not,' asked the woman, 'long to throw yourself down, and mingle with your mother earth?' 'No,' I replied."[44] This is a stony answer to the effusiveness that affected some female travellers of the time. Martineau does not dwell on what twentieth-century travel theorist Christopher Mulvey calls "the fall into insanity and the plunge into bathos that would have left her damned before her public."[45] Instead of making *herself* an object of curiosity, Martineau turns to a fellow (female) tourist and makes her that.

As a coda to this interesting development, another writer after Harriet Martineau found an equally unique way of using his female companion as a register of the complex feelings incited by Niagara. Walter Henry, an internationally known Irish-born doctor, challenged the idea that Niagara should be "done" alone.[46] Whereas Frances Trollope, Nathaniel Hawthorne, Caroline Gilman, Anna Jameson, Charles Dickens, and Margaret Fuller all deprived themselves of companionship or struggled for solitude, in his memoir *Events of a Military Life: Being Recollections after Service in the Peninsular War, Invasion of France, the East Indies, St. Helena, Canada, and Elsewhere* (1843) Henry suggests that every tourist needs a female companion in order to process the sublime:

I have visited the Falls of Niagara four times; and on three of these occasions in company with ladies—for the view of anything grand or sublime in nature or art is not worth two pence in selfish solitude, or rude male companionship, unembellished by their sex, and I have noticed that the predominant feeling at first is the inadequacy of language to express the strength of the emotion.[47]

Henry faces the same barriers as the other travel writers: he feels inadequate and he cannot describe the emotions induced by Niagara's sublimity. But he finds a way of overcoming these problems. He turns away from the scene and looks at another who is experiencing Niagara as Frances Trollope and Martineau's fellow sightseer did: "One of the ladies alluded to, of a refined mind and ingenuous nature, after gazing for the first time, with a long and fixed expression, on the sublime object before her, looked for an instant in my face and burst into tears" (187). While he is not deficient in human sympathy, the sensations that Henry writes about are vicarious ones. For him, sublimity is not tested with instruments, but through the emotional outbursts of women: "There are others so constituted as to be fascinated by the spectacle to such a dangerous and overpowering extent, as to feel a strong desire to throw themselves into the abyss" (ibid.). The implied loss of control exhibited by his companions makes these females into spectacles. Martineau sensed this, and in her writing she masters these impulses and does not give rein to the feelings. But, for Henry, the sublime is a rhetoric that seems to aestheticize the emotions and the women too: "A lady of good sense and mature age assured me, that as she stood on the edge of the Table Rock, this impulse became so strong and overmastering, that she was obliged to recede rapidly from the brink, for fear of the consequences" (187). While women weep and become distressed, he avoids losing control by reflecting on how Niagara affects others: "I am of a calm and subdued temperament, the result of long effort and much reflection on the silliness of giving the rein to strong feelings and emotions" (ibid.). The suppression of "strong feelings and emotions" is the painful part for Henry: it is easier to "give the rein" to them than to act with restraint. This illustrates the tension that exists in Burke's system between irrational and volitional reactions. Henry ends his account by belittling his companions, by calling their impulses "silly," showing that he (and Martineau) can shift into an empirical state, whereas his female companions (and Frances Trollope) are stuck in the realm of emotion.

OVER A PERIOD OF ONE HUNDRED YEARS, a number of original experiments in the natural world and in the realm of rhetoric led to participants measuring the Falls, testing their mettle, and witnessing the effect of Niagara on others. Previously in this book, we saw how particular eighteenth- and nineteenth-century images that aestheticized the Indian figure were defined in terms of current imperial ideologies and current aesthetic concepts of nature. We also saw that historical events influenced the way in which the human element appeared in paintings. To look at how some writers, such as Harriet Martineau and Walter Henry, aestheticized their fellow (female) travellers at the Falls, we outlined the refined code of judgment (the Burkean sublime) that advocated certain responses to the experience: feelings of terror for women and a sort of objective analysis on the part of men. Martineau was an exception to this. Using a more detached spirit of connoisseurship, she had the objectivity to observe another's experience of Niagara as "beyond all power of words" without being mastered by it herself. At this turning point in the history of sublimity, an almost separate, paradoxical attitude toward aspects of nature began to emerge. This new rhetoric—another attempt at mastery—saw the subordination of nature to human use and improvement. In the remainder of this chapter, I look at descriptions of Niagara that engaged with a new kind of sublime. This examination of Niagara as a site of technology and development begins with reflections on the first illumination of the Falls in Nicholas Woods's account of the Prince of Wales's 1860 visit, and on reports about the 1870s debates on whether Niagara was a mecca for hydroelectric power generation or a natural wonder. At this interesting point in the "story" of the waterfalls, too, there is a slight detour that outlines the conflict between scenic preservation, tourism, and industrialization. This countermovement between preservationists and capitalists led to calls for state control and the "Free Niagara" campaign. In their efforts to explain their undertakings, the promoters of technology at Niagara drew upon such familiar words as "tamed" and "harnessed" and freely mixed the metaphors of conquest and triumph to convey the power required to accomplish their task. This is an example of how debates over the technology-based paradigms of progress and development can be placed in the context of the imperialist enterprise. After governments intervened, there followed the process of "emparking," landscaping, and "harnessing" Niagara (in the 1880s). This brings us to the twentieth century, to the new age of hydroelectricity—the "manifest destiny of white men"[48]—and to H.G. Wells, who judged Niagara's "wildness" by its machines (and not by his feelings). He saw the hydro-generation plants not as a boil on the landscape, but as the epitome of infinite force and power.

Illuminating and Engineering Niagara

NICHOLAS WOODS, a special correspondent for *The Times,* was one of a number of journalists accompanying the Prince of Wales on his 1860 tour of the Canadian colony. His newspaper accounts were collected and reprinted one year later as *The Prince of Wales in Canada and the United States* (1861). Acknowledging in the "Dedication" that his audience was "the English public," Woods, the official voice of the Palace, sets the stage by describing the waterfalls as a "black and gloomy" backdrop.[49] Where Gilman saw God, Dickens imagined faces, and Fuller conjured an Indian, Woods brings on the Prince (and an illumination):

> The first view which the Prince got of the cataracts was on the evening of his arrival, when he saw them as no man had ever seen them before, and as they will probably never be seen again—he saw the Falls of Niagara illuminated! At the first idea it seems about as feasible to light up the Atlantic...[but] about 50 or 60 [Bengal lights] were placed in a row under the cliffs, beneath Clifton House, and facing the American Fall; 50 or 60 more were placed under Table Rock, and 50 or 60 behind the sheet of water itself...at ten o'clock at night they were all lit, and their effect was something grand, magical, brilliant, and wonderful beyond all power of words to pourtray [*sic*]. (245)

Part of the marvel was the amazing effort of lighting up Niagara to give the Prince a view that "no man had ever seen...before." This is what Fuller thought Hennepin had experienced when he came upon an untamed Niagara. For the late nineteenth-century journalist, technology could deliver a similar experience, which was also "beyond all power of words."

During the 1860s, Niagara was seen as a source of unlimited "horsepower," and geologists and engineers mused about harnessing it. While the scientists claimed that diverting water for power generation would modify the alarming rate of recession and thereby control the destructive force of the river, others argued that hydraulic projects would lead to Niagara's ultimate ruin.[50] Articles about the negative effects of expanding industries and increased tourism began to appear with increasing regularity during the 1870s.[51] The growing list of complaints called for the government to confiscate the land, to strip off the ugly accumulations, and to "redesign" Niagara aesthetically. The famous

American painter Frederic Edwin Church helped to organize the campaign, which became known as the "Free Niagara" movement.[52] He lobbied politicians and encouraged a letter-writing campaign. Church helped to determine how an aesthetically designed landscape was to appear, and his actions proved that his vision of Niagara did not exist independently of the social world. What Church proposed was styled like his canvases—highly sanitized and free of all references to development, industrialization, and communication:

> the natural formation of the rocks seemed to invite some artistic treatment especially by cutting channels for the purpose of forming picturesque cascades which would not only greatly enrich and diversify certain portions but also do much toward harmonizing the general effect.[53]

The aesthetician cuts channels for picturesque effect; the scientist, on the other hand, digs aqueducts to power the machines.

In 1878, Church approached Frederick Law Olmsted (known for his design of Central Park in New York City in the late 1850s) with his ideas. Both men went to Lord Dufferin, the Governor General of Canada, with their proposal for an international park.[54] By this time, a number of state surveys had been conducted to determine the physics of the Niagara River. Church and Olmsted chose C.B. Comstock's *United States Lake Survey* (1875) and James T. Gardner's *New York State Survey on the Preservation of the Scenery of Niagara Falls* (1879) to support their claims. In 1879, Lord Dufferin took Church's and Olmsted's advice, assessed the surveys, viewed the scene, and contacted the Governor of New York, Lucius Robinson, to inquire "about the possibility of cooperating in efforts to restore the site as an international park."[55] Following this query, Church and Olmsted conducted an inspection in 1880 and advised Dufferin and Robinson to confiscate the land.

In 1882, the other instigator of the "Free Niagara" movement, J.B. Harrison, wrote a series of newspaper articles that argued for a park that would uplift the "higher powers of the mind" and in turn help to civilize, and thus control, the lower classes. According to twentieth-century tourism critic John Sears, part of the effort to save the Falls was "an attempt to assert the values of upper middle-class society in the name of raising the moral tone of democratic life."[56] Science and a version of Kantian aesthetics were invaluable tools in this struggle. When the Niagara Parks Committee was formed in 1882, the Governors appointed Church and Olmsted to it. In turn, they hired American geologist James T. Gardner to survey the area again. Two other assessments followed: Thomas Evershed's *New York State Survey* (1883) and G.F. Wright's diagram of the lower Niagara gorge (1884), which calculated the effects of cliff erosion and provided insights into the river's future "behaviour."

In his book on travel theory, Dean MacCannell has argued that the tourist industry organizes all tourist attractions, even natural wonders or, as he calls them, "thrills of nature," into "sacred sites." The first stage of this process occurs when the place is marked off as worthy of preservation: "sometimes an act of Congress is necessary, as in the official designation of a national park or historical shrine."[57] Hence, the state of New York bought up the lands and buildings around the Falls (412 acres, 300 of which were underwater). The money came from taxpayers: "this was the first time in American history that a state of the Union had used public money to expropriate property for purely aesthetic purposes."[58] The "emparking" of the Falls, then, was an attempt not only to civilize nature and control the lower classes, but also to ritualize sightseeing into a state-approved collective activity.

Since the movement to establish a park was to protect the Falls from commercial and industrial "desecrations" (and from the wrong kind of tourist), all the mills, factories, tourist shops, and hotels were torn down. Next, to preserve nature from "itself" (i.e., to prevent recession and erosion) the cliff sides were bolstered up and the extraneous rubble was removed. Then, the whole area was landscaped and replanted.

Olmsted, the architect of America's Niagara, rejected all forms of sublimity from which he felt the desecration of the Falls had sprung. He concluded that most of the tourists who visited the cascades had "poor taste," were in a hurry, and were too easily led to the "astonishing arrangements" instead of pensively contemplating Niagara's beauty. Hence, Olmsted set out to "redesign" not only the landscape, but also tourists' expectations. In a reflection of his philosophy of the beautiful, Olmsted generally resisted the inclusion of anything obviously human-made in the preserve, including statues, monuments, and, especially, floral arrangements.[59] The New York State Reservation at Niagara was opened on July 15, 1885, and 75,000 people attended the ceremonies.

Canada's side of the Falls took another three years to landscape. The act that incorporated the Queen Victoria Niagara Falls Park stipulated that the park had to be self-funding, but the only sources of revenue available were souvenir, transportation, and tourist services concessions.[60] In order for the Canadian government to reclaim 118 acres along the riverfront, contracts that had allowed businesses to operate those very franchises (souvenir, transportation and other tourist services) on crown lands since the turn of the century were terminated.[61] The stairs, buildings and drainage pipes along the bank were declared unauthorized and torn down. Then, the Parks Commissioners (Sir Casimir S. Gzowski, John W. Langmuir, and John G. MacDonald) hired Roderick Cameron, a graduate of the Royal Botanic Garden in Edinburgh, as chief gardener. The Commissioners asked Cameron to preserve the natural beauty as much as possible and to augment it by creating a unique botanical garden.[62] Queen Victoria Niagara Falls Park was opened on Victoria Day, May 24, 1888.

In name and in style, Canada's Niagara was fashioned like a British park.[63] It was enclosed and well groomed. While the banks of the river separated grass and water, a wall of brick and iron along this natural edge made the delineation more ornamental. In addition, a parallel footpath (a "perambulation") along the river road added to the overall feeling of order and balance, even as it confined people to the park area. Entrances on either end of the promenade (in the form of modified triumphal arches), horticultural displays planted in a style called "gardenesque," and topiary avenues forming an "axial" approach to the waterfalls all suggested that Niagara was measured and shaped in the picturesque tradition.[64]

Niagara Parks Commissions in Canada and in the United States controlled developments along the land and the river. Business people, politicians, and speculators needed the Commissioners' permission to build toll roads, staircases, railways, bridges, hotels, and factories. Not long after the area was "naturalized," though, local entrepreneurs pushed for the most immediate financial returns. On the American side, the Commission's board rehabilitated the Falls' reputation as industrialized: iron foundries, tanneries, and paper mills were built on the shores above the waterfalls again. Within a few years, the Niagara Parks Commission on the Canadian side was selling snacks and souvenirs and leasing out tourist attractions—museums, sideshows, and hotels—all of which made Niagara Falls, Ontario a tourist mecca. Travellers still complained of harassment, and local business people began asking why it was all right for the state to profit from tourism but morally repugnant for them to do so.[65]

The so-called "preservation" of Niagara was short-lived. The dilemma presented by the attempt to create an exemplary park without either an admission charge or provincial/state assistance eventually induced the Commissioners to enter into what one twentieth-century Niagara historian calls "the most lucrative concession of all—the hydro-electric business."[66] Yet again, Niagara bore the promise of greatness: the "white coal" of falling water brought to Canada and the United States a constant source of power that could fuel new manufacturing processes.[67] By 1889, five hydro-generation companies had taken the advice of geologists to develop hydroelectric industries on the American side, and within a few years three other American companies had built plants on the Canadian side (to take advantage of the river's tilt). The early part of the twentieth century was also a period of intense development. The American-owned Canadian Niagara Power Company went into operation in 1905, and all the energy created there was sent over to the United States. The Canadian-owned Ontario Power Co. was built in 1906 to supply Toronto (see figure 17). Designed along classical Italian Renaissance lines, this power plant was located below the Horseshoe Falls:

A wide colonnade, supported by massive stone columns, extended along the entire 462-foot front of the structure, and from this colonnade visitors would be able to view, through large plate glass windows, the massive machinery which included eleven generators, each weighing about 386,359 pounds. The floor space, incidentally, was large enough to accommodate five regulation-sized hockey rinks.[68]

The very magnitude and mystery of turbines, generators, and, of course, the waterfalls themselves were enough to captivate the public imagination. Public tours of the powerhouses made them as popular as Niagara.[69] Because of their importance, whole sections around the waterfalls were engineered to keep these "palaces" of power in operation. In 1906, the Commissioners on the Canadian side did some remedial work on the exposed flanks of the riverbed near Table Rock. They took the soil and rocks excavated from the Canadian Niagara Power Company tunnel and filled almost 400 feet of the crest line of the Horseshoe Falls. These "adjustments" were thought to benefit industry and tourism because they added to the park area and made available views of the Falls hitherto unobtainable.[70]

After the powerhouses were built, one-quarter of the flow was siphoned off, considerably reducing the amount of water reaching the brink of the Falls and making the "preservationists" fear that Niagara would become a mere trickle if diversions of the river continued.[71]

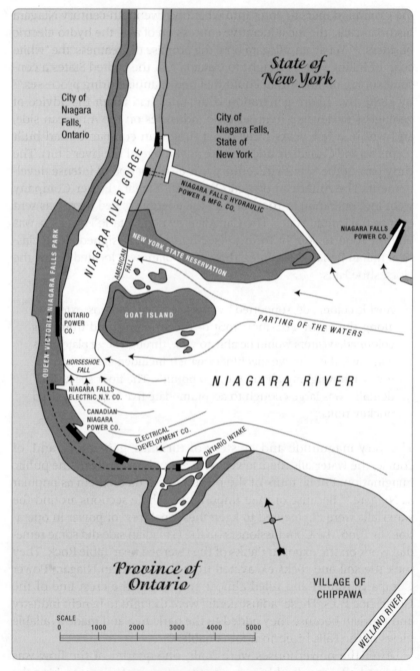

Figure 17: *Power Works at Niagara Falls* (1906) in Ronald L. Way,
Ontario's Niagara Parks: A History (1946), 70 (opposite).
Niagara Parks Commission.

Treaties between the two countries set quotas specifying the amount of water each could divert, but the power demands increased over the years, leading to massive reductions in flow.

H.G. Wells arrived in the midst of all these transformations. During the first decade of the twentieth century when Wells visited, terrestrial scientists were publishing their concerns about attrition, saying that land erosion due to water diversion, and not tourism or industry, was destroying Niagara. Wells also thought that the river's power could be put to better use. He added to the deluge of writing to argue against the "waste" of Niagara and, in the process, subverted the aesthetic and the scientific traditions in a new version of the "electrical" technological sublime.[72]

H. G. Wells

HERBERT GEORGE WELLS went to the Falls in 1906 and, in his initial impression, he states that the buildings interested him far more than the natural landscape:

> The real interest of Niagara for me, was not in the water-fall but in the human accumulations about it. They stood for the future, threats and promises, and the water-fall was just a vast reiteration of falling water. The note of growth in human accomplishment rose clear and triumphant above the elemental thunder.[73]

This is not orthodox sublime rhetoric. Wells is not awestruck by nature, but by the technological sublime; not caught in the immediacy of the moment, but looking to the future; not paralyzed by the impulse of the senses, but able to find pattern and sense in the built structures around the waterfalls. For Wells, the "human accomplishment"—the combination of gigantic proportions and technological complexity—actually saves Niagara from a type of "natural" sordidness:

> The dynamos and turbines of the Niagara Falls Power Company, for example, impressed me far more profoundly than Behind the Sheet; are indeed, to my mind, greater and more beautiful than that accidental eddying of air beside a downpour. (54)

In comparison with the waterfalls, Wells considers the powerhouses ideal—ordered, clean, and efficient: "all the clatter and tumult of the early age of machinery is past and gone here; there is no smoke, no coal grit, no dirt at all" (55). These ideas had a basis in the climate of his time. Science, applied in conjunction with "good" taste, produced beauty.[74] Wells also finds the powerplant's aural sensations to be aesthetically pleasing. He compares the sound inside the machine with a "cloister" and evokes the qualities that other respondents sought in nature, but never found because the noise of Niagara was too overpowering: "The wheel-pit into which one descends has an almost cloistered quiet about its softly humming turbines" (ibid.). Basil Hall, Frederic Church, Anthony Trollope, and Henry James, tried to block these structures out. For them, the pits, turbines, and powerhouses were sordid because only natural phenomena made aesthetic sense. This divergence in values shows how Wells differed from the aesthetic commentators when it came to objective and subjective levels of experience, to the realms of "function" and emotion, and to the rhetorics of science and art.

In resolving that a "harnessed" Niagara was aesthetically pleasing, Wells entered the controversy between industrialists and preservationists, between those who advocated an unlimited use of Niagara power regardless of the grandeur of the Falls and those who, while believing in a proper use of this power for economic purposes, still wanted restrictions to preserve Niagara's beauty.[75] Yet, in Wells's view, the debate went beyond economics and aesthetics because it was a moral issue:

> There is much discussion about Niagara at present. It may be some queer compromise, based on the pretence that a voluminous waterfall is necessarily a thing of incredible beauty, and a human use is necessarily a degrading use, will "save" Niagara and the hack-drivers and the souvenir-shops for a series of years yet, "a magnificent monument to the pride of the United States in a glory of nature," as one journalistic savior puts it. It is, as public opinion stands, a quite conceivable thing. (57)

For Wells, the problem is the waste of electric power, not the waste of revenue or nature. Between these two issues there must be a "queer compromise." As part of the method of looking at the world scientifically, commentators had engaged in inductive thinking about such compromises (change and progress). Wells's writing, which alternates between the hope and despair of Niagara's future, provides both a warning and an incentive to action:

This electric development may be stopped after all, and the huge fall of water remain surrounded by gravel paths and parapets and geranium-beds, a starting-point for dull wonder, a crown for a day's excursion, a thunderous impressive accessory to the vulgar love-making that fills the surrounding hotels, a Titanic imbecility of wasted gifts. (57–58)

This is typical Wellsian rhetoric: a mistrust of the power of those in control in tension with a need for humans to institute order and efficiency. He had that in common with most of the scientific commentators. Because of their training/experience/backgrounds, they desired to control that which caused anxiety. They did this through feats of physical endurance and through their rhetoric.

One of the common themes in this chapter is how the science writers outdid each other. The competition among the earliest observers at Niagara was not unrelated to the intense national rivalries between imperialist cultures in North America. Pehr Kalm set out to "better" Hennepin, and his emphasis on moving beyond the "lies," on shifting from the marvellous to the measured, was linked to the dynamics of meaning-making on the frontier. So too the "ladder tournament," a kind of "tribal" rite that saw men deliberately venturing into hazardous, marginal areas to flirt with danger and death. They may have been seeking the qualities of the sublime set out throughout Burke's *Enquiry,* or they may have been engaging at a more subconscious level with their own cultural "expansionist" enterprises.

As the feats got wilder (climbing down rickety ladders, finding a foothold from which to throw rocks, withstanding intense pressures inside the cavern) and the technology more sophisticated, the scientific respondents tended to aestheticize their equipment and to test Niagara's phenomena with these instruments (not with their emotions). This was part of the male aesthetic. Thomas Hamilton's experiment with firing a musket augments Kalm's account, but not through self-glorification. Scientific writers like Hamilton were less likely to dramatize their internal processes, such as anticipation, disappointment, or sensual discomfort. And, instead of describing the depth of their own suffering, they were more likely to observe and report this in others. Harriet Martineau's little story about the "overwhelmed" makes a spectacle of another tourist. She uses this other woman to deflect her own unease and to undermine the "breathless" tradition. Martineau's was definitely a commercial venture—she needed to satisfy the reader's expectation of "original" description. Her approach is to incorporate "hot" topics (such as politics and geology) into a popular narrative, and then to undercut the didactic nature of this male discourse by showing how it is inserted knowledge. Because of this subversion, her writing is part of the feminine aesthetic.

Commentators at Niagara who were self-controlled did not act overwhelmed, but they described that feeling in others. Hence, another common factor among scientific authors is that they were not as interested in experiencing Niagara in solitude. Pehr Kalm and Harriet Martineau decided beforehand to ask everyone in their parties for their impressions before venturing their own opinions. The military surgeon Walter Henry aestheticizes his female companion (as others aestheticized the ladder or their equipment) and reasserts his (male) strength of mind. In a final evolution in the second half of the nineteenth century, writers began to aestheticize "the machine." Nicholas Woods describes how technology delivered an "untamed" experience "beyond all power of words." And, during the first decade of the twentieth century, H.G. Wells presented the turbines, dynamos, and power plants as more beautiful than "sordid" nature. Woods and Wells were writing for publication (perhaps Hamilton and Hall were too). In any case, whether the scientific writers are marvelling about the technical possibilities, initiating new itineraries, describing the scene through similes, combining interesting aesthetic and scientific narratives, or creating sets of laws to both explain and predict the phenomena, their presentations make Niagara into a wonder—of nature, of endurance, and, finally, of technology.

To conclude with Wells in the early 1900s is to end this study of Niagara with a "queer compromise" that prioritizes industry over nature. Yet, like many of the depictions over the centuries, this one shows how the Falls can be a touchstone for understanding the connection between humans, the world, and all the complicated cultural issues that are still relevant to the Niagara of our era.

Conclusion

We must have new combinations of language to describe the Fall of Niagara.

Thomas Moore (1804)[1]

*T*HE FIRST COMMENTATOR ON NIAGARA, Louis Hennepin (1697), reacted with horror and awe, but he felt unfit for the task of describing the Falls because he did not want to disappoint his readers. This is not a comment on his ability as a writer; rather, it is a condition of the aesthetic he was using. Hennepin was influenced by mid-seventeenth-century concepts of nature, and his report, along with the engraving based on that presentation, constructs a world of reaction to the awesomeness of Niagara. At different times, the Niagara tour seemed to be surrounded and regulated by Hennepin's report and the image based on it. Faced with the challenges of painting or describing Niagara, artists and writers turned with remarkable consistency to the seminal European image codified by Hennepin. I have not intended to suggest that they were simply imitating or mechanically reproducing Hennepin's discourse, however. Hennepin, I have suggested, was invoked mainly as a gesture and as a point of departure for other imaginative and ideological projects. According to Mary Louise Pratt, these later artists and writers were "transculturating" European materials, "selecting and deploying them in ways that do not simply reproduce the hegemonic visions of Europe or simply legitimate the designs of European capital."[2] Instead, painters after Hennepin used his scenery as an imaginary stage of war, peace, nation-building, and industrialization. And writers who appropriated Hennepin transformed his discourse into quests for self-realization or for God, or created specific relationships to North American expansionism and forms of imperial authority. As such, they designed new visual and rhetorical "combinations" to describe Niagara Falls.

Pehr Kalm (1750) illustrates the varied profile of science-related writing on the frontier of European expansion. As part of his "double journey" (to use Michel Butor's term), Kalm's narrative, which measures and catalogues knowledge of a new land, revisits the original pattern of representation (Hennepin's) and documents Europe's current ideologies, especially when Kalm describes Indians as childlike and wedded to a way of life that is seen as unprogressive. Elizabeth Simcoe (1794) also read Hennepin's account, yet she does not accede to his particular response. Her enjoyment, excitement, and curiosity are confined in their applications to descriptions of nature (as picturesque beauty), not to her emotional state. These two writers typify thinking in two converse traditions (the scientific and the aesthetic); hence, their different rhetorical emphases.

The great popularity of Kalm arose from his promised veracity, yet he was unable to distance himself from Hennepin's tendency to exaggeration (even though he set out to do that). Kalm initiates a response that involves two different kinds of expression: the wild and the marvellous, associated with emotions and with an Indian legend; and the civilized and mastered, associated with colonialism and with science.

In another eighteenth-century visual based on Hennepin, Henry Fuseli (1776) links Niagara with the marvellous when he paints a gun-toting Indian figure at the Falls. A new fine arts valuation of nature as a primordial wilderness (and the aboriginal as the "noble savage") placed this view within the aesthetic of the sublime. The literary sublime at Niagara evolved later than the visual one and incorporated within it feelings of fear and terror. Margaret Fuller's (1844) chronicle of Niagara as haunted by a similar Indian and her tropes which reduce that figure to savagery are based on what Philip Deloria calls two interlocked American traditions: one of self-criticism, the other of conquest.[3] While Fuller had set out to plead for the victimized Indian—she had read extensively in the field of philanthropic writings about vanishing tribes—she ended up using the uncomplimentary rhetoric that she had set out to resist when she describes the Indian as a threat to civilized woman. The biases of popular American culture, as much as the aesthetics of sublimity, also pervade Fuller's thinking. And, while she claims to disapprove of the image of the naked savage (after all, it came to her "unbidden"), he nevertheless serves as an oppositional figure against whom she might imagine a civilized national self.

While the legends abound, indigenous voices are never quoted, reproduced, or even invented. Instead, they are glimpsed through anecdotes by Kalm and through "traces" left on the landscape: the Indian ladder, the ghost-like figures of naked warriors in Fuller. These writings and images produce the indigenous peoples and then abstract them from the history that is being made. This is balanced by the kind of writing that Mary Louise Pratt would call "anti-conquest"—a strategy of representation whereby the "colonizing" protagonist strikes a tone of innocence and vulnerability.[4] What matters for the "anti-conquest" is not the contribution to scientific knowledge or to art, but rather the simple fact of having braved the extremes, of having climbed down to the edge of a cultural, psychological, or physical otherness, and having lived to tell about it. Basil Hall (1827) and Thomas Hamilton (1830) made some interesting discoveries during their "quest-tests": the task of experimenting with air pressure and noise induced more awe than the natural scenery or the emotional response. Others discharged guns—the human-made equivalent of real thunder—to unleash more noise and make Niagara sound louder. The rituals of the male aesthetic through which they proved their mettle made the place seem dangerous and wild.

Representations of Niagara before and after the aesthetic influence of the sublime are properly distinctions between the projection of an idea upon nature and the process of the mind discovering itself through nature. Writers at Niagara who inflected the sublime submitted to sensory inundations or deprivations during which they stood in mute rapture—an experience that was far from liberating. When the "translation" came, it did so through the rhetorical process. The intensity of Frances Trollope's (1832) "breathless" internal drama makes her incapable of describing nature and only able to record her emotions. To protest inexpressibility was another essential Niagara experience. While both Hennepin and Kalm apologized—the missionary because he could not hope to satisfy the reader's curiosity (even though he did!) and the botanist because his description would not astonish (even though it did!)—Trollope's confession is about the impossibility of language, as if Niagara is so wild that civilized discourse cannot hope to account for it. Her narrative initiates the idea of an experience "beyond the power of words." This allowed Trollope and others to get past the many aspects of Niagara that were disappointing, tame, or ugly.

Some writers achieved this "deeper-than-words" experience by focusing on the sound of Niagara. The first artifact to emerge from a European vision showed the spectators distracted by the noise of the Falls, which may have piqued Kalm's interest. His assessment that Nia-

gara was not as loud as normal levels of conversation was followed by
Basil Hall's (1827) comparison of Niagara with millstones and Thomas
Hamilton's (1830) with thunder. For these scientific commentators
(Kalm, Hall, and Hamilton), sound variations could be analyzed without them succumbing to aural or other inundations. When Nathaniel
Hawthorne (1835) and Caroline Gilman (1838) reacted to the noise
(in the mode of the sublime), they suffered acutely. Hawthorne seems
to fall back on the first explorer's reaction—he feels unworthy and is
disappointed with himself. Once he stops expecting the scene to look
like one of its wild images (in reality, it seems too "tasteful"), Hawthorne
becomes attuned to something beyond his ken and he is able to
recover lost feelings of awe. So, too, when Anthony Trollope (1862)
says that Niagara is melodious and soft, yet loud as thunder. Again, this
somewhat paradoxical description is another attempt to write the marvellous. As such, it met the expectations of the reader—desires that had
been formed by well-established schemata and by a body of literature
expressing the indescribable.

The overall feeling of inadequacy—Hennepin's word—shifted from
the unpreparedness of the spectator to the ugliness of the object and
back to the spectator's lack of exaltation, enthusiasm, and wonder.
Anna Jameson (1838) locates herself within this latter vision and uses
mocking words to account for the fact that Niagara does not live up
to its exaggerated representations. She does not blame others (as Kalm
does); instead, like Hennepin and Hawthorne, she blames herself. Her
reaction codifies the aesthetics of her day in that it is both a self-
effacement and a response to nature. Jameson is not out to prove others wrong; rather, she is there to evaluate her own disillusionment.
The circumstances of her trip abroad also had something to do with
her state of mind and her choice of diction: she needed to write a
highly personal account that was frank about her "unacceptable" choice
of lifestyle (she was separated from her husband). To accommodate her
transgression, and the views that disappoint, her writing often veers
toward a satiric denunciation, as when she confesses to feeling weak
and miserable and then patronizes herself in a counternarrative voice,
or as when she is satisfied that the "real" Niagara (that depresses her)
can finally be replaced by an imitative vision. This type of self-translation—not a trope, but a manipulation of genres in which the writer
is not only the object of change, but also the agent of change—leads
to a kind of doubleness, or polyvocality, that critics such as Mary
Mason, Bina Friewald, Rachel Blau DuPlessis, and Thomas Gerry call
the feminine aesthetic.

The feminine aesthetic was also in operation through accounts that played up the unease to the point at which the inundations or deprivations became indescribable. Then they went on to present the experience as something beyond the limits of civilized language. This rhetorical strategy of gaining intellectual control over the Niagara phenomenon was a Romantic recuperation. Each writer managed to revive the reverie in a unique way—after all, these stories were written to sell. Other kinds of discourse had respondents recovering a sense of mastery (and not a sense of sublimity).

Harriet Martineau (1838) and Walter Henry (1843) measured the awe of Niagara not through instruments but through their human companions. Like the other impecunious women writers who turned to writing to support themselves and their families (such as Anna Jameson, Frances Trollope, and Margaret Fuller), Martineau travelled to Niagara, the most popular spot for tourists, to sell more books. And, like her contemporaries, Martineau worked within fields of rhetoric—in her case, the sublime, and the geological—to assess the qualities of Niagara and of human nature. When Martineau describes how another female spectator quivers with fear, we get a unique portrait of a woman writer mastering her own emotions and adopting an attitude of superiority over the "common" female viewer.

Even as the writers were being transported to the edge of a new consciousness, where there was a sense of being observed, there was also a sense of inferiority. Frances Trollope becomes aware of the proximity of Thomas Hamilton, and Margaret Fuller of her "imaginary" Indian; even the women who make spectacles of themselves break from "being sublimed" by Niagara to notice Harriet Martineau and Walter Henry watching them experience the dread. This is another example of a "dominant" group "mirroring" itself: any emotions approximating the sublime ideal were judged sufficiently irrational to be included in the sketch. Other common themes were the various put-downs of national "types"—Americans (by the British) and Canadians (by an American). And Anthony Trollope's (1862) censure of tourists, and of the amenities that catered to them, was meant to prove that the prescribed view or activity was somehow inappropriate to a person of his demeanour. His criticism was also levelled at those who attempted to exploit nature for financial gain, like the businessman portrayed later in Arthur Lumley's (1873) drawing.

While most travellers of the nineteenth century complained that Niagara did not so much have an affect as be an effect, they actually welcomed the advances made possible by technology—roads, canals, bridges, railways, and tourist facilities—but disapproved of the way in which nature had been ruined by development. (It was standard practice to denigrate the human-built structures, but not to put down the "common" viewer. That is why the descriptions by Harriet Martineau, Walter Henry, Anthony Trollope, and Henry James are unique.) In the history of responses to tourism and development, Isaac Weld was the first to complain that the facilities at Niagara were not suitable— for women. Basil Hall (1827), one of the first to utilize new scientific equipment, also cries out against the mills and factories. As an antidote to the complaints about the ruined landscape, and perhaps as a different way of talking about Niagara's marvels, Christian Schultz (1807) demands better facilities because he sees Niagara as a tourist place that needs to be tamed. And Caroline Gilman (1838) offers advice on the construction of better walkways because she is afraid of the apparent danger and is impatient for Niagara to be made more accessible.

But why did travellers continue to go to a place promoted in the literature as unsuitable for women (Weld), as dangerous to both men and women (Bigelow), and as aesthetically inappropriate (Schultz, Gilman, Anthony Trollope, and James)? Over the centuries, they travelled to Niagara to recuperate a sense of the marvellous, of the dangerous, or to prove their own value and superior taste. The earliest travel writers had to get beyond their feelings of fear, the Victorians beyond their disappointment. On the other hand, the scientists of the eighteenth century and well into the nineteenth managed to gain satisfaction by mastering either the landscape or their emotions. But, during the last half of the nineteenth century, the feat for most respondents (fine arts, literary, and scientific) was to get past the "common" view in order to recover an "untamed" Niagara. When travel theorist Christopher Mulvey writes about this process of detachment from sober reality, he calls it a "Niagarized" effect.[5] Some chose to ignore the "carnival" of tourists and developments and transform the landscape into a sublime wilderness again (Frederic Church in 1856). On the other hand, James managed a type of transcendence by switching aesthetics to celebrate Niagara's "classical" beauty and not its sublimity.

Hennepin expatiated on the wonders of nature; toward the end of the nineteenth century and into the twentieth, Nicholas Woods (1860) and H.G. Wells (1906) were impressed by the wonders of technology. According to Woods, science delivers a wild experience, "beyond all power of words." Similarly, Wells sees Niagara as sublime, yet he considers the natural world sordid. This in itself shows how discourse about nature had circled in on itself. While Wells's ideology had its foundation in the electrical technological sublime, which called for the conquest of nature, it also echoed pre-eighteenth-century pre-sublime ideas about the natural world as ugly and chaotic. (And, as predicted, Niagara did usher in the age of electricity: the term "Niagarics" represents the development of hydroelectric power at all waterfalls.[6])

As a coda to all that came before, in this final phase of Niagara the "hydro myth" imparted a new romantic aura. Even as the rhetoric surrounding hydroelectric development was one of conquest and triumph over the forces of nature, representations of the Falls alternated between ruined or evolving landscapes. Twentieth-century scientists were still concerned with controlling nature, not with their experience of it. During this era, they deemed the river's actions to be self-destructive so geologists and engineers intervened to "save" the waterfalls from future attrition and transformation. In the 1950s, bolts were inserted in the cliff face, honeycombed walls were plugged, and the crest lines of the two waterfalls were reconstructed to prevent further erosion and rock slides. In the early 1970s, "invisible" current deflectors were placed upriver, making it impossible for the water to gather in the centre of the Horseshoe. But the ways in which scientists made use of nature affected the visuals. Tourists came to Niagara expecting to see a deluge, but as a result of the improvements most of the river's flow was channelled to the power plants and not allowed down the gorge. Whether nature is a force to be controlled or a locus for tourism, technology, or spiritual regeneration, the interconnected maze of cultural reflections on Niagara's "betwixt- and betweenness" offers a fantasy of unresolved dualities (of civilization vs. wildness, of artifice vs. nature) similar to that of the Indian figure, who represents both dependence and rebellion, both naturalness and savagery.

We began with William Gass's, Isabel Colegate's, and Al Purdy's disappointment—or, no yelps of surprise—followed by André Brink's struggle to see Niagara as an untamed power ("despite all the efforts to spoil it"). It is clear that Brink's perception of tourism and development as ruining nature (and not as preserving it or making it more aesthetic) operates within the ideology of the late twentieth century. To end here, with disapproving writers bemoaning the river's spoiled potential, shows that the patterns of experience and the modes of literary production that have been established continue to inform how people are "Niagarized" to this day.

Notes

Introduction

1 André Brink is quoted in Elizabeth Renzetti, "Writers Opt for Bus, Not Barrel," The *Globe and Mail* (Oct. 31, 1996): C3.

2 While there is no "proof," the notable Niagara historian Charles Mason Dow believes that other French explorers may have "discovered" Niagara around the time Champlain was in the vicinity. In his extensive study of travel to the frontier, Dow argues that the Franciscan missionary Dallion may have been the first to reach the Niagara River as early as 1626 (although he left no records of that journey). Similarly, Brébeuf and Chaumonot were close to the river in the winter of 1640–41, but they did not write of the cascades. Lalemant, another Jesuit, mentions the river in 1641, but not the Falls. And nine years before the European missionary Louis Hennepin travelled with La Salle's second exploration party and wrote of his visit to the cascades, René Brehan de Galinée, a Sulpician missionary who went to the Niagara area in 1669 in the company of Dollier de Casson and La Salle, wrote a hearsay account of waterfalls. This list of seventeenth-century explorers is gleaned from Charles Mason Dow's *Anthology and Bibliography of Niagara Falls* (Albany, NY, 1921), Vol. 1, 49, fn. 1.

3 The earliest known Natives in the Niagara area were the Mound Builders who travelled up from the Ohio Valley. They settled around the river in 1000 AD and by 1300 AD had been replaced by the Neutrals. Then in 1643, the Neutral Nation was exterminated by the Senecas, one of the most important tribes in the Confederacy of the Iroquois. The Senecas settled both banks of the Niagara, fought under England in the War of Independence, and were later relocated to the Grand River Reservation, to areas in New York State, and to territories as far west as Oklahoma. For more on the complex history of the Neutrals and the Senecas, see Robert Higgins, *The Niagara Frontier: Its Place in U.S. and Canadian History* (Kitchener, ON: Upney Editions, 1996), 21–23.

4 Louis Hennepin, *Description of Louisiana* (1683) in Dow, *Anthology and Bibliography of Niagara Falls,* Vol. 1, 23.

5 Some of the French priests/soldiers/explorers at Niagara during the pre-Revolutionary period, and the post-Revolutionary British soldiers/

natural historians/literary travellers included Pierre François Xavier de Charlevoix (1721), Paul Dudley (1721), Joseph Pierre de Bonnecamps (1749), Pehr Kalm (1750), M. de la Lande (1751), J.C. Bonnefons (1753), Captain François Pouchot (1755–60), Robert Rogers (1765), Ralph Izard (1765), Captain Jonathan Carver (1766), Hector St. John de Crévecoeur (1785), Captain Enys (1787), Ann Powell (1789), Robert McCauslin (1789), François Auguste René Chateaubriand (1791), Duncan Ingraham (1792), Elizabeth Simcoe (1792), Isaac Weld (1796), and La Rochefoucault Liancourt (1796). This list of eighteenth-century visitors is gleaned from Dow, *Anthology and Bibliography of Niagara Falls*, Vol. 1, 32–43, 62–109.

6 The British Grand Tour "to celebrate Upper Canada's survival" took in the springs, the lakes, Upper and Lower Canada, and the New England states. The American Northern Tour followed a similar itinerary, but celebrated a different victory. Patricia Jasen, *Wild Things: Nature, Culture and Tourism in Ontario, 1790–1914* (Toronto, ON: University of Toronto Press, 1995), 298.

7 As early as 1791, a log hut situated on the high bank above the Horseshoe Falls served as an inn. "It was described as the only place of accommodation for travellers of the day to refresh themselves. The Duke of Kent, Queen Victoria's father, visited the inn on his journey to the Falls of Niagara in 1791." George A. Seibel, *Ontario's Niagara Parks: A History*, 2nd ed. (Niagara Falls, ON: Niagara Parks Commission, 1991), 6.

8 W.B. Turner, "The Early Settlement of Niagara," *Niagara's Changing Landscapes*, ed. Hugh J. Gayler (Ottawa, ON: Carleton University Press, 1994), 189.

9 Pierre Berton, *Niagara: A History of the Falls* (Toronto, ON: McClelland and Stewart, 1992), 80.

10 Many excellent studies of the nineteenth- and twentieth-century focus on Niagara's Honeymoon phenomenon (also called "Honey-Lunacy"). For scholarly/conventional discussions about honeymooning, see Karen Dubinsky's *The Second Greatest Disappointment: Honeymooning and Tourism at Niagara Falls* (Toronto, ON and New Brunswick, NJ: Between the Lines and Rutgers University Press, 1999); Elizabeth McKinsey's *Niagara Falls: Icon of the American Sublime* (Cambridge, MA: Harvard University Press, 1985), 178–88; and John Sears's first and last chapters in *Sacred Places: American Tourist Attractions in the 19th Century* (New York: Oxford University Press, 1989). Select chapters in Jasen's *Wild Things* examine the history of the Canadian honeymoon as it pertains to tourism, and Peter Ward's *Courtship, Love and Marriage in Nineteenth-Century English Canada* (Montreal and Kingston: McGill-Queen's University Press, 1990) questions whether Canadians ever "demonstrated the passion for a wedding trip to Niagara Falls so characteristic of [Americans]" (116). Other more general studies on honeymooning conventions include Ellen K. Rothman's *Hands and Hearts: A History of Courtship in America* (New York: Basic Books, 1984), 82, 175, which contains some information about Niagara; and Rob Shields's *Places on the Margin: Alternative Geographies of Modernity* (London: Routledge, 1991) a British-based study also contains information on Niagara but focuses only on American issues and events. Berton's *Niagara,* Patrick McGreevy's *Imagining Niagara:*

The Meaning and Making of Niagara Falls (Amherst, MA: University of Massachusetts Press, 1994), 93–99, and Dwight Whalen's *Lover's Guide to Niagara Falls* (Niagara Falls, ON: Horseshoe Press, 1990), tend to present the cultural myths about Niagara Falls and "Honey-Lunacy" without questioning what the phenomena may mean, or how the honeymoon has been constructed/scripted/reproduced. As a final note, a recent "scientific" study of the honeymoon phenomenon suggests that Niagara has a biological effect on the reproductive organs. According to engineer Fred Soyka and business executive Alan Edmonds, waterfalls are surrounded by a "beneficial load" of charged particles: "neg-ions [negative ions] produce a sense of well-being [which] may be the reason why Niagara has been a honeymooners' paradise for almost as long as the area has been accessible." *The Ion Effect: How Electricity Rules Your Life and Health* (Toronto, ON: Lester and Orphen, 1977), 27.

11 Dubinsky, *The Second Greatest Disappointment,* 56–57.

12 Berton, *Niagara,* 198.

13 For more on how the working-class holiday affected tourism at Niagara, see Jasen, *Wild Things,* 21; and Michael J. Piva, *The Condition of the Working Class in Toronto, 1900–1921* (Ottawa, ON: University of Ottawa Press, 1979), 89.

14 Hugh J. Gayler, "Introduction to Niagara," in Gayler, ed., *Niagara's Changing Landscapes,* 89.

15 The one-hour weekly crime series, *Taking the Falls,* aired for a season on Canada's CTV in 1995. Other television series have included the CBC's real-life stories of people in the tourist business, *Niagara* (2000). Popular movies set at the Falls include *Canadian Bacon* (1994), starring John Candy, and *Niagara* (1952), starring Marilyn Munroe and Joseph Cotten. Documentaries include Kevin McMahon's *The Falls: An Irreverent Portrait of Niagara Falls* (National Film Board of Canada, 1991), and Robert Borgatti's and Paul Lamont's *Fading in the Mist* (MediaGeist Productions, 1996). Fiction includes Eudora Welty's "The Key," in *The Collected Stories of Eudora Welty* (New York: Harcourt Brace Jovanovich, 1980), 29–37; Margaret Atwood's "The Whirlpool Rapids," *Redbook* (Nov. 1986): 51–57; Sandra Birdsell's "Niagara Falls," in *Agassiz Stories* (Winnipeg, MB: Turnstone Press, 1987), 217–36; Michel Butor's *6810000 litres d'eau par second; étude stéréophonique* (Paris: Gallimard, 1965), later translated by Elinor S. Miller as *Niagara: A Novel* (Chicago, IL: H. Regnery, 1969); Ishmael Reed's *Flight to Canada* (New York: Random House, 1976); Jane Urquhart's *The Whirlpool* (Toronto, ON: McClelland and Stewart, 1986); Tom Marshall's *Voices on the Brink: A Border Tale* (Toronto, ON: Macmillan, 1988); Suzette Mayr's *The Widows* (Edmonton, AB: NeWest Press, 1998); Colin Bateman's *Maid of the Mist* (Toronto and New York: HarperCollins, 1999); Lauren Belfer's *City of Lights* (New York: The Dial Press, 1999); Patricia Seaman's *The Nightingales* (Toronto, ON: Coach House Books, 2001); and Camilla Gibb's *The Petty Details of So-and-So's Life* (Toronto, ON: Doubleday Canada, 2002).

16 The Web site address is http://www.fallsview.com. Cameras mounted on top of the Sheraton Fallsview Hotel on the Canadian side offer many live still shots of the Falls.

17 W. Rhys Roberts, *Longinus on the Sublime* (Cambridge: Cambridge University Press, 1935), 247.

18 For information on the five editions of *Peri Hupsous,* see Marjorie Hope Nicolson, *Mountain Gloom and Mountain Glory: The Development of the Aesthetics of the Infinite* (New York: W.W. Norton, 1959), 30–31, 143; Samuel H. Monk, *The Sublime: A Study of Critical Theories in XVIII-Century England* (New York: MLA, 1935), 20; and Jan Cohn and Thomas H. Miles, "The Sublime: In Alchemy, Aesthetics and Psychoanalysis," *Modern Philology* (Feb. 1977), 293, fn. 9.

19 Monk, *The Sublime,* 45.

20 Nicolson, *Mountain Gloom and Mountain Glory,* 278. On this distinction (between the sublime and the beautiful) there is disagreement among modern scholars. Monk (*The Sublime,* 54) contends that it was not Dennis but Joseph Addison who established the sublime as antithetical to beauty.

21 Anthony Ashley Cooper Shaftesbury, *The Moralists: A Philosophical Rhapsody* (1709). Republished as *Treatise V of Characteristicks of Men, Manners, Opinions, Times, etc.,* Vol. 2, ed. John M. Robertson (London, 1900), 125.

22 Monk, *The Sublime,* 54.

23 Jerome Stolnitz, "Beauty: Some Stages in the History of an Idea," *Journal of the History of Ideas* 22 (Apr.–June 1961): 189.

24 Nicolson, *Mountain Gloom and Mountain Glory,* 300–301; and Stolnitz, "Beauty," 191.

25 Nicolson, *Mountain Gloom and Mountain Glory,* 29, 113. While Elizabeth McKinsey groups the pre-sublime writers (i.e. Dennis, Shaftesbury, and Addison) under the aesthetics of the infinite (*Niagara Falls,* 16), Marjorie Hope Nicolson suggests that the aesthetics of the infinite was better represented by Thomas Burnet (*Mountain Gloom and Mountain Glory,* 29). I follow Nicolson and consider the pre-sublime writers as different from Thomas Burnet in the practice of the aesthetics of the infinite.

26 Edmund Burke, *A Philosophical Enquiry into the Origin of Our Ideas of the Sublime and Beautiful,* ed. J.T. Boulton (Notre Dame, IN: University of Notre Dame Press, 1968), 58.

27 Frances Ferguson, "The Sublime of Edmund Burke, or the Bathos of Experience," in *Glyph 8: Johns Hopkins Textual Studies,* Ed. Walter Benn Michaels (Baltimore, MD: Johns Hopkins University Press, 1981), 62–78; Monk, *The Sublime,* 84–100; and Thomas Weiskel, *The Romantic Sublime: Studies in the Structure and Psychology of Transcendence* (Baltimore, MD: Johns Hopkins University Press, 1976), 85–97.

28 McKinsey, *Niagara Falls,* 31.

29 Ibid., 56.

30 McKinsey, who is vague in her definition of "sentimentalization," sets up a metonymical chain of associations linking the term to literature, the feminine, women, and domestication: "sentimental literature locates Niagara in the realm of the feminine. This is not to say that men were never sentimental; indeed, the bulk of such poetry and fiction was written by men. But even male writers emphasized Niagara's aesthetic connection with femininity; as its image was domesticated and sentimentalized, its

meaning was read in terms of social or life-cycle matters (for example, calmly accepting death as the entrance to the afterlife) that were included in the popular mind within 'woman's sphere'" (*Niagara Falls,* 170–71). Later in her book, McKinsey adds the beautiful, commercialization, and honeymoons to this list of associations anchored by the term "sentimental."

31 James Buzard, *The Beaten Track: European Tourism, Literature, and the Ways to Culture, 1800–1918* (Oxford: Clarendon Press, 1993), 16. Interestingly, Buzard codes the picturesque as male, whereas McKinsey would equate it with femaleness (if only because it is "lesser" than the sublime).

32 Uvedale Price, *An Essay on the Picturesque: As Compared with the Sublime and the Beautiful; And, on the Use of Studying Pictures, for the Purpose of Improving Real Landscape* (1794; reprint, Farnborough, UK: Gregg, 1971), Vol. 2, 103.

33 Richard Payne Knight, *The Landscape: A Didactic Poem in Three Books,* 2nd ed. (1795; reprint, Farnborough, UK: Gregg, 1972).

34 Susan Glickman, *The Picturesque and the Sublime: A Poetics of the Canadian Landscape* (Montreal and Kingston: McGill-Queen's University Press, 1998), 11.

35 Cohn and Miles, "The Sublime," 298.

36 James B. Twitchell, *Romantic Horizons: Aspects of the Sublime in English Poetry and Painting, 1770–1850* (Columbia, MO: University of Missouri Press, 1983), 61.

37 Shields, *Places on the Margin,* 117.

38 Dubinsky, *The Second Greatest Disappointment,* 22.

39 Patricia Jasen's earlier article, "Romanticism, Modernity and the Evolution of Tourism on the Niagara Frontier, 1790–1850," *Canadian Historical Review* 72 (1991): 283–318, forms the backbone of the first chapter, "Taming Niagara," in *Wild Things,* 29–54.

40 Other popular histories include: Gordon Donaldson, *Niagara! The Eternal Circus* (Toronto, ON: Doubleday, 1979) and Ralph Greenhill and Thomas D. Mahoney, *Niagara* (Toronto, ON: University of Toronto Press, 1969).

41 Susan Joan Wood, *The Land in Canadian Prose, 1840–1945* (Ottawa, ON: Carleton University Press, 1988), 15.

42 Glickman, *The Picturesque and the Sublime,* vii.

43 Michel Butor, "Travel and Writing," trans. John Powers and K. Lisker, *Mosaic* 8 (1974): 1.

44 William W. Stowe, *Going Abroad: European Travel in Nineteenth-Century American Culture* (Princeton, NJ: Princeton University Press, 1994), 13.

45 Daniel J. Boorstin, *The Image: A Guide to Pseudo-Events in America* (New York: Harper Colophon Books, 1961), 78–99. The relationship between the tourist and the traveller is the subject of much debate among travel theorists. See Boorstin, 84–85; Paul Fussell, *Abroad: British Literary Traveling Between the Wars* (New York: Oxford University Press, 1980), 39; Buzard, *The Beaten Track,* 1–4; Dean MacCannell, *The Tourist: A New Theory of the Leisure Class* (New York: Schocken Books, 1976), 1–2; and John Urry, *The Tourist Gaze: Leisure and Travel in Contemporary Societies*

(London: Sage, 1990), 2–3. For a sample of this discussion, I turn to another travel critic, Ian Ousby, who argues that the word "tourist" was not, as Boorstin supposed, a creation of the railway age. It first came into currency (according to the *Oxford English Dictionary*) in the 1780s and meant someone pursuing a serious inquiry, but by the 1830s the word had developed negative connotations and was defined as a traveller who was merely passing sights and impressions. See Ian Ousby, *The Englishman's England: Taste, Travel and the Rise of Tourism* (Cambridge: Cambridge University Press, 1990), 18–19. Buzard (*The Beaten Track*, 82) even goes so far as to "gender" the terms, calling the traveller (who has "authentic" experience) male and the tourist (who only takes in "the dupe of fashion") female.

46 Mary Louise Pratt, *Imperial Eyes: Travel Writing and Transculturation* (London and New York: Routledge, 1992), 4.

47 Sixteenth-century French explorers used the word "sauvage" to describe Native people. British explorers translated that to "savage," and English usage mixed both "savage" and "Indian" (a word based on Christopher Columbus's "los Indios," introduced in 1493). See Robert F. Berkhofer, *The White Man's Indian: Images of the American Indian from Columbus to the Present* (New York: Knopf, 1978), 5 and 199, fn. 2; and Olive Patricia Dickason, *Canada's First Nations: A History of the Founding Peoples from Earliest Times* (Toronto, ON: McClelland and Stewart, 1992), 83. I use the term "Indian" to discuss images or descriptions of Native peoples.

Chapter 1

1 Marjorie Hope Nicolson, *Mountain Gloom and Mountain Glory: The Development of the Aesthetics of the Infinite* (New York: W.W. Norton, 1959), 138–43.

2 Samuel de Champlain, *Des Sauvages, ou Voyage fait en la France Nouvelle* (Paris, 1604).

3 Champlain's *Carte de la Nouvelle France* (1612) was reprinted in 1632. It was also reproduced in the frontispiece of E.B. O'Callaghan's *Documentary History of the State of New York*, Vol. 3. (Albany, 1849), 13. Reported in Charles Mason Dow, *Anthology and Bibliography of Niagara Falls* (Albany, NY, 1921), Vol. 2, 849.

4 Between 1663 and 1763, the French traded 200,000 flintlocks to Indians; see Merilyn Simonds, "Code of Arms," *Canadian Geographic* (Mar./Apr. 1996), 46, 48.

5 Le Sieur Gendron, *Quelques Particularitez du pays des Hurons en la Nouvelle France* (Paris, 1645), in Dow, *Anthology and Bibliography of Niagara Falls*, Vol. 1, 20.

6 N. Sanson's map was published in *Le Canada, ou Nouvelle France* (Paris, 1656) and René Brehan de Galinée's map in *Exploration of the Great Lakes, 1669–1670*, trans. James H. Coyne, (Toronto, ON: The Ontario Historical Society, 1903), Vol. 4, 38–41 (Dow, *Anthology and Bibliography of Niagara Falls*, Vol. 2, 849; Vol. 1, 21).

7 De Galinée, *Exploration of the Great Lakes 1669–1670* (Dow, *Anthology and Bibliography of Niagara Falls,* Vol. 1, 21–22).

8 Meursium's map was printed in Amsterdam and Joliet's was lithographed in Paris (Dow, *Anthology and Bibliography of Niagara Falls,* Vol. 2, 850–51).

9 Since both La Salle expeditions were sponsored by the king of France, and since copies of relevant maps and manuscripts accompanied the king's cartographer on every journey into the interior, La Salle's map-maker would have known about the previous reports by Champlain, Le Sieur Gendron, Ragueneau, Bressani, Sanson, and de Galinée. These documents were issued to the king's officials by the "compilers" Jean-Baptiste-Louis Franquelin and map-maker Louis Joliet. They sent updated information from the colony to France and it was returned to them in published form through their office in Quebec. See Conrad E. Heidenreich, "The French Mapping of North America in the Seventeenth Century," in *The Map Collector* (Berkhamsted, UK: Abacus Press, 1982), 8.

10 Mary Louise Pratt, *Imperial Eyes: Travel Writing and Transculturation* (London and New York: Routledge, 1992), 202.

11 Charles P. De Volpi, *The Niagara Peninsula: A Pictorial Record, 1697–1880* (Montreal, QC: Dev-Sco, 1966), 3.

12 The movement of First Nations peoples in what was to become south-western Ontario during the time of early contact is a complex study in itself. For a window onto this period in Canadian history, see E. Reginald Good, "Mississauga-Mennonite Relations in the Upper Grand River Valley," *Ontario History* 87 (2) (June 1995): 155–72.

13 Hennepin's *Description* (1683) was published in Paris, and his *A New Discovery* (1697) in Utrecht by Chez Guillaume Brodelet. A second version of *A New Discovery*, based on the Paris and Utrecht publications, was produced in Holland in 1697. Dedicated to "His Majesty K. William," the sponsor of the expedition, this revised edition became Hennepin's most widely disseminated version. By 1699, it had been translated into English, German, and Spanish. All subsequent quotations from Hennepin will be from the 1699 English translation of the 1697 Dutch publication which is reproduced in Dow, *Anthology and Bibliography of Niagara Falls,* Vol. 1, and will have paginal notations.

14 I follow most art critics in referring to Hennepin's engraver as anonymous. However, George Seibel attributes the etching to J. Van Vienan in *300 Years Since Father Hennepin: Niagara Falls in Art 1678–1978* (Niagara Falls, ON: Niagara Falls Heritage Foundation, 1992), 49; and Victoria Dickenson attributes it to the Dutch engraver Jan van Vianen (1660–1726) in *Drawn from Life: Science and Art in the Portrayal of the New World* (Toronto, ON: University of Toronto Press, 1998), 108.

15 For a close reading of the two Hennepin versions (1683 and 1697), see Elizabeth McKinsey, *Niagara Falls: Icon of the American Sublime* (Cambridge, MA: Harvard University Press, 1985), 8–13. McKinsey also investigates another debate concerning *A New Discovery*—whether Hennepin went on to make a trip to the lower Mississippi, or whether he plagiarized his description from another missionary's account (284, fn. 7).

16 John Dennis, *Miscellanies in Verse and Prose in Critical Works,* Vol. 2, ed. Edward Niles Hooker (Baltimore, MD: Johns Hopkins University Press, 1943), 380.

17 Nicolson, *Mountain Gloom and Mountain Glory*, viii, 71–72, 82–83.

18 Ibid., 200. Burnet first published his work in Latin as *Telluris Theoria Sacra* in 1681 and issued his first English version, *The Sacred Theory of the Earth,* in 1684. For more on Thomas Burnett, see Ian Ousby, *The Englishman's England: Taste, Travel and the Rise of Tourism* (Cambridge: Cambridge University Press, 1990), 130–31, 142; and Simon Schama, *Landscape and Memory* (New York/Toronto: A.A. Knopf/Random House of Canada, 1995), 451–52.

19 Nicolson, *Mountain Gloom and Mountain Glory,* 138–40, 155–56.

20 Hennepin, *A New Discovery* (1697), in Dow, *Anthology and Bibliography of Niagara Falls,* Vol. 1, 29.

21 The easterly waterfall in the Hennepin-based picture was first named the Schlosser Falls, after a German mercenary officer in the British army, Col. John J. Schlosser. By the 1820s, this cascade was more commonly called the American Falls. Goat Island was named in 1770. According to legend, the American settler John Stedman cleared a portion of the land and placed on the island a number of animals, including a male goat. By the spring of 1770, all but the goat were dead, and the goat's survival is thought to be celebrated in the name. The widest waterfall has been variously called the Horseshoe Falls, the Montmorency Falls, the British Falls, and the Canadian Falls. In his 1721 *Journal of a Voyage to North-America*, Father Pierre François Xavier de Charlevoix was the first to use the term "horseshoe" to describe it. And finally, the cross-stream beside the Horseshoe Falls may be an imaginary feature, because topographical maps from the seventeenth and eighteenth centuries do not include it.

22 There were nine Italian editions of Cesare Ripa's *Iconologia* and it was translated into other European languages.

23 Schama, *Landscape and Memory,* 456. For more on Salvator Rosa, see ibid., 453–56; Elizabeth Wheeler Manwaring, *Italian Landscape in Eighteenth Century England: A Study Chiefly of the Influence of Claude Lorrain and Salvator Rosa on English Taste 1700–1800* (1925; London: Frank Cass, 1965), 54; Charlotte Klonk, *Science and the Perception of Nature: British Landscape Art in the Late Eighteenth and Early Nineteenth Centuries* (New Haven, CT: Yale University Press, 1996), 9; and Susan Glickman, *The Picturesque and the Sublime: A Poetics of the Canadian Landscape* (Montreal and Kingston: McGill-Queen's University Press, 1998), 8, 11. For more on Cesare Ripa, see McKinsey, *Niagara Falls*, 14–16. For more on Claude Lorrain, see Manwaring, *Italian Landscape in Eighteenth Century England,* 4; and Glickman, *The Picturesque and the Sublime,* 8, 10. For more on Gaspard Dughet, see McKinsey, *Niagara Falls,* 14.

24 Cartographers such as Caspar Luken in *Niagara* (1697), Tomas Campanius Holm in *View of the Falls of Niagara* (1702), and Henry Popple in *A Map of the British Empire in America* (1733) included insets of the Hennepin engraving on their maps.

25 Paul Dudley, "An Account of the Falls of the River Niagara, Taken at Albany, October 10, 1721, from Monsieur Borassaw, a French Native of Canada," in Dow, *Anthology and Bibliography of Niagara Falls,* Vol. 1, 36. In that same year, Pierre François Xavier de Charlevoix, a geographer sent under the auspices of the French king, measured the waterfall and sent a series of letters to the Duchess of Lesdiguieres that were published as *Journal of a Voyage to North-America. Undertaken by order of the French King. Containing the Geographical Description and Natural History of that Country, Particularly Canada* (London: R. and J. Dodsley, 1761). However, the visual correction that supplemented his description has not survived.

26 Dudley, who was born in Roxbury, Massachusetts in 1675, studied law in England. Known chiefly as the founder of the "Dudleian Lecture" on Religion at Harvard, he had served as Attorney General of the Massachusetts Government and Council and was appointed judge in the Massachusetts Superior Court of Judicature in 1718 (three years before he travelled to Niagara Falls). See "Dudley, Paul," in *Who Was Who in America* (Chicago, IL: Mercer, 1967), Vol. 1, 227.

27 Swedish botanist and taxonomist Karl von Linné (1707–78), known more commonly through his writings as Carolus Linnaeus, was considered the founder of the binomial system of nomenclature and the originator of modern scientific classification of plants and animals. Linnaeus named some flora and fauna found at Niagara after Kalm: an evergreen bush (*Kalmia latifolia*) and two wildflowers (the *Lobelia Kalmianum* and the *Hypericum Kalmii,* a species of St. John's wort). See Nils William Olsson, *Pehr Kalm and the Image of North America* (Minneapolis, MN: The Associates of the James Ford Bell Library, 1970), 3.

28 Pehr Kalm, "Letter" (1750) (in Dow, *Anthology and Bibliography of Niagara Falls,* Vol. 1, 53). All subsequent quotations from Kalm will be from this text and will have paginal notations.

29 Olsson, *Pehr Kalm and the Image of North America,* 8.

30 When the Tuscaroras were admitted to the League of Five Nations the title Six Nations was adopted.

31 The enormous fir trees are probably another imaginary feature. Historians and scientists have documented that, at the time of early European exploration, the whole Niagara Peninsula was a deciduous forest dominated by broad-leaved trees such as oak, maple, and beech. See Michael R. Moss, "Forests in the Niagara Landscape: Ecology and Management," in *Niagara's Changing Landscapes,* ed. Hugh J. Gayler (Ottawa, ON: Carleton University Press, 1994), 142, 146.

32 There is a debate about the origins of the word "race." The zoologist Cedric Dover claimed in 1951 that the word came from the Arabic *ras,* meaning "chief head, origin or beginning," and entered Spanish as *raza* "meaning a kinship group or follower of a headman." However, anthropologist J.C. Trevor argued that "race" derived from the Latin *ratio,* meaning "species, kind, nature," and then entered Italian as *razza* and spread from there into other related languages. See Audrey Smedley, *Race in North America: Origin and Evolution of a Worldview* (Boulder, CO: Westview Press, 1993), 37.

33 J.S. Slotkin, *Readings in Early Anthropology* (London: Methuen, 1965), 43.

34 François Bernier, "A New Division of the Earth," from *Journal des Scavans* (April 24, 1684), in *Memoirs Read Before the Anthropological Society of London (1863–64)*, trans. T. Bendyshe, n.p., Vol. 1, 361.

35 Smedley, *Race in North America,* 235.

36 The first "missing link" theory was developed in 1699 when the British physician Edward Tyson argued that a "pygmie" (in reality, a chimpanzee) was the intermediate between man and monkey. One century later, the Manchester physician Charles White introduced the concept of the Negro as the connecting link between the white man and the ape. See Nancy Stepan, *The Idea of Race in Science: Great Britain, 1800–1960* (Hamden, CT: Archon Books, 1982), 7–8.

37 Stephen Jay Gould, *The Mismeasure of Man* (New York: Norton, 1996), 22.

38 Pratt, *Imperial Eyes,* 25; Robert F. Berkhofer, *The White Man's Indian: Images of the American Indian from Columbus to the Present* (New York: Knopf, 1978), 39–40.

39 In dealing with North American Natives, the British were more organized than the French. They established an Office of Indian Affairs, run through the British Indian Department. And, unlike the French, the British acknowledged marriage alliances between Indian women and British men. One of the most famous examples is that of the Superintendent of Indian Affairs, Sir William Johnson, who married Molly Brant, the sister of Mohawk leader Joseph Brant. This alliance greatly influenced other tribes, especially during the War of Independence, when Chief Brant and his brother-in-law, Superintendent Johnson, led the British-affiliated Six Nations Indians against the American revolutionaries. See Barbara Graymond, "The Six Nations Indians in the Revolutionary War," in *Sweet Promises: A Reader on Indian-White Relations in Canada,* ed. J.R. Miller (Toronto, ON: University of Toronto Press, 1991), 107.

40 Fuseli's illustration first appeared in *Le Voyage des Quatre Parties du Monde de M. Henri Vernon, Anglais.* See Seibel, *300 Years since Father Hennepin,* 42.

41 McKinsey, *Niagara Falls,* 22, 25.

42 Charles W. Jeffreys, ed., *Canadiana and Americana: A Catalogue of the Sigmund Samuel Collection at the Royal Ontario Museum* (Toronto, ON: Ryerson Press, 1948), 14.

43 On the other hand, in eighteenth-century popular American imagery, the Indian was a bloodthirsty foe. See McKinsey, *Niagara Falls,* 24; and James Doyle, *North of America: Images of Canada in the Literature of the United States, 1775–1900* (Toronto, ON: ECW Press, 1983), 92.

44 Immanuel Kant, *Observations on the Feeling of the Beautiful and Sublime,* trans. John T. Goldthwait (1764; Berkeley, CA: University of California Press, 1960), 111.

45 The land-treaty negotiations between the British government, the First Nations peoples and the founding peoples of Canada are a complex study in themselves. For an excellent overview of the issues involved, see Olive Patricia Dickason, *Canada's First Nations: A History of the Founding Peoples from Earliest Times* (Toronto, ON: McClelland and Stewart, 1992); Arthur J. Ray, *I Have Lived Here since the World Began: An Illustrated*

History of Canada's Native People (Toronto, ON: Lester/Key Porter, 1996); and Bruce G. Trigger, *Natives and Newcomers: Canada's "Heroic Age" Reconsidered* (Montreal and Kingston: McGill-Queen's University Press, 1985).

46 "Robert Hancock," in *The Dictionary of Art,* ed. Jane Turner (London: Macmillan, 1996), Vol. 14, 132.

47 Robert Hancock, *The Waterfall of Niagara in North America* (London: Laurie & Whittle, 1794), in Dow, *Anthology and Bibliography of Niagara Falls,* Vol. 2, 879.

48 Naomi Zack, *Philosophy of Science and Race* (New York and London: Routledge, 2002), 18.

49 Immanuel Kant's "Of the Different Human Races" (1775), in Robert Bernasconi, et al., *The Idea of Race* (Indianapolis, IN: Hackett, 2000), 8–22.

50 Jean-Jacques Rousseau, *Essay on the Origin of Languages,* trans. John T. Scott. Vol. 7 of the *Collected Writings of Rousseau* (1781; Hanover, NH: University Press of New England, 1999), 133.

51 Walter George Strickland, ed., *A Dictionary of Irish Artists* (New York: Hacker Art Books, 1968), Vol. 1, 232.

52 Weld's and Henn's pictures were composed at a time when Natives across North America were succumbing to disease, starvation, alcoholism, and the remorseless ebb and flow of civilizations. The "fact" that they were a dying race made them more attractive symbols. The movement to portray Native tribes before they "vanished" became an urgent mission in the late eighteenth to mid-nineteenth century—a number of non-Native artists went onto reservations to document their lives, including the American painter George Catlin and the Canadian painter Paul Kane. For more on these artists, see Daniel Francis, *The Imaginary Indian: The Image of the Indian in Canadian Culture* (Vancouver, BC: Arsenal Pulp Press, 1992), 16–25.

53 Jeremy Elwell Adamson, "Nature's Grandest Scene in Art," in *Niagara: Two Centuries of Changing Attitudes, 1697–1901,* ed. Jeremy Elwell Adamson (Washington, DC: Corcoran Gallery of Art, 1985), 48, 79, fn. 131.

54 McKinsey, *Niagara Falls,* 311, fn. 12. The Hudson River School was the first American group to concentrate exclusively on landscapes instead of portraits. Its more famous members included the following painters who, at one time or another, made Niagara their subject matter: Robert W. Weir, Thomas Chambers, John Frederick Kensett, Jasper Francis Cropsey, George Inness, Albert Bierstadt, and Louis Remy Mignot.

55 For a critical analysis of the American "frontier thesis" see Martin Ridge, "Introduction," in Frederick Jackson Turner, *History, Frontier, and Section: Three Essays* (Albuquerque, NM: University of New Mexico Press, 1891; reprint 1993); and Sacvan Bercovitch, *The American Jeremiad* (Madison, WI: University of Wisconsin Press, 1978).

56 On how the policy of manifest destiny resulted in the decimation of America's Native tribes, see Richard Drinnon, *Facing West: The Metaphysics of Indian-Hating and Empire-Building* (Minneapolis, MN: University of Minnesota Press, 1980).

57 Richard Slotkin, *Regeneration through Violence: The Mythology of the American Frontier, 1600–1860* (Middletown, CT: Wesleyan University Press, 1973), 62.

58 Other sketches of the event show this paddleboat. One is a coloured engraving, *The* Caroline *Steam boat Precipitated over the Falls of Niagara* by an unknown artist, (ca. 1838), and the other is a sketch by Henry J. Morgan, *The Cutting out of the* Caroline, reprinted in *Sketches of Celebrated Canadians* (Quebec, 1862).

59 Adamson, "Nature's Grandest Scene in Art," 62.

60 *Niagara Falls by Moonlight* may be one of Church's 1856 oils.

61 Franklin Kelly, "A Passion for Landscape: The Paintings of F.E. Church," in *Frederic Edwin Church,* ed. Franklin Kelly, et al. (Washington, DC: National Gallery of Art and the Smithsonian Institution Press, 1989), 51.

62 McKinsey, *Niagara Falls,* 243.

63 Adamson, ed., *Niagara,* 14.

64 Ibid., 15.

65 Deborah Rindge, "Chronology," in Kelly, et al., eds., *Frederic Edwin Church,* 163. Rindge adds that the chromolithograph sold in 1861 for $5,000. Church also received a share of the subscription revenue.

66 Adamson, "Nature's Grandest Scene in Art," 65.

67 Ibid., 51.

68 The Mignot painting was discovered in 1995 in the basement of the Brooklyn Museum. See William Grimes, "11 Almost-Masters from the Vaults," *The New York Times* (Feb. 5, 1995): 42.

69 Adamson, "Nature's Grandest Scene in Art," 69.

70 Ibid., 70.

71 Ibid., 80, fn. 234.

72 In the 1860s, the American side was a conglomeration of mills, hotels, factories, stairways, and bridges, and these tourist facilities were built on the land where Church "imagined" the solitary lookout. In trying to control the image as sublime, he had to leave these out.

73 Arthur Lumley, *Niagara Seen with Different Eyes, Harper's Weekly* 17 (Aug. 9, 1873): 698.

74 The Irish-born Lumley, who had emigrated to New York City in 1847, studied illustration and painting at the National Academy of Design and became a freelance cartoonist with papers in the United States and in Europe. See "Arthur Lumley," in *Who Was Who in American Art* ed. Peter Hastings Falk (Madison, CT: SoundView Press, 1985), 383.

75 Alison Adburgham, *A Punch History of Manners and Modes, 1841–1940* (London: Hutchinson, 1961), 17.

76 In chapter 3, I will discuss the dispute between industrialists and preservationists during the latter part of the nineteenth century. Some of these arguments are examined in William R. Irwin, *The New Niagara: Tourism, Technology and the Landscape of Niagara Falls, 1776–1917* (University Park, PA: Pennsylvania State University Press, 1996), 55–75.

77 The term "Uncle Sam," a nickname for the US government, was fashioned and used derisively by the members of the 1812 Peace Party. The first image of Uncle Sam appeared in 1834. In this picture, he is a young man, dressed in street clothes. Another evolution during the Civil War period had the figure sporting whiskers and grey hair and dressed in revolutionary-style striped pants, bootstraps, and a beaver hat. Lumley may

have borrowed this caricature, which was created by Thomas Nash and Charles G. Bush, two contemporary illustrators on staff at *Harpers Weekly*. The term "John Bull," also a nickname, was first used in the 1600s. The image of John Bull did not appear until 1712, when John Arbuthnot, a Scottish writer, published a figure of a jolly farmer in a pamphlet advocating the end of the War of the Spanish Succession. Bull featured in magazines too. Drawn in the early 1800s (by Sir John Teaniel) as a more dignified gentleman, the figure evolved again in the latter part of the nineteenth century (under the pen of Sir Francis Carruthers Gould) into a man wearing a "tile" hat and swallowtail coat, with his trousers tucked into riding boots. The British flag often appears on his waistcoat. This is the version Arthur Lumley relied upon when he drew this British icon at Niagara Falls. See Charles Press, *The Political Cartoon* (Rutherford, NJ: Fairleigh Dickinson University Press, 1981), 218–19, 230.

78 The cartoon of Johnny Canuck first appeared in the pages of *Grinchuckle*, a Montreal journal, in 1869. This personification of Canada was young and in military uniform. The caricature of Miss Canada began to appear in Britain's *Punch* magazine in the 1870s.

79 See Stepan, *The Idea of Race in Science*, 11–19.

80 Studies of how other disciplines were influenced by racial theories include Philip F. Rehbock's *The Philosophical Naturalists: Themes in Early Nineteenth-Century British Biology* (Madison, WI: University of Wisconsin Press, 1983); and John C. Greene's *Science, Ideology and World View* (Berkeley, CA: University of California Press, 1981).

81 Charles Darwin's *Diary* was first published as *Journal of Researches into the Natural History and Geology of the Countries Visited during the Voyage Round the World of HMS 'Beagle'* (1839) and later called *The Voyage of the Beagle* (1845).

82 For an analysis of Darwin's racial ideologies, see Robert J.C. Young, *Colonial Desire: Hybridity in Theory, Culture and Race* (London and New York: Routledge, 1995), 11–19.

83 While John Stuart Mill's essay "Nature" was written between 1850 and 1858, it was published posthumously, in *Three Essays on Religion: Nature, the Utility of Religion, Theism* (1873).

Chapter 2

1 Edmund Burke, *A Philosophical Enquiry into the Origin of Our Ideas of the Sublime and Beautiful*, ed. J.T. Boulton (Notre Dame, IN: University of Notre Dame Press, 1968), 57.

2 Frances Ferguson, "The Sublime of Edmund Burke, or the Bathos of Experience," in *Glyph* 8: *Johns Hopkins Textual Studies*, ed. Walter Benn Michaels (Baltimore, MD: Johns Hopkins University Press, 1981), 62–78; Samuel H. Monk, *The Sublime: A Study of Critical Theories in XVIII-Century England* (New York: MLA, 1935), 84–100; and Thomas Weiskel, *The Romantic Sublime: Studies in the Structure and Psychology of Transcendence* (Baltimore, MD: Johns Hopkins University Press, 1976), 85–97.

3 Burke, *Enquiry*, 113.

4 Ferguson, "The Sublime of Edmund Burke," 69, 72, 77.

5 Ibid., 73.

6 Ibid., 69.

7 William Gilpin, *Observations on the Western Parts of England, Relative Chiefly to Picturesque Beauty, To Which Are Added a Few Remarks on the Picturesque Beauties of the Isle of Wight* (1798; Richmond, UK: Richmond, 1973), 328.

8 Immanuel Kant, "Analytic of the Sublime," in *Second Book of Critique of Judgement,* trans. J.C. Meredith (Oxford: Oxford University Press, 1932), 106.

9 James B. Twitchell, *Romantic Horizons: Aspects of the Sublime in English Poetry and Painting, 1770–1850* (Columbia, MO: University of Missouri Press, 1983), 61.

10 Mary Louise Pratt, *Imperial Eyes: Travel Writing and Transculturation* (London and New York: Routledge, 1992), 105–106.

11 Mary Quayle Innis, "Introduction," in *Mrs. Simcoe's Diary [1791–96],* ed. Mary Quayle Innis (Toronto, ON: Macmillan, 1965), 4. All subsequent quotations from Simcoe's *Diary* will be from this edition and will have paginal notations.

12 Duke de La Rochefoucault Liancourt, *Travels through the United States of North America, the country of the Iroquois, and Upper Canada, in the years 1795, 1796, and 1797; with an authentic account of Lower Canada* (London: Phillips, 1799).

13 Simcoe's diaries were "discovered" by John Ross Robertson in 1911 and published that same year. Mary Quayle Innis's *Mrs. Simcoe's Diary* (1965), a revision of the Robertson edition, contains the "rough" and "polished" versions, as well as selected maps, drawings, and letters.

14 Innis, "Introduction," 20.

15 The maps inserted into the "polished" diary show the Lieutenant-Governor's proposed towns. These maps, along with thirty-two water-colours and drawings, were donated posthumously to the Prince Regent (on behalf of King George III) and later divided up and housed in the British Museum and in the Province of Ontario Archives. See Marian Fowler, *The Embroidered Tent: Five Gentlewomen in Early Canada* (Toronto, ON: Anansi, 1982), 47.

16 Sometime in May 1794, Simcoe wrote a note explaining that the fifteen-month-old girl had gone into spasms because she had "been feverish two or three days cutting teeth" (125). The baby, who died when John Simcoe, Thomas Talbot (Simcoe's second-in-command), and the family doctor were away, was buried near Fort Niagara on April 17, 1794.

17 Indians and canoes were enduring icons for the Simcoes. When they left Upper Canada in 1796, they took two important souvenirs: a painting of their son Francis dressed as an Indian and a birchbark canoe.

18 William Gilpin, *Observations on the River Wye, and Several Parts of South Wales Relative Chiefly to Picturesque Beauty; Made in the Summer of the Year 1770* (1782; Richmond, UK: Richmond, 1973), 18.

19 William Gilpin, *Observations, Relative Chiefly to Picturesque Beauty, Made in the Year 1772, on Several Parts of England; Particularly the Mountains,*

and Lakes of Cumberland, and Westmoreland (1786; Richmond, UK: Richmond, 1973), Vol. 1, 188.

20 Ibid., Vol. 1, 96.

21 William W. Stowe, *Going Abroad: European Travel in Nineteenth-Century American Culture* (Princeton, NJ: Princeton University Press, 1994), 11.

22 Frances Trollope, *Domestic Manners of the Americans,* ed. Donald Smalley (1832; London: The Folio Society, 1974), 28. All subsequent quotations from Frances Trollope's work will be from this text and will have paginal notations.

23 Biographical information from Frances Trollope's trip to North America is from Helen Heineman, *Frances Trollope* (Boston, MA: Twayne, 1984), 2–3 and Johanna Johnston, *The Life, Manners, and Travels of Fanny Trollope: A Biography* (New York: Hawthorn Books, 1978), 103. The Bazaar was not demolished until 1881.

24 Ian Ousby, *The Englishman's England: Taste, Travel and the Rise of Tourism* (Cambridge: Cambridge University Press, 1990), 2.

25 Walter John Hipple, Jr., *The Beautiful, the Sublime and the Picturesque in Eighteenth-Century British Aesthetic Theory* (Carbondale, IL: Southern Illinois University Press, 1957), 13.

26 In a footnote, Trollope identifies that other person—"himself"—as "the accomplished author of *Cyril Thornton*" (279, fn. 1). A further insight into this fellow traveller/author is provided by Donald Smalley, editor of *Domestic Manners*: "Thomas Hamilton, author of the novel *Cyril Thornton* (1827), which enjoyed much popularity in its day, had come to the United States in the fall of 1830 to gather material for a book upon America" (279, fn. 2). In the next chapter, I discuss the way in which Hamilton depicts Niagara and the reasons why he is *not* silenced by Trollope's presence or "held back" from describing the scene.

27 Gilpin, *Observations on ... Several Parts of England,* Vol. 2, 68.

28 Burke, *Enquiry*, 18.

29 Hipple, *The Beautiful, the Sublime and the Picturesque,* 89.

30 Trollope's reference to the "moist atmosphere" inside the "appalling cavern" may also be a response to Basil Hall's account of extremely low air pressure behind the sheet of water. In the next chapter, we will see how this male traveller measured the innermost pressure with a barometer in order to conquer his fear (and respiratory discomfort).

31 Yordas Cave, in Kingsdale, near Ingleton, in the Yorkshire Dales, consisted of a large limestone cavern and small "closets" including Yordas Bedchamber and Yordas Oven. The Devil's Arse, located in the Peak District village of Castleton in Derbyshire, contained a Great Cave, a subterranean river called the River Styx, and a smaller cavern called Pluto's Dining Room. See the Web site http://www.showcaves.com.

32 Nathaniel Hawthorne, "My Visit to Niagara," in *The Snow-Image and Uncollected Tales,* Vol. 11 (Columbus, OH: Ohio State University Press, 1974), 281. All subsequent quotations from Hawthorne will be from this text and will have paginal notations.

33 Arlin Turner, *Nathaniel Hawthorne: A Biography* (New York: Oxford University Press, 1980), 73.

34 Hawthorne's letter to Franklin Pierce is quoted in *The Letters, 1813–1843*, ed. Thomas Woodson et al. (Columbus, OH: Ohio State University Press, 1984), Vol. 1, 224.

35 Hawthorne's "The Gray Champion" was also printed in *The New England Magazine* in January 1835. See *Hawthorne's Journals*, ed. Newton Arvin (New York: Barnes and Noble, Inc., 1929), 303.

36 William Wordsworth, "Lines Composed a Few Miles above Tintern Abbey, on Revisiting the Banks of the Wye during a Tour. July 13, 1798," in *The Prose Works of William Wordsworth*, ed. W.J.B. Owen and Jane Worthington Smyser (Oxford: Clarendon Press, 1974), 1: 116–20, lines 22–24 and 47–49. All subsequent quotations from this poem will be from this edition and will have line references.

37 Caroline Gilman, *The Poetry of Travelling in the United States. With Additional Sketches by a Few Friends; and A Week among Autographs*, by Rev. S. Gilman (New York: S. Colman, 1838; Upper Saddle, NJ: Literature House, 1970), 205. All subsequent quotations from Gilman will be from this text and will have paginal notations.

38 Marjorie Hope Nicolson, *Mountain Gloom and Mountain Glory: The Development of the Aesthetics of the Infinite* (New York: W.W. Norton, 1959), 306.

39 James Buzard, *The Beaten Track: European Tourism, Literature, and the Ways to Culture, 1800–1918* (Oxford: Clarendon Press, 1993), 10.

40 Anna Brownell Jameson, *Winter Studies and Summer Rambles in Canada* (London: Saunders and Otley, 1838; Toronto, ON: McClelland and Stewart, 1990), 16. All subsequent quotations from Jameson will be from this text and will have paginal notations.

41 Lorraine M. York, "'Sublime Desolation': European Art and Jameson's Perception of Canada," *Mosaic* 19 (2) (Spring 1986): 43, 46.

42 According to nineteenth-century niece/biographer Gerardine Macpherson, the Jameson marriage was not successful because Anna was "too strong-minded, independent and outspoken." When the husband was sent to Dominica, the wife stayed in England. When he was offered the post in Upper Canada in 1833, she waited three years before joining him. See Gerardine Macpherson, *Memoirs of the Life of Anna Jameson* (Boston, MA: Roberts Brothers, 1878), 19.

43 Clara Thomas, "Afterword," in Jameson, *Winter Studies and Summer Rambles in Canada*, 544.

44 Mary G. Mason, "The Other Voice: Autobiographies of Women Writers," *Autobiography: Essays Theoretical and Critical*, ed. James Olney (Princeton, NJ: Princeton University Press, 1980), 231.

45 Sara Mills, "Knowledge, Gender, and Empire," in *Writing Women and Space: Colonial and Postcolonial Geographies*, ed. Alison Blunt and Gillian Rose (New York and London: Guilford Press, 1994), 40.

46 Bina Friewald, "Femininely Speaking: Anna Jameson's *Winter Studies and Summer Rambles in Canada*," in *A Mazing Space: Writing Canadian Women Writing*, ed. Shirley Neuman and Smaro Kamboureli (Edmonton, AB: NeWest Press, 1986), 68.

47 According to twentieth-century biographer Marian Fowler (*The Embroidered Tent*, 146), Ottilie von Goethe was the widow of Goethe's son

August. Anna Jameson spent two years with her in Germany, and was reluctant to leave for Canada because she wanted to protect von Goethe and her illegitimate child. The letters sent back and forth cemented their relationship, and Jameson eventually went back to Germany to live with von Goethe.

48 Alexander Henry, Scottish fur trader and author of *Travels and Adventures in Canada and the Indian Territories* (1809), served as Anna Jameson's "Ulysses of these parts." See W.J. Keith, *Literary Images of Ontario* (Toronto, ON: Ontario Historical Studies Series, 1992), 124.

49 Mason, "The Other Voice," 220; Friewald, "Femininely Speaking," 69; Rachel Blau DuPlessis, "For the Etruscans," in *The New Feminist Criticism: Essays on Women, Literature and Theory,* ed. Elaine Showalter (New York: Pantheon, 1985), 280; Thomas M.F. Gerry, "'I Am Translated': Anna Jameson's Sketches and *Winter Studies and Summer Rambles in Canada*," *Journal of Canadian Studies* 25 (4) (Winter 1990–91): 38.

50 Stowe, *Going Abroad,* 222.

51 Fowler, *The Embroidered Tent,* 164.

52 Although I have used York's terminology, she does not agree that Jameson escapes from the paradox of sublime desolation. In her argument, Jameson's "inner" image of the Falls—based on landscapes moulded into art—is too different from the Niagara landscape which refuses to be "composed." In the end, York argues, the poignant note struck is "the utter impossibility of matching the external landscape to the imagined picture" (York, "'Sublime Desolation,'" 54).

53 Jerome Meckier, *Innocent Abroad: Charles Dickens's American Engagements* (Lexington, KY: University Press of Kentucky, 1990), 75.

54 Dickens had a copy of Lyell's book in his library. See Peter Ackroyd, *Dickens* (London: Sinclair-Stevenson, 1990), 663.

55 Charles Dickens, *American Notes for General Circulation* (London: Chapman and Hall, 1850), Vol. 2, 137. All subsequent quotations from Dickens will be from this edition and will have paginal notations.

56 For an in-depth study of how Dickens's *American Notes* imitates Frances Trollope's *Domestic Manners of the Americans* on such topics as the vulgarity of Americans, see Meckier, *Innocent Abroad,* 75–132.

57 On the copyright controversy, see Meckier, *Innocent Abroad,* 39–74.

58 Ackroyd, *Dickens,* 353.

59 Mary Hogarth spent long periods of time with Charles and Catherine Dickens. Dickens grieved her death intensely and wrote of a desire to be buried in her grave. See John Forster, *The Life of Charles Dickens* (London: Chapman and Hall, 1872), Vol. 1, 199.

60 "Letter to Mrs. George Hogarth," May 8, 1843, in *The Letters of Charles Dickens,* ed. Madeline House and Graham Storey (Oxford: Clarendon Press, 1974), Vol. 3, 484.

61 David Spurr, *The Rhetoric of Empire: Colonial Discourse in Journalism, Travel Writing, and Imperial Administration* (Durham and London: Duke University Press, 1993), 153.

62 Margaret Fuller, James Freeman Clarke, and his sister, Sarah Freeman Clarke, made the trip to the American West to follow in the footsteps of the thousands of emigrants who had travelled overland in ox-drawn cov-

ered wagons. See Annette Kolodny, *The Land Before Her: Fantasy and Experience of the American Frontiers, 1630–1860* (Chapel Hill, NC: University of North Carolina Press, 1985), 112.

63 Margaret Fuller, *Summer on the Lakes in 1843,* ed. Madeleine B. Stern (Boston, MA: Charles C. Little & James Brown, 1844; Nieuwkoop: De Graff, 1972), 3. All subsequent quotations from Fuller will be from this text and will have paginal notations.

64 Stowe, *Going Abroad*, 106–107, 113.

65 Madeleine B. Stern, "Introduction," in Fuller, *Summer on the Lakes in 1843,* 12. One of these friends was Henry Thoreau, who was also an important influence on Fuller's writing. After she returned home from her westward "migration," he "listened attentively to descriptions of her summer adventures and encouraged her plans to turn journal notes into a book." See Arthur W. Brown, *Margaret Fuller* (New York: Twayne, 1964), 69.

66 Fuller went to Sault Ste. Marie to visit Anna Jameson's friend and guide, Mrs. Schoolcraft. But, unlike Jameson, Fuller did not travel with the Indian woman to the falls of St. Mary's. Instead, she ventured south and then west to America's Indian frontier. After her journey to Niagara Falls, the Great Lakes, and the Illinois prairie, she travelled to Europe (in 1846). This pleasure tour abroad ended with her shipwrecked off Fire Island in July 1850.

67 For a detailed discussion of Fuller's interpretations of the Indian as destined to his/her fate, see Christina Zwarg, "Footnoting the Sublime: Margaret Fuller on Black Hawk's Trail," *American Literary History* 5 (4) (1993): 616–42.

68 Pratt, *Imperial Eyes,* 7, 60.

69 The image of an Indian raising a tomahawk occurs twice in *Summer on the Lakes*. In the second scene, Fuller defends the Indian as having acted "the Roman or the Carthaginian part of heroic and patriotic self-defense when he wielded his tomahawk against the Europeans who took possession of this country" (234–35). This is a different kind of rhetoric: the Indian, a patriotic hero, is the ultimate victim and not Fuller's female narrator.

70 In his *Observations on the Feeling of the Beautiful and Sublime* (trans. John T. Goldthwait [1764; Berkeley, CA: University of California Press, 1960], 111) Immanuel Kant writes: "among all the savages there is no nation that displays so sublime a mental character as those of North America."

71 Pratt, *Imperial Eyes,* 185.

72 Zwarg, "Footnoting the Sublime," 618.

73 Anthony Trollope, *North America,* ed. Donald Smalley and Bradford Allen Booth (1862; New York: Alfred A. Knopf, 1951), 95. All subsequent quotations from Trollope will be from this text and will have paginal notations.

74 While Trollope's *The West Indies and the Spanish Main* was published as a book in 1859, the section about Niagara Falls (chapter 13) is reprinted in *North America*, Appendix C. Trollope's first impression of the waterfalls is found on page 538.

75 Catherine Hall, "Going a-Trolloping: Imperial Man Travels the Empire," in *Gender and Imperialism*, ed. Clare Midgley (Manchester, UK: Manchester University Press, 1998), 181.

76 Smalley and Booth, "Introduction," *North America*, 7.

77 Hall, "Going a-Trolloping," 191.

78 In his preface (19–20), Anthony Trollope provides a lengthy explanation of how his writing is different from his mother's: "She saw with a woman's keen eye, and described with a woman's light but graphic pen, the social defects and absurdities which our near relatives had adopted into their domestic life. All that she told was worth the telling, and the telling, if done successfully, was sure to produce a good result. I am satisfied that it did so. But she did not regard it as a part of her work to dilate on the nature and operation of those political arrangements which had produced the social absurdities which she saw, or to explain that though such absurdities were the natural result of those arrangements of their new-ness, the defects would certainly pass away, while the political arrange-ments, if good, would remain. Such a work is fitter for a man than for a woman."

79 Trollope's defence of the Union met with some criticism in *Blackwood's Magazine*. Because of this, Chapman and Hall (his English publishers) did not reprint the travel book. See J.W. Ward, "Introduction," in Trollope, *North America* (1862; Toronto, ON: Penguin Books, 1992), 8.

80 L.J. Swingle, *Romanticism and Anthony Trollope* (Ann Arbor, MI: University of Michigan Press, 1990), 53.

81 Trollope's reference to America as "a savage country" is quoted in Ward, "Introduction," 9.

82 Smalley and Booth, "Introduction," *North America*, 5.

83 Stowe, *Going Abroad*, 12, 55.

84 Buzard, *The Beaten Track*, 153.

85 William Wordsworth, "Book VII: Residence in London" of *The Prelude, or Growth of a Poet's Mind*, ed. Ernest de Selincourt, 2nd ed. revised by Helen Darbishire (Oxford: Clarendon Press, 1959), lines 685–88. All sub-sequent quotations from *The Prelude* will be from this edition and will have line references.

86 Jameson, *Winter Studies and Summer Rambles in Canada*, 218.

87 Ousby, *The Englishman's England*, 133.

88 Henry James, "Niagara Falls," in *Portraits of Places* (Boston, MA: James R. Osgood, 1883), 364. All subsequent quotations from James will be from this text and will have paginal notations.

89 Stowe, *Going Abroad*, 171–74.

90 Francis Parkman's exotic and popular histories of early settlement in the New World include two "frontiers": the American (*The Oregon Trail* [1847]) and the Canadian (*The Jesuits in North America in the Seventeenth Century* [1867]). For a detailed examination of Parkman's distinctions between the types of frontiersmen in Oregon and in Quebec, see James Doyle, *North of America: Images of Canada in the Literature of the United States, 1775–1900* (Toronto, ON: ECW Press, 1983), 27–28, 57–71.

91 Harry T. Moore, *Henry James and His World* (London: Thames and Hudson, 1974), 15, 31.

92 Henry James, "Quebec City," in *The Wild Is Always There: Canada through the Eyes of Foreign Writers*, ed. Greg Gatenby (Toronto, ON: Alfred A. Knopf, 1993), 117.

Chapter 3

1 Pehr Kalm, "Letter" (1750), in Charles Mason Dow, *Anthology and Bibliography of Niagara Falls* (Albany, NY, 1921), Vol. 1, 53–54. All subsequent quotations from Kalm will be from this text and will have paginal notations.

2 Much of the information on seventeenth- and eighteenth-century theories about how the earth works is based on the lengthy discussions found in Charles Coulston Gillispie's *Genesis and Geology: A Study in the Relations of Scientific Thought, Natural Theology, and Social Opinion in Great Britain, 1790–1850* (Cambridge, MA: Harvard University Press, 1951), 41–55; and in Morris Zaslow's *Reading the Rocks: The Story of the Geological Survey of Canada, 1842–1972* (Toronto, ON: Macmillan, in association with the Department of Energy, Mines and Resources and Information Canada, 1975), 3–27.

3 Gillispie, *Genesis and Geology*, 41. Throughout *Genesis and Geology*, Gillispie refers to the Neptunist formulations as "imaginative exercises" and to Vulcanist treatises as more logical, scientific "syntheses."

4 Edmund Burke, *A Philosophical Enquiry into the Origin of Our Ideas of the Sublime and Beautiful*, ed. J.T. Boulton (Notre Dame, IN: University of Notre Dame Press, 1968), 110.

5 Ibid., 135.

6 Frances Ferguson, "The Sublime of Edmund Burke, or the Bathos of Experience," in *Glyph 8: Johns Hopkins Textual Studies,* ed. Walter Benn Michaels (Baltimore, MD: Johns Hopkins University Press, 1981), 69.

7 Burke, *Enquiry*, 40.

8 Ibid., 25.

9 Immanuel Kant, *Observations on the Feeling of the Beautiful and Sublime,* trans. John T. Goldthwait (1763; Berkeley, CA: University of California Press, 1960), 79.

10 David Spurr, *The Rhetoric of Empire: Colonial Discourse in Journalism, Travel Writing, and Imperial Administration* (Durham and London: Duke University Press, 1993), 159.

11 David E. Nye, *American Technological Sublime* (Cambridge, MA: MIT Press, 1994), 14, 22.

12 Keith J. Tinkler, "The Idea of a History and the History of an Idea," *Geomorphology* 1 (1987): 73.

13 P. Pouchot, *Memoir upon the Late War in North America, between the French and English 1755–60; followed by Observations upon the Theatre of Actual War, and by New Details Concerning the Manners and Customs of the Indians; with Topographical Maps* (Switzerland, 1781; reprint, Roxbury, MA: W. Elliot Woodward, 1866) (Dow, *Anthology and Bibliography of Niagara Falls*, Vol. 1, 43–47).

14 Ibid., 46.

15 The letter published in the *Antigua Gazette* was signed "A.B." According to Keith Tinkler ("The Idea of a History," 73), "A.B.'s identity is a mystery although there is a chance that he was Anthony Bacon (1717–1786), a Manxman long employed as a British Secret Service agent working in North America." Twentieth-century historian Suzanne Zeller identifies

"A.B." as "Capt. F.H. Baddeley of the Royal Engineers," who published a series of "hints" on a geological survey of the province of Upper Canada. See Suzanne Zeller, *Inventing Canada: Early Victorian Science and the Idea of a Transcontinental Nation* (Toronto, ON: University of Toronto Press, 1987), 28.

16 Although Maclay's 1790 notion that the earth was over 55,000 years old lengthens the scriptural date of 5,700 years, it does not come close to what James Hutton proposed five years later when he estimated the earth as 450 million years old.

17 Dow, *Anthology and Bibliography of Niagara Falls,* Vol. 1, 495–520.

18 Isaac Weld, *Travels Through the States of North America, and the provinces of Upper and Lower Canada, during the years 1795, 1796, and 1797* (London: Stockdale, 1799) (Dow, *Anthology and Bibliography of Niagara Falls*, Vol. 1, 97). All subsequent quotations from Weld will be from this text and will have paginal notations.

19 Mary Quayle Innis, ed., *Mrs. Simcoe's Diary* (1791–96) (Toronto, ON: Macmillan, 1965), 162.

20 Mary Louise Pratt, *Imperial Eyes: Travel Writing and Transculturation* (London and New York: Routledge, 1992), 64.

21 Timothy Bigelow, *Journal of a Tour to Niagara Falls in the Year 1805* (Boston, MA: John Wilson and Son, 1876) (Dow, *Anthology and Bibliography of Niagara Falls,* Vol. 1, 132). All subsequent quotations from Bigelow will be from this text and will have paginal notations.

22 Ian Ousby, *The Englishman's England: Taste, Travel and the Rise of Tourism* (Cambridge: Cambridge University Press, 1990), 131–32.

23 Christian Schultz, *Travels on an Inland Voyage through the States of New-York, Pennsylvania, Virginia, Ohio, Kentucky and Tennessee, and through the Territories of Indians, Louisiana, Mississippi and New-Orleans; performed in the years 1807 and 1808; including a tour of nearly six thousand miles,* 2 vols. (New York: Isaac Riley, 1810) (Dow, *Anthology and Bibliography of Niagara Falls,* Vol. 1, 144).

24 Immanuel Kant, *Observations on the Feeling of the Beautiful and Sublime,* 48–49.

25 Pratt, *Imperial Eyes,* 7, 56.

26 Captain Basil Hall, *Travels in North America in the Years 1827 and 1828* (Edinburgh: Cadell, 1829) (Dow, *Anthology and Bibliography of Niagara Falls,* Vol. 1, 164). All subsequent quotations from Hall will be from this edition and will have paginal notations.

27 Quoted in Marjorie Hope Nicolson, *Mountain Gloom and Mountain Glory: The Development of the Aesthetics of the Infinite* (New York: W.W. Norton, 1959), 291.

28 For more on the connection between Newton and the pre-sublime, see F.E.L. Priestley, "Newton and the Romantic Concept of Nature," *The University of Toronto Quarterly* 4 (July 1948): 323–36.

29 Quoted in Nicolson, *Mountain Gloom and Mountain Glory,* 302–303.

30 Biographical information on Thomas Hamilton comes from Christopher Mulvey, *Anglo-American Landscapes: A Study of Nineteenth-Century Anglo-American Travel Literature* (Cambridge: Cambridge University Press, 1983), 198.

31 Thomas Hamilton, *Men and Manners in America* (Edinburgh and London, 1833) (Dow, *Anthology and Bibliography of Niagara Falls,* Vol. 1, 525–26). All subsequent quotations from Hamilton will be from this text and will have paginal notations.

32 William Gilpin, *Observations, Relative Chiefly to Picturesque Beauty, Made in the Year 1772, on Several Parts of England; Particularly the Mountains, and Lakes of Cumberland, and Westmoreland* (1786; Richmond, UK: Richmond, 1973), Vol. 2, 61.

33 Ousby, *The Englishman's England,* 151.

34 Harriet Martineau, *Retrospect of Western Travel* (London: Saunders and Otley, 1838; New York: Greenwood Press, 1969), Vol 1., 152. All subsequent quotations from Martineau will be from this text and will have paginal notations.

35 Gillian Thomas, *Harriet Martineau* (Boston, MA, Twayne, 1985), 2; and Valerie Sanders, *Reason Over Passion: Harriet Martineau and the Victorian Novel* (Sussex, UK: Harvester Press, 1986), 130.

36 For example, George Fairholme's "On the Falls of Niagara, with Some Observations on the Distinct Evidence which they Bear to the Geological Character of the North American Plains," published in the *London and Edinburgh Philological Magazine* in 1834, promotes the Neptunist theory that Niagara was formed after the Flood (Dow, *Anthology and Bibliography of Niagara Falls,* Vol. 1, 527).

37 Tinkler, "The Idea of a History," 78.

38 Ibid..

39 Robert Bakewell's *Bird's-Eye View, Niagara Gorge and Surrounding Country* was published in *Loudon's Magazine of Natural History* in January 1830 (Dow, *Anthology and Bibliography of Niagara Falls,* Vol. 1, 520). Like the Hennepin print, Bakewell's *Bird's-Eye View* spawned many copies. It was made into a lithograph by D.W. Kellogg & Co. and included in a reprint of Bakewell's first monograph, *An Introduction to Geology* (1838). Later, the American geologist James Hall used the picture as the basis for his own "bird's-eye sketch" in *Geology of New York* (1843).

40 The other female writer who approached the subject of geological speculation was Isabella Lucy Bird, who reserves two lines at the end of her description of Niagara to state: "It would be out of place to enter upon the numerous geological speculations which have arisen upon the structure and recession of Niagara. It seems as if the faint light which science has shed upon the abyss of bygone ages were but to show that its depths must remain for ever unlighted by human reason and research." See Isabella Lucy Bird, *The Englishwoman in America* (1856; Toronto, ON: University of Toronto Press, 1966), 236.

41 Harriet Martineau later went on to write an article entitled "Dress and Its Victims" for the periodical *Once a Week* (1859). In it, Martineau claims that women are "murdered" by their costumes and other feminine paraphernalia—tight and cumbersome outfits affect the human frame; clothing catches fire; makeup causes illnesses. Even milliners and shop workers are "worn out and killed off in the cause of dress." Perhaps owing to her discomforts at Niagara, in this article Martineau also advises that all women wear practical hats, and not bonnets or brimless "chimney-pot hats." See

Gayle Graham Yates, ed., *Harriet Martineau on Women* (New Brunswick, NJ: Rutgers University Press, 1985), 229–38.

42 Catherine Hall, "Going a-Trolloping: Imperial Man Travels the Empire," in *Gender and Imperialism,* ed. Clare Midgley (Manchester, UK: Manchester University Press, 1998), 192.

43 Unlike Martineau, women who came to Niagara after her were frightened by the guide. When they refer to him as "the Phlegethon of waters," "a grinning demon," and "a black imp," he is given a sinister grandeur. At this point, the sublimity at Niagara depends as much on its human occupant as on its natural scenery. See Emma C. Embury, "Niagara," *Ladies Companion* (Sept. 1841): 251; Alexander Dunlop, *The New World Journals of Alexander Graham Dunlop,* ed. D. Sinclair and G. Warkentin (1845; Toronto: Dundurn Press, 1976), 49; and Bird, *The Englishwoman in America,* 233.

44 Harriet Martineau, *Society in America* (London: Saunders and Otley, 1837; New York: Greenwood Press, 1969), Vol. 3, 81.

45 Mulvey, *Anglo-American Landscapes,* 197.

46 Dr. Walter Henry published a famous account of the autopsy he performed on Napoleon before he emigrated to Canada (in 1827). Between 1827 and 1841, Henry served as an army surgeon in the 66th Regiment in Halifax, Kingston, Quebec, and Montreal. He was also an officer of the Quebec Literary and Historical Society. See Mary Lu MacDonald, *Literature and Society in the Canadas, 1817–1850* (Queenston, ON: Edwin Mellen Press, 1992), 309–10.

47 Walter Henry, *Events of a Military Life: Being Recollections after Service in the Peninsular War, Invasion of France, the East Indies, St. Helena, Canada, and Elsewhere* 2 Vols. (London: W. Pickering, 1843) (Dow, *Anthology and Bibliography of Niagara Falls,* Vol. 1, 187). All subsequent quotations from Henry will be from this text and will have paginal notations.

48 Karen Dubinsky, *The Second Greatest Disappointment: Honeymooning and Tourism at Niagara Falls* (Toronto, ON and New Brunswick, NJ: Between the Lines and Rutgers University Press, 1999), 102.

49 Nicholas A. Woods, *The Prince of Wales in Canada and the United States* (London: Bradbury and Evans, 1861), 238. All subsequent quotations from Woods will be from this text and will have paginal notations.

50 As early as 1789, respondents were disputing the rate of recession. Robert McCauslin estimated the rate as "not very fast" in his paper delivered to the American Philosophical Society. The next year, William Maclay wrote an account that computed it at less than one foot a year (see page 181, note 16). Charles Lyell's assessment sparked the most debate. In 1843, he proposed "a probable recession of more than one foot in a year; though part of the Fall may go back faster than this." Lyell also gave a warning about the future of the waterfalls, taking into account data which suggested that "the cataracts were once far down-stream, and twice their present height." And, if the landscape continued to erode at this rate, the once-mighty cataract would eventually be a smallish waterfall: "If it recedes one foot in a year, then in about five thousand years it would recede a mile...Thus, at the end of 10,000 years, when the Falls shall have receded two miles, they would be eighty feet high." (Dow, *Anthology and Bibliography of Niagara Falls,* Vol. 1, 495, 501; Vol, 2, 45).

51 Some of the writings of the 1870s and 1880s that called for a cleanup of the whole Niagara landscape are found in Henry James's article, "Free Niagara" in *The Nation* (1871); Charles R. Edwards, *A Story of Niagara, To Which are Appended Reminiscences of a Custom House Officer* (Buffalo, NY: Breed, Lent, 1870); and *Royal Commission to Inquire into Alleged Abuses Occurring in the Vicinity of Niagara Falls* (Toronto, ON: The Archives of Ontario, 1873) and the New York (State) Commissioners of the State Reservation at Niagara, *Five Annual Reports, 1884–1889* (New York: Troy Press, 1885–89).

52 Other public-spirited New Yorkers devoted to the "Free Niagara" movement included landscape architect Frederick Law Olmsted and journalist Jonathan Harrison (Dubinsky, *The Second Greatest Disappointment,* 88).

53 The letter from Frederic Edwin Church to Thomas V. Welch, first superintendent of the State Reservation at Niagara, quoted in Ronald L. Way, *Ontario's Niagara Parks: A History* (Niagara Falls, ON: Niagara Parks Commission, 1946), 17.

54 According to Olmsted's "Notes" on the Report of the New York State Survey for 1879, Church had approached him about "freeing" Niagara as early as 1868. Quoted in Way, *Ontario's Niagara Parks,* 16.

55 Alfred Runte, "The Role of Niagara in America's Scenic Preservation," in *Niagara: Two Centuries of Changing Attitudes, 1697–1901,* ed. Jeremy Elwell Adamson (Washington, DC: Corcoran Gallery of Art, 1985), 122.

56 John Sears, *Sacred Places: American Tourist Attractions in the 19th Century* (New York: Oxford University Press, 1989), 188–89.

57 Dean MacCannell, *The Tourist: A New Theory of the Leisure Class* (New York: Schocken Books, 1976), 81.

58 Pierre Berton, *Niagara: A History of the Falls* (Toronto, ON: McClelland and Stewart, 1992), 192. For a discussion of the human-built features that had to be removed from the American side, see Elizabeth McKinsey, *Niagara Falls: Icon of the American Sublime* (Cambridge, MA: Harvard University Press, 1985), 253–82.

59 Sears, *Sacred Places,* 186–88; Runte, "The Role of Niagara," in *Niagara,* ed. Adamson, 124.

60 Roland Barnsley, *The Public Gardens and Parks of Niagara* (St. Catharines, ON: Vanwell, 1989), 10.

61 Since 1786, when the area was first surveyed by Augustus Jones, the Crown surveyor, "a strip of land one chain in width was reserved all along the gorge bank as the property of the Crown (a chain is equivalent to 20 m or 66 ft.). It was referred to by various names, the Chain Reserve, Crown Reserve, and Military Reserve." See George A. Seibel, *Ontario's Niagara Parks: A History,* 2nd ed. (Niagara Falls, ON: Niagara Parks Commission, 1991), 7.

62 Barnsley, *The Public Gardens and Parks of Niagara,* 11.

63 Queen Victoria Niagara Falls Park was named after the first publicly funded park, the Royal Victoria Park in Bath (opened by Princess Victoria in 1830). For a history of British parks, see Susan Lasdun, *The English Park: Royal, Private and Public* (London: Andre Deutsch, 1991).

64 Ibid., 1–18, 61–128, 161–85.

65 Dubinsky, *The Second Greatest Disappointment*, 94.

66 H.V. Nelles, *The Politics of Development: Forests, Mines and Hydro-Electric Power in Ontario* (Toronto, ON: Macmillan, 1974), 32–33.

67 Ibid., 216.

68 Carlie Oreskovich, *Sir Henry Pellatt: The King of Casa Loma* (Toronto, ON: McGraw-Hill Ryerson, 1982), 61.

69 Tours cost twenty-five cents. During the first fourteen years that the Niagara Falls Electric N.Y. Co. charged for tours (1904–18), it collected $46,441. See William Irwin, *The New Niagara: Tourism, Technology, and the Landscape of Niagara Falls, 1776–1917* (University Park, PA: Pennsylvania State University Press, 1996), 130.

70 Seibel, *Ontario's Niagara Parks,* 169.

71 Runte, "The Role of Niagara," in *Niagara,* ed. Adamson, 125.

72 The term "electrical" technological sublime was coined by Nye, *American Technological Sublime,* 171.

73 H.G. Wells, *The Future in America: A Search after Realities* (New York and London: Harper & Brothers, 1906), 54. The account of his visit to Niagara Falls was also published separately in *Harper's Weekly* (July 21, 1906): 108–20. (In a 1907 edition of *The Future in America,* published in Leipzig by Bernhard Tauchnitz, Wells called the account of his visit "The End of Niagara.") All subsequent quotations from Wells will be from the Harper and Brothers text and will have paginal notations.

74 Roslynn D. Haynes, *H.G. Wells: The Discoverer of the Future* (London: Macmillan Press, 1980), 15.

75 For details of the controversy between industrialists and preservationists during the first decade of the twentieth century, see Irwin, *The New Niagara,* 55–75.

Conclusion

1 Letter from Thomas Moore to his mother, quoted in James B. Twitchell, *Romantic Horizons: Aspects of the Sublime in English Poetry and Painting, 1770–1850* (Columbia, MO: University of Missouri Press, 1983), 38, fn. 44.

2 Mary Louise Pratt, *Imperial Eyes: Travel Writing and Transculturation* (London and New York: Routledge, 1992), 188.

3 Philip J. Deloria, *Playing Indian* (New Haven and London: Yale University Press, 1998), 4.

4 Pratt, *Imperial Eyes,* 56.

5 Christopher Mulvey, *Anglo-American Landscapes: A Study of Nineteenth-Century Anglo-American Travel Literature* (Cambridge: Cambridge University Press, 1983), 204. According to Mulvey, the word "Niagarized" was first coined by Lady Emmeline Wortley in her *Travels in the United States* (1851).

6 William R. Irwin, *The New Niagara: Tourism, Technology and the Landscape of Niagara Falls, 1776–1917* (University Park, PA: Pennsylvania State University Press, 1996), 12.

Bibliography

Abrams, Ann Uhry. *The Valiant Hero: Benjamin West and Grand-Style History Painting*. Washington, DC: Smithsonian Institution Press, 1988.

Abrams, M.H. *The Mirror and the Lamp: Romantic Theory and the Critical Tradition*. New York: Oxford University Press, 1953.

Ackroyd, Peter. *Dickens*. London: Sinclair-Stevenson, 1990.

Adamson, Jeremy Elwell, ed. *Niagara: Two Centuries of Changing Attitudes, 1697–1901*. Washington, DC: Corcoran Gallery of Art, 1985.

Adburgham, Alison. *A Punch History of Manners and Modes, 1841–1940*. London: Hutchinson, 1961.

Addison and Steele and Others. *The Spectator in Four Volumes*. Ed. Gregory Smith. London: J.M. Dent & Sons, 1961.

Addison, Joseph. *Essays Moral and Humorous: Also Essays on Imagination and Taste*. Edinburgh: W. and R. Chambers, 1839.

Aldridge, Alexandra. *The Scientific World View in Dystopia*. Ann Arbor, MI: UMI Research Press, 1978.

Alexander, J.E. *Transatlantic Sketches: Comprising Visits to the Most Interesting Scenes in North and South America, and the West Indies, with Notes on Negro Slavery and Canadian Emigration*. 2 vols. London: Richard Bentley, 1833.

Alexander, Jeb. *Jeb and Dash: A Diary of Gay Life, 1918–1945*. Ed. Ina Russell. Boston, MA: Faber and Faber, 1994.

Altick, Richard D. *Victorian People and Ideas*. New York: W.W. Norton, 1973.

Andrews, Malcolm. *The Search for the Picturesque: Landscape Aesthetics and Tourism in Britain, 1760–1800*. Aldershot, UK: Scolar, 1989.

Arensberg, Mary, ed. *The American Sublime*. Albany, NY: State University of New York Press, 1986.

Atwood, Margaret. *Days of the Rebels, 1815–1840*. Toronto, ON: Natural Science of Canada, 1977.

———. "The Whirlpool Rapids." *Redbook* (Nov. 1986): 51–57.

Bail, Murray. "Victoria and Niagara." *Brick* 45 (1993): 72–74.

Baird, Robert. *Impressions and Experience of the West Indies and North America in 1849*. Philadelphia: Lea & Blanchard, 1850.

Bannister, Robert C. *Social Darwinism: Science and Myth in Anglo-American Social Thought*. Philadelphia: Temple University Press, 1979.

Bannon, Anthony. *The Taking of Niagara: A History of the Falls in Photography*. Buffalo, NY: Media Study, 1982.

Barbier, Carl Paul. *William Gilpin: His Drawings, Teaching, and Theory of the Picturesque*. Oxford: Clarendon Press, 1963.

Barnes, Trevor J., and James S. Duncan, eds. *Writing Worlds: Discourse, Text and Metaphor in the Representation of Landscape*. New York: Routledge, 1991.

Barnett, Louise K. *The Ignoble Savage: American Literary Racism, 1790–1890*. Rev. ed. London: Methuen, 1987.

Barnsley, Roland. *The Public Gardens and Parks of Niagara*. St. Catharines, ON: Vanwell, 1989.

Barrell, John. *The Dark Side of the Landscape*. Cambridge: Cambridge University Press, 1980.

———. *The Idea of Landscape and the Sense of Place, 1730–1840: An Approach to the Poetry of John Clare*. Cambridge: Cambridge University Press, 1972.

Bartlett, William. *Bartlett's Canada: A Pre-Confederation Journey*. Toronto, ON: McClelland and Stewart, 1968.

Bateman, Colin. *Maid of the Mist*. Toronto and New York: HarperCollins, 1999.

Baxandall, Michael. *Patterns of Intention: On the Historical Explanation of Pictures*. New Haven, CT: Yale University Press, 1985.

Beckett, Sr. Wendy. *The Story of Painting*. Boston and Toronto: Little Brown, in association with the National Gallery of Art, Washington, 1994.

Belfer, Lauren. *City of Lights*. New York: Dial Press, 1999.

Bell, Rev. Adam. "An Account of the Trip from the Head of the Lake to the Falls of Niagara and Hence to Buffalo, State of New York (1823)." In *Travellers Accounts from the Clearwater Collection in the Niagara Falls (New York) Public Library*. Collected by George A. Seibel. Microfilm #15. Niagara Falls, ON: Niagara Falls Public Library, 1982. 4 pp.

Bercovitch, Sacvan. *The American Jeremiad*. Madison, WI: University of Wisconsin Press, 1978.

———. *The Rites of Ascent: Transformations in the Symbolic Construction of America*. New York: Routledge, 1993.

Berger, Carl. *Science, God and Nature in Victorian Canada*. Toronto, ON: University of Toronto Press, 1983.

———. *The Sense of Power: Studies in the Ideas of Canadian Imperialism, 1867–1914*. Toronto, ON: University of Toronto Press, 1970.

———. *The Writing of Canadian History: Aspects of English-Canadian Historical Writing Since 1900*. 2nd ed. Toronto, ON: University of Toronto Press, 1986.

Berkhofer, Robert F. *The White Man's Indian: Images of the American Indian from Columbus to the Present*. New York: Knopf, 1978.

Bermingham, Ann. *Landscape and Ideology: The English Rustic Tradition, 1740–1860*. Berkeley, CA: University of California Press, 1986.

Bernasconi, Robert, et al. *The Idea of Race*. Indianapolis, IN: Hackett, 2000.

Berton, Pierre. *Niagara: A History of the Falls*. Toronto, ON: McClelland and Stewart, 1992.

———. *A Picture Book of Niagara Falls*. Toronto, ON: McClelland and Stewart, 1993.

Best, Joel, ed. *Images of Issues: Typifying Contemporary Social Problems.* New York: Aldine de Gruyter, 1989.

Bigelow, Timothy. *Journal of a Tour to Niagara Falls in the Year 1805.* Boston, MA: J. Wilson, 1876.

Bird, Isabella Lucy. *The Englishwoman in America.* 1856; Toronto, ON: University of Toronto Press, 1966.

Birdsell, Sandra. "Niagara Falls." In *Agassiz Stories.* Winnipeg, MB: Turnstone Press, 1987, 217–36.

Birkett, Dea. *Spinsters Abroad: Victorian Lady Explorers.* Oxford: Basil Blackwell, 1989.

Blaise, Clark. *The Border as Fiction.* Borderlands Monograph Ser. 4. Orono, ME: Borderlands Project, 1990, 1–12.

Blunt, Alison, and Gillian Rose, eds. *Writing Women and Space: Colonial and Postcolonial Geographies.* New York and London: Guilford Press, 1994.

Boorstin, Daniel J. *The Image: A Guide to Pseudo-Events in America.* New York: Harper Colophon Books, 1961.

Bremer, Fredrika. *The Homes of the New World.* 2 vols. London: Chapman & Hall, 1850.

British Autobiographies. Hamden, CT: Archon Books, 1968.

Brown, Arthur W. *Margaret Fuller.* New York: Twayne, 1964.

Brown, Wallace. "First Impressions: Through British North America with Canada's First Tourists." *The Beaver* (Apr./May 1988): 4–20.

Brunsden, Denys, and John C. Doornkamp, eds. *The Unquiet Landscape.* Bloomington, IN: Indiana University Press, 1974.

Bryan's Dictionary of Painters and Engravers. 5 vols. Port Washington, NY: Kennikat Press, 1904.

Buell, Lawrence. *Literary Transcendentalism: Style and Vision in the American Renaissance.* Ithaca, NY: Cornell University Press, 1973.

Buffalo Fine Arts Academy. *Three Centuries of Niagara Falls: Oils, Watercolors, Drawings, Prints.* Ed. Ursula N. Eland. Buffalo, NY: Albright-Knox Art Gallery, 1964.

"Bugle." "A Letter from the Falls of Niagara." *Littell's Spirit of the Magazine* (1839): 256–60.

Burke, Andrew. *Burke's Descriptive Guide or Visitor's Companion to Niagara Falls for 1851.* Buffalo, NY: n.p., 1851.

Burke, Edmund. *A Philosophical Enquiry into the Origin of Our Ideas of the Sublime and Beautiful.* Ed. J.T. Boulton. 1757; Notre Dame, IN: University of Notre Dame Press, 1968.

Burnet, Thomas. *The Sacred Theory of the Earth.* 1684; London: Centaur, 1965.

Butor, Michel. *6810000 litres d'eau par seconde; étude stéréophonique.* Paris: Gallimard, 1965. Translated as *Niagara, a novel.* Trans. Elinor S. Miller. Chicago, IL: H. Regnery, 1969.

———. "Travel and Writing." Trans. John Powers and K. Lisker. *Mosaic* 8(1) (1974): 1–16.

Buzard, James. *The Beaten Track: European Tourism, Literature, and the Ways to Culture, 1800–1918.* Oxford: Clarendon Press, 1993.

Campbell, Henry C., ed. *Bartlett's Canada: A Pre-Confederation Journey.* Toronto, ON: McClelland and Stewart, 1968.

Canadian Letters, Description of a Tour thro' the Provinces of Lower and Upper Canada [1792–93]. Montreal, 1912.

Carlyle, Thomas. *Shooting Niagara: And After?* London: Chapman and Hall, 1867.

Carter, Paul. *The Road to Botany Bay: An Exploration of Landscape and History.* New York: Alfred A. Knopf, 1988.

Catton, Bruce. "The Thundering Water." *American Heritage* 15(6) (1964): 256–60.

Clark, Kenneth. *Landscape into Art.* New York: Harper & Row, 1976.

Cohn, Jan, and Thomas H. Miles. "The Sublime: In Alchemy, Aesthetics and Psychoanalysis." *Modern Philology* (Feb. 1977): 289–304.

Conrad, Peter. *Imagining America.* London: Routledge and Kegan Paul, 1980.

Cosgrove, Denis, and Stephen Daniels, eds. *The Iconography of Landscape.* Cambridge: Cambridge University Press, 1988.

Costa, Richard Haver. *H.G. Wells.* Boston, MA: Twayne, 1985.

Cruikshank, Julia. *Whirlpool Heights: The Dream-House on the Niagara River.* London: George Allen & Unwin, 1915.

Culler, Jonathan. "The Semiotics of Tourism." In *Framing the Sign: Criticism and Its Institutions.* Oxford: Basil Blackwell, 1988, 153–67.

Cutter, Charles. *Pan-American Buffalo and Niagara Falls: A Picturesque Souvenir.* Niagara Falls, NY: Charles Cutter, 1901.

———. *Cutter's Guide to Niagara Falls and Adjacent Points of Interest.* 6th ed. Niagara Falls, NY: Charles Cutter, 1905.

Davidson, Arnold E., ed. *Studies on Canadian Literature: Introductory and Critical Essays.* New York: The Modern Language Association of America, 1990.

DeBolla, Peter. *The Discourse of the Sublime: Readings in History, Aesthetics and the Subject.* Oxford: Basil Blackwell, 1989.

Debus, Allen G., ed. *World Who's Who in Science.* Chicago, IL: n.p., 1968.

Deloria, Philip J. *Playing Indian.* New Haven and London: Yale University Press, 1998.

De Luca, Vincent Arthur. *Words of Eternity: Blake and the Poetics of the Sublime.* Princeton, NJ: Princeton University Press, 1991.

Dennis, John. *Critical Works,* Vol. II. Ed. Edward Niles Hooker. Baltimore, MD: Johns Hopkins University Press, 1943.

De Pencier, Honor. "The Artist's Niagara: The Falls from the 1690s to the 1890s." *Rotunda* 12(2) (1979): 5–11.

De Roos, Lieut. the Hon. Fred. Fitzgerald. *Personal Narrative of Travels in the United States and Canada in 1826.* London: William Harrison Ainsworth, 1827.

De Volpi, Charles P. *The Niagara Peninsula: A Pictorial Record, 1697–1880.* Montreal, QC: Dev-Sco, 1966.

Dickason, Olive Patricia. *Canada's First Nations: A History of the Founding Peoples from Earliest Times.* Toronto, ON: McClelland and Stewart, 1992.

Dickens, Charles. *American Notes for General Circulation.* 2 vols. London: Chapman and Hall, 1842.

———. *The Letters of Charles Dickens.* Ed. Madeline House and Graham Storey. 8 vols. Oxford: Clarendon Press, 1974.

Dickenson, Victoria. *Drawn from Life: Science and Art in the Portrayal of the New World*. Toronto, ON: University of Toronto Press, 1998.

Dippie, Brian W. *The Vanishing American: White Attitudes and U.S. Indian Policy*. Middletown, CT: Wesleyan University Press, 1982.

Donaldson, Gordon. *Niagara! The Eternal Circus*. Toronto, ON: Doubleday, 1979.

Dow, Charles Mason. *Anthology and Bibliography of Niagara Falls*. 2 vols. Albany, NY, 1921.

Doyle, James. *North of America: Images of Canada in the Literature of the United States, 1775–1900*. Toronto, ON: ECW Press, 1983.

Drinnon, Richard. *Facing West: The Metaphysics of Indian-Hating and Empire-Building*. Minneapolis, MN: University of Minnesota Press, 1980.

Dryden, John. *Essays*. Ed. W.P. Ker. 2 vols. 1900; New York: Russell & Russell, 1961.

Dubinsky, Karen. *The Second Greatest Disappointment: Honeymooning and Tourism at Niagara Falls*. Toronto, ON and New Brunswick, NJ: Between the Lines and Rutgers University Press, 1999.

Dunlop, Alexander. *The New World Journals of Alexander Graham Dunlop*. Ed. D. Sinclair and G. Warkentin. 1845; Toronto, ON: Dundurn Press, 1976.

DuPlessis, Rachel Blau. "For the Etruscans." In *The New Feminist Criticism: Essays on Women, Literature and Theory,* ed. Elaine Showalter. New York: Pantheon, 1985, 271–91.

Eagleton, Terry. *The Ideology of the Aesthetic*. Oxford: Basil Blackwell, 1990.

Edel, Leon. *Henry James: A Life*. New York: Harper and Row, 1985.

Edwards, Charles R. *A Story of Niagara, To Which Are Appended Reminiscences of a Custom House Officer*. Buffalo, NY: Breed, Lent, 1871.

Embury, Emma C. "Niagara." *Ladies Companion* (Sept. 1841): 250–51.

Endo, Paul. "'Mont Blanc,' Silence, and the Sublime." *English Studies in Canada* 21(3) (1995): 283–300.

Errington, Jane. *The Lion, the Eagle and Upper Canada: A Developing Colonial Ideology*. Montreal and Kingston: McGill-Queen's University Press, 1987.

Fading in the Mist. Writers and Dirs. Robert Borgatti and Paul Lamont. MediaGeist Productions, 1996.

Falk, Peter Hastings, ed. *Who Was Who in American Art*. Madison, CT: Sound View Press, 1985.

The Falls: An Irreverent Portrait of Niagara Falls. Writer and Dir. Kevin McMahon. The National Film Board of Canada, 1991.

Ferguson, Frances. "The Sublime of Edmund Burke, or the Bathos of Experience." In *Glyph* 8: *Johns Hopkins Textual Studies,* ed. Walter Benn Michaels. Baltimore, MD: Johns Hopkins University Press, 1981, 62–78.

Ferree, J.W. *The Falls of Niagara and Scenes Around Them*. New York: A.S. Barnes, 1876.

Fidler, Rev. Isaac. *Observations on the Professions, Literature, Manners and Emigration in the United States and Canada Made during a Residence There in 1832*. New York: J. & J. Harper, 1832.

Finley, Gerald E. *George Heriot, 1759–1839*. Ottawa, ON: National Gallery of Canada, 1979.

Fisher, Robin, and Kenneth Coates, eds. *Out of the Background: Readings on Canadian Native History*. Toronto, ON: Copp Clark Pitman, 1988.

Forster, John. *The Life of Charles Dickens.* 3 vols. London: Chapman and Hall, 1872–74.

Fowler, Marian. *The Embroidered Tent: Five Gentlewomen in Early Canada.* Toronto, ON: Anansi, 1982.

Francis, Daniel. *The Imaginary Indian: The Image of the Indian in Canadian Culture.* Vancouver, BC: Arsenal Pulp Press, 1992.

Francis, David. "The Golden Dreams of the Social Constructionist." *Journal of Anthropological Research* 50(2) (Summer 1994): 97–108.

Fraser, Marian Botsford. *Walking the Line: Travels along the Canadian/American Border.* San Francisco: Sierra Club Books, 1989.

Freedman, Jonathan. *Professions of Taste: Henry James, British Aestheticism, and Commodity Culture.* Stanford, CA: Stanford University Press, 1990.

Friewald, Bina. "Femininely Speaking: Anna Jameson's *Winter Studies and Summer Rambles in Canada.*" In *A Mazing Space: Writing Canadian Women Writing,* ed. Shirley Neuman and Smaro Kamboureli. Edmonton, AB: NeWest Press, 1986.

Frye, Northrop. *Reading the World: Selected Writings, 1935–76.* New York: Peter Lang, 1990.

Fryer, Mary Beacock. *Elizabeth Postuma Simcoe, 1762–1850: A Biography.* Toronto, ON: Dundurn Press, 1989.

Fuller, Margaret. *The Essential Margaret Fuller.* Ed. Jeffrey Steele. New Brunswick, NJ: Rutgers University Press, 1995.

———. *The Letters of Margaret Fuller.* Ed. Robert N. Hudspeth. 5 vols. Ithaca, NY: Cornell University Press, 1988.

———. *Summer on the Lakes in 1843.* Ed. Madeleine B. Stern. Boston, MA: Charles C. Little & James Brown, 1844; Nieuwkoop: De Graff, 1972.

Fussell, Paul. *Abroad: British Literary Traveling between the Wars.* New York: Oxford University Press, 1980.

Gardner, Helen. *Art through the Ages.* 5th ed. New York: Harcourt, Brace & World, 1970.

Gardner, James T. *New York State Survey on the Preservation of the Scenery of Niagara Falls and Fourth Annual Report on the Triangulation of the State.* Buffalo, NY: 1879.

Gatenby, Greg, ed. *The Very Richness of That Past: Canada through the Eyes of Foreign Writers.* Vol. II. Toronto, ON: Vintage Canada, 1996.

———. *The Wild Is Always There: Canada through the Eyes of Foreign Writers.* Vol. I. Toronto, ON: Alfred A. Knopf, 1993.

Gayler, Hugh J., ed. *Niagara's Changing Landscapes.* Ottawa, ON: Carleton University Press, 1994.

Gentilcore, R.L. *Ontario's History in Maps.* Ottawa, ON: Ministry of Citizenship and Culture, 1984.

Gerry, Thomas M.F. "'I Am Translated': Anna Jameson's Sketches and Winter Studies and Summer Rambles in Canada." *Journal of Canadian Studies* 25(4) (Winter 1990–91): 34–49.

Gibb, Camilla. *The Petty Details of So-and-So's Life.* Toronto, ON: Doubleday Canada, 2002.

Gibbins, Roger. *Canada as a Borderlands Society.* Borderlands Monograph Ser. 2. Orono, ME: Borderlands Project, 1989, 1–17.

Gidley, Mick, Robert Lawson-Peebles, and Leo Marx, eds. *Views of American Landscapes*. Cambridge: Cambridge University Press, 1989.

Gillispie, Charles Coulston. *Genesis and Geology: A Study in the Relations of Scientific Thought, Natural Theology, and Social Opinion in Great Britain, 1790–1850*. Cambridge, MA: Harvard University Press, 1951.

Gillmor, Don. "Promised Land." *Canadian Geographic* (July/Aug. 1995): 46–55.

Gilman, Caroline. *The Poetry of Travelling in the United States. With Additional Sketches by a Few Friends; and A Week among Autographs by Rev. S. Gilman*. New York: S. Colman, 1838; Upper Saddle, NJ: Literature House, 1970.

Gilpin, William. *An Essay upon Prints*. 4th ed. 1768; London: R. Blamire, 1892.

———. *Observations on the River Wye, and Several Parts of South Wales Relative Chiefly to Picturesque Beauty; Made in the Summer of the Year 1770*. 1782; Richmond, UK: Richmond, 1973.

———. *Observations on the Western Parts of England, Relative Chiefly to Picturesque Beauty, To Which Are Added a Few Remarks on the Picturesque Beauties of the Isle of Wight*. 1798; Richmond, UK: Richmond, 1973.

———. *Observations, Relative Chiefly to Picturesque Beauty, Made in the Year 1772, on Several Parts of England; Particularly the Mountains, and Lakes of Cumberland, and Westmoreland*. 1786; Richmond, UK: Richmond, 1973.

———. *Three Essays: On Picturesque Beauty; on Picturesque Travel; and on Sketching Landscape: to Which is Added a Poem, On Landscape Painting*. 2nd ed. 1792; London: R. Blamire, 1794.

Glickman, Susan. *The Picturesque and the Sublime: A Poetics of the Canadian Landscape*. Montreal and Kingston: McGill-Queen's University Press, 1998.

Goldie, Terry. *Fear and Temptation: The Image of the Indigene in Canadian, Australian, and New Zealand Literature*. Montreal and Kingston: McGill-Queen's University Press, 1989.

Gombrich, E.H. *Art and Illusion: A Study in the Psychology of Pictorial Representation*. Princeton, NJ: Princeton University Press, 1960.

Good, E. Reginald. "Mississauga-Mennonite Relations in the Upper Grand River Valley." *Ontario History* 87(2) (June 1995): 155–72.

Goode, Patrick, et al. *The Oxford Companion to Gardens*. Oxford: Oxford University Press, 1986.

Gould, Stephen Jay. *The Mismeasure of Man*. New York: Norton, 1996.

Greenfield, Bruce. *Narrating Discovery: The Romantic Explorer in American Literature, 1790–1855*. New York: Columbia University Press, 1992.

Greenhill, Ralph, and Thomas D. Mahoney. *Niagara*. Toronto, ON: University of Toronto Press, 1969.

Grimes, William. "11 Almost-Masters from the Vaults." *The New York Times* (Feb. 5, 1995): 42.

Grossberg, Lawrence, Cary Nelson, and Paula A. Treichler, eds. *Cultural Studies*. New York: Routledge, 1992.

Guillet, Edwin C. *Early Life in Upper Canada*. Toronto, ON: Ontario Publishing, 1933.

Hall, Basil. *Travels in North America in the Years 1827 and 1828*. Vol. 1. Edinburgh: Cadell, 1829, 177–208, 351–54.

Hall, Catherine. "Going a-Trolloping: Imperial Man Travels the Empire." In *Gender and Imperialism*, ed. Clare Midgley. Manchester, UK: Manchester University Press, 1998, 180–99.

Hamilton, Thomas. *Men and Manners in America*. 2 vols. Edinburgh, 1833.

Harper, J. Russell. *Painting in Canada: A History*. 2nd ed. Toronto, ON: University of Toronto Press, 1972.

Hartt, Frederick. *Art: A History of Painting, Sculpture, Architecture*. Englewood Cliffs, NJ: Prentice-Hall, 1985.

Hawthorne, Nathaniel. *Hawthorne's Journals*. Ed. Newton Arvin. New York: Barnes and Noble, 1929.

————. *The Letters, 1813–1843*. Ed. Thomas Woodson, et al. Vol. 1. Columbus, OH: Ohio State University Press, 1984.

————. "My Visit to Niagara." In *The Snow-Image and Uncollected Tales*, Vol. 11. Columbus, OH: Ohio State University Press, 1974, 281–88.

Haynes, Roslynn D. *H.G. Wells: The Discoverer of the Future*. London: Macmillan Press, 1980.

Hedlam, Bruce. "Sleight of Mind." *Saturday Night* 107(4) (1992): 24–25.

Heidenreich, Conrad E. "The French Mapping of North America in the Seventeenth Century." In *The Map Collector*. Berkhamsted, UK: Abacus Press, 1982, 2–11.

Heineman, Helen. *Frances Trollope*. Boston, MA: Twayne, 1984.

Henry, Walter Dr. *Events of a Military Life: Being Recollections after Service in the Peninsular War, Invasion of France, the East Indies, St. Helena, Canada, and Elsewhere*. 2 vols. London: W. Pickering, 1843.

Heriot, George. *Travels through the Canadas*. 2 vols. London, 1807; Toronto, ON: Coles, 1971.

Hertz, Neil. *The End of the Line: Essays on Psychoanalysis and the Sublime*. New York: Columbia University Press, 1985.

Higgins, Robert. *The Niagara Frontier: Its Place in U.S. and Canadian History*. Kitchener, ON: Upney Editions, 1996.

Hillegas, Mark R. *The Future as Nightmare: H.G. Wells and the Anti-Utopians*. Carbondale, IL: Southern Illinois University Press, 1974.

Hipple, Walter John, Jr. *The Beautiful, the Sublime and the Picturesque in Eighteenth-Century British Aesthetic Theory*. Carbondale, IL: Southern Illinois University Press, 1957.

Holder, Thomas. *A Complete Record of Niagara Falls and Vicinage being Descriptive, Historical and Industrial; containing a Complete Guide Book, Local History, Manufacturing Facilities, Biographical Sketches*. Niagara Falls, NY: n.p., 1882.

Holley, George W. *The Falls of Niagara and Other Famous Cataracts*. London: Hodder and Stoughton, 1882.

Holstein, James A., and Gale Miller, eds. *Reconsidering Social Constructionism: Debates in Social Problems Theory*. Hawthorne, NY: Aldine De Gruyter, 1993.

Hough, Jack L. *Geology of the Great Lakes*. Urbana, IL: University of Illinois Press, 1958.

Housley-Simpson, Paul, ed. *A Few Acres of Snow: Literary and Artistic Images of Canada*. Toronto, ON: Dundurn, 1992.

Howells, William Dean, et al. *The Niagara Book*. 2nd ed. New York: Doubleday, 1901.

Hunt, John Dixon. *The Figure in the Landscape: Poetry, Painting, and Gardening During the Eighteenth Century*. Baltimore, MD: Johns Hopkins University Press, 1976.

Hunter, William S. *Chisholm's Panoramic Guide from Niagara Falls to Quebec*. Montreal, QC: C.R. Chisholm, 1869.

———. *Hunter's Panoramic Guide from Niagara Falls to Quebec*. Boston, MA: John P. Jewett, 1857.

Hussey, Christopher. *The Picturesque: Studies in a Point of View*. London: G.P. Putnam's Sons, 1927; Hamden, CT: Archon Books, 1967.

Hutton, James. *System of the Earth* (1785); *Theory of the Earth* (1788); *Observations on Granite* (1794). Foreword by George White. Darien, CT: Hafner, 1970.

Ingraham, Joseph Wentworth. *A Manual for the Use of Visitors to the Falls of Niagara*. Buffalo, NY: Charles Faxon, 1834.

Innis, Mary Quayle, ed. *Mrs. Simcoe's Diary [1791–96]*. Toronto, ON: Macmillan, 1965.

Irwin, William R. *The New Niagara: Tourism, Technology and the Landscape of Niagara Falls, 1776–1917*. University Park, PA: Pennsylvania State University Press, 1996.

Izard, Ralph. "A Trip to Niagara in 1765." *Knickerbocker* (1845): 1–2.

James, Henry. *Portraits of Places*. Boston, MA: James R. Osgood, 1883.

Jameson, Anna Brownell. *Early Canadian Sketches by Mrs. Jameson*. Toronto, ON: Burns and MacEachern, 1958.

———. *Winter Studies and Summer Rambles in Canada*. London: Saunders and Otley, 1838; Toronto, ON: McClelland and Stewart, 1990.

Janson, H.W. *History of Art*. New York: Harry N. Abrams, 1995.

Jasen, Patricia. "Romanticism, Modernity and the Evolution of Tourism on the Niagara Frontier, 1790–1850." *Canadian Historical Review* 72(3) (1991): 283–318.

———. *Wild Things: Nature, Culture and Tourism in Ontario, 1790–1914*. Toronto, ON: University of Toronto Press, 1995.

Jeffreys, Charles W., ed. *Canadiana and Americana: A Catalogue of the Sigmund Samuel Collection at the Royal Ontario Museum*. Toronto, ON: Ryerson, 1948.

Johnston, Johanna. *The Life, Manners, and Travels of Fanny Trollope: A Biography*. New York: Hawthorn Books, 1978.

Jordan, David M. *New World Regionalisms: Literature in the Americas*. Toronto, ON: University of Toronto Press, 1994.

Josipovici, Gabriel. *The World and the Book*. London: Macmillan Press, 1971.

Kant, Immanuel. "Analytic of the Sublime." In *The Second Book* of *Critique of Judgement*. Trans. J.C. Meredith. 1790; Oxford: Oxford University Press, 1932.

———. *Observations on the Feeling of the Beautiful and Sublime*. Trans. John T. Goldthwait. 1763; Berkeley, CA: University of California Press, 1960.

———. "Of the Different Human Races" (1775) in Robert Bernasconi, et al., *The Idea of Race*. Indianapolis: Hackett, 2000, 8–22.

Keith, W.J. *Literary Images of Ontario*. Toronto, ON: Ontario Historical Studies Series, 1992.

Kelly, Franklin, et al., eds. *Frederic Edwin Church and the National Landscape.* Washington, DC: Smithsonian Institution Press, 1988.

———. *Frederic Edwin Church.* Washington, DC: National Gallery of Art and Smithsonian Institution Press, 1989.

King, Thomas, et al. *The Native in Literature.* Toronto, ON: ECW Press, 1987.

Kirschke, James J. *Henry James and Impressionism.* Troy, NY: Whitston, 1981.

Kline, Marcia B. *Beyond the Land Itself: Views of Nature in Canada and the US.* Cambridge, MA: Harvard University Press, 1970.

Klonk, Charlotte. *Science and the Perception of Nature: British Landscape Art in the Late Eighteenth and Early Nineteenth Centuries.* New Haven, CT: Yale University Press, 1996.

Knight, Richard Payne. *The Landscape: A Didactic Poem in Three Books.* 2nd ed. 1795; reprint, Farnborough, UK: Gregg, 1972.

Kohl, J.G. *Travels in Canada and through the States of New York and Pennsylvania.* Trans. Mrs. Percy Sinnett. London: George Manwaring, 1861, Vol. 1, 128–85.

Kolodny, Annette. *The Land before Her: Fantasy and Experience of the American Frontiers, 1630–1860.* Chapel Hill, NC: University of North Carolina Press, 1984.

Krasner, James. *The Entangled Eye: Visual Perception and the Representation of Nature in Post-Darwinian Narrative.* New York: Oxford University Press, 1992.

Kunitz, Stanley J., ed. *British Authors of the Nineteenth Century.* New York: H.W. Wilson, 1936.

"Lady Travellers." *Blackwoods Edinburgh Magazine* 160 (1896): 49–66.

Lane, Christopher W. *Impressions of Niagara: The Charles Rand Penney Collection of Prints of Niagara Falls and the River Niagara from the Sixteenth to the Early Twentieth Century.* Philadelphia: The Philadelphia Print Shop, 1993.

Lasdun, Susan. *The English Park: Royal, Private and Public.* London: Andre Deutsch, 1991.

Lawrence, Karen R. *Penelope Voyages: Women and Travel in the British Literary Tradition.* Ithaca and London: Cornell University Press, 1994.

Leslie, Miss. "Niagara." *Godey's Lady's Book & Magazine* (1845): 230–37.

Levine, George. *Darwin and the Novelists: Patterns of Science in Victorian Fiction.* Cambridge, MA: Harvard University Press, 1988.

Liancourt, Duke de La Rochefoucault. *Travels through the United States of North America, the country of the Iroquois, and Upper Canada, in the years 1795, 1796, and 1797; with an authentic account of Lower Canada.* London: Phillips, 1799.

Lipset, Seymour Martin. *North American Cultures: Values and Institutions in Canada and the United States.* Borderlands Monograph Ser. 3. Orono, ME: Borderlands Project, 1990, 1–50.

Lord, Barry. *The History of Painting in Canada: Toward a People's Art.* Toronto, ON: NC Press, 1974.

Ludlow, Fitz Hugh. *The Hasheesh Eater.* 1857; Upper Saddle River, NJ: Literature House, 1970.

Lyell, Charles. *On North American Geology.* Ed. Hubert C. Skinner. New York: Greeley & McElrath, 1843; New York: Arno Press, 1978.

————. *Principles of Geology: Being an Attempt to Explain the Former Changes of the Earth's Surface by References to Causes Now in Operation.* 3 vols. 1830–33; New York: Johnson Reprint, 1969.

————. *Travels in North America, in the Years 1841–42, with Geological Observations on the United States, Canada, and Nova Scotia.* Vol. 1. New York: Wiley and Putnam, 1845.

Lyell, Mrs. *Life, Letters and Journals of Sir Charles Lyell, Bart.* London: John Murray, 1881.

MacCannell, Dean. *The Tourist: A New Theory of the Leisure Class.* New York: Schocken Books, 1976.

MacDonald, Mary Lu. *Literature and Society in the Canadas, 1817–1850.* Queenston, ON: Edwin Mellen Press, 1992.

————. "The Natural World in Early Nineteenth-Century Canadian Literature." *Canadian Literature* 111 (Winter 1986): 48–65.

Macpherson, Gerardine. *Memoirs of the Life of Anna Jameson.* Boston, MA: Roberts Brothers, 1878.

Maid of the Mist and Other Famous Niagara News Stories. Niagara Falls, ON: The Kiwanis Club of Stamford, 1971.

Mainiero, Lina, ed. *American Women Writers.* 4 vols. New York: Frederick Ungar, 1980.

Manwaring, Elizabeth Wheeler. *Italian Landscape in Eighteenth Century England: A Study Chiefly of the Influence of Claude Lorrain and Salvator Rosa on English Taste 1700–1800.* 2nd ed. 1925; London: Frank Cass, 1965.

Marshall, Tom. *Voices on the Brink: A Border Tale.* Toronto, ON: Macmillan, 1988.

Martineau, Harriet. *Illustrations of Political Economy.* 13 vols. London: C. Fox, 1832–33.

————. *Retrospect of Western Travel.* 3 vols. London: Saunders and Otley, 1838; New York: Greenwood Press, 1969.

————. *Society in America.* 3 vols. London: Saunders and Otley, 1837; New York: Greenwood Press, 1969.

Martling, James Abraham. "The Hermit of Niagara." In *Poems of Home and Country.* Boston, MA: James H. Earle, 1886, 363–65.

Marx, Leo. *The Machine in the Garden: Technology and the Pastoral Ideal in America.* New York: Oxford University Press, 1964.

Mason, Mary G. "The Other Voice: Autobiographies of Women Writers." In *Autobiography: Essays Theoretical and Critical,* ed. James Olney. Princeton, NJ: Princeton University Press, 1980, 210–31.

Mason, Philip Dudley. *A Guide to the Niagara Frontier with Maps and Photographs.* Niagara Falls, ON: Travelpic Publications, 1965.

————. *Niagara and the Daredevils.* Niagara Falls, ON: Travelpic, 1969.

Mayr, Suzette. *The Widows.* Edmonton, AB: NeWest Press, 1998.

McConnell, Frank. *The Science Fiction of H.G. Wells.* New York: Oxford University Press, 1981.

McGreevy, Patrick. "The End of America: The Beginning of Canada." *The Canadian Geographer* 32(4) (1988): 307–18.

————. *Imagining Niagara: The Meaning and Making of Niagara Falls.* Amherst, MA: University of Massachusetts Press, 1994.

————. "Reading the Texts of Niagara Falls: The Metaphor of Death." In *Writing Worlds: Discourse, Text and Metaphor in the Representation of Landscape,* ed. Trevor J. Barnes et al. New York: Routledge, 1991, 50–72.

————. *The Wall of Mirrors: Nationalism and Perceptions of the Border at Niagara Falls.* Borderlands Monograph Ser. 5. Orono, ME: Borderlands Project, 1991, 1–18.

McGregor, Gaile. *The Wacousta Syndrome: Explorations in the Canadian Langscape.* Toronto, ON: University of Toronto Press, 1985.

McKinsey, Elizabeth. *Niagara Falls: Icon of the American Sublime.* Cambridge, MA: Harvard University Press, 1985.

McKinsey, Lauren, and Victor Konrad. *Borderlands Reflections: The United States and Canada.* Borderlands Monograph Ser. 1. Orono, ME: Borderlands Project, 1989, 1–37.

McMullen, Lorraine, ed. *Re(dis)covering Our Foremothers: Nineteenth-Century Canadian Women Writers.* Ottawa, ON: University of Ottawa Press, 1990.

Meckier, Jerome. *Innocent Abroad: Charles Dickens's American Engagements.* Lexington, KY: University Press of Kentucky, 1990.

Meinig, D.W., ed. *The Interpretation of Ordinary Landscapes: Geographical Essays.* New York: Oxford University Press, 1979.

————. *The Shaping of America: A Geographical Perspective on 500 Years of History. Vol. 2: Continental America, 1800–1867.* New Haven, CT: Yale University Press, 1993.

Mellow, James R. *Nathaniel Hawthorne in His Times.* Boston, MA: Houghton Mifflin, 1980.

Merrit, Chris. *Crossing the Border: The Canada-United States Boundary.* Borderlands Monograph Ser. 4. Orono, ME: Borderlands Project, 1991, 19–55.

Middleton, Dorothy. *Victorian Lady Travellers.* London: Routledge & Kegan Paul, 1965.

"The Mighty Niagara of Souls." *The War Cry & Official Gazette of the Salvation Army in Canada & Newfoundland* 12 (6) (Nov. 9, 1895): 1, 4.

Mill, John Stuart. *Three Essays on Religion: Nature, the Utility of Religion, Theism.* London: Longmans, Green, Reader & Dyer, 1873.

Miller, J.R., ed. *Skyscrapers Hide the Heavens: A History of Indian-White Relations in Canada.* Toronto, ON: University of Toronto Press, 1989.

————. *Sweet Promises: A Reader on Indian-White Relations in Canada.* Toronto, ON: University of Toronto Press, 1991.

Mills, Sara. *Discourses of Difference: An Analysis of Women's Travel Writing and Colonialism.* London and New York: Routledge, 1991.

Minh-ha, Trinh T. "Other Than Myself/My Other Self." In *Travellers' Tales: Narratives of Home and Displacement,* ed. George Robertson, et al. London and New York: Routledge, 1994, 9–26.

Mitchell, Lee Clark. *Witness to a Vanishing America: The Nineteenth-Century Response.* Princeton, NJ: Princeton University Press, 1981.

Mitchell, W.J.T., ed. *Landscape and Power.* Chicago, IL: University of Chicago Press, 1994.

Monk, Samuel H. *The Sublime: A Study of Critical Theories in XVIII-Century England.* New York: MLA, 1935.

Moodie, Susanna. *Life in the Clearings versus the Bush.* 1853; Toronto, ON: McClelland and Stewart, 1989.

Moore, Harry T. *Henry James and His World*. London: Thames and Hudson, 1974.

Moorman, David T. "Where Are the English and the Americans in the Historiography of Upper Canada?" *Ontario History* 88(1) (Mar. 1996): 65–69.

Morden, James. *Falls View Bridges and Niagara Ice Bridges*. Niagara Falls, ON: F.H. Leslie, 1938.

Moriyama & Teshima Planners Limited. *Ontario's Niagara Parks: Planning the Second Century—A 100-Year Vision, A 20-Year Plan*. Toronto, ON: The Niagara Parks Commission, 1988.

Mottram, Eric, ed. *The Penguin Companion to Literature*. 4 vols. London: Penguin, 1971.

Moyles, R.G., and Doug Owram. *Imperial Dreams and Colonial Realities: British Views of Canada, 1880–1914*. Toronto, ON: University of Toronto Press, 1988.

Mulvey, Christopher. *Anglo-American Landscapes: A Study of Nineteenth-Century Anglo-American Travel Literature*. Cambridge: Cambridge University Press, 1983.

Nelles, H.V. *The Politics of Development: Forests, Mines and Hydro-Electric Power in Ontario*. Toronto, ON: Macmillan, 1974.

Nemeth, Mary. "Romancing the Falls." *Maclean's* June 28, 1993, 42.

A New Guide to Niagara Falls and Vicinity. New York: Rand & McNally, 1893.

New York (State) Commissioners of the State Reservation at Niagara. *Five Annual Reports, 1884–1889*. New York: Troy Press, 1885–89.

"Niagara 1805–1875: By an Old Resident." In *Travellers Accounts from the Clearwater Collection in the Niagara Falls (New York) Public Library*. Collected by George A. Seibel. Microfilm #15. Niagara Falls, ON: Niagara Falls Public Library, 1982. 14 pp.

Nicolson, Marjorie Hope. *Mountain Gloom and Mountain Glory: The Development of the Aesthetics of the Infinite*. New York: W.W. Norton, 1959.

Nodine, Calvin F., ed. *Perception and Pictorial Representation*. New York: Praeger, 1979.

Nye, David E. *American Technological Sublime*. Cambridge, MA: MIT Press, 1994.

O'Brien, Andy. *Daredevils of Niagara*. Toronto, ON: Ryerson, 1964.

Olsson, Nils William. *Pehr Kalm and the Image of North America*. Minneapolis, MN: The Associates of the James Ford Bell Library, 1970.

Oreskovich, Carlie. *Sir Henry Pellatt: The King of Casa Loma*. Toronto, ON: McGraw-Hill Ryerson Press, 1982.

Osborne, Harold, ed. *The Oxford Companion to Art*. Oxford: Clarendon Press, 1970.

Ousby, Ian. *The Englishman's England: Taste, Travel and the Rise of Tourism*. Cambridge: Cambridge University Press, 1990.

Owahyah. *Birch Bark Legends of Niagara, Founded on Traditions among the Iroquois, or Six Nations*. St. Catharines, ON: Journal Printing, 1884.

Pardue, Jeff. "'There is no land unhabitable, nor sea innavigable': British Geography and Empire, from the Elizabethan Era to the Turn of the Nineteenth Century." Diss. University of Waterloo, 1995.

Parkman, Francis. *The Jesuits in North America in the Seventeenth Century*. 1867; Boston, MA: Little, Brown, 1895.

Parry, Ellwood. *The Image of the Indian and the Black Man in American Art, 1590–1900*. New York: Braziller, 1974.

Peacock, Shane. "The Falls Guy." *Saturday Night* 108(3) (1993): 46–48.

Percy, Walker. "The Loss of the Creature." In *The Message in the Bottle: How Queer Man Is, How Queer Language Is, and What One Has to Do with the Other*. New York: Farrar, Straus and Giroux, 1975, 46–63.

Petrie, Francis J. *Roll Out the Barrel: The Story of Niagara's Daredevils*. Erin, ON: Boston Mills Press, 1985.

Pfahl, John. *Arcadia Revisited: Niagara River and Falls from Lake Erie to Lake Ontario*. Albuquerque, NM: University of New Mexico Press, 1988.

Phillips, David. *The Day Niagara Falls Ran Dry!: Canadian Weather Facts and Trivia*. Toronto, ON: Key Porter Books, 1993.

Pierce, Patricia. *Canada—The Missing Years*. Don Mills, ON: Stoddart, 1985.

Piva, Michael J. *The Condition of the Working Class in Toronto, 1900–1921*. Ottawa, ON: University of Ottawa Press, 1979.

Porteous, J. Douglas. "Bodyscape: The Body-Landscape Metaphor." *The Canadian Geographer* 30(1) (1986): 2–12.

Porter, Peter. *Goat Island*. Niagara Falls, NY: Niagara Frontier Historical Society, 1900.

———. *Official Guide to Niagara: Falls, River, Frontier*. Buffalo, NY: Matthews-Northrup Works, 1901.

Pratt, Mary Louise. *Imperial Eyes: Travel Writing and Transculturation*. London and New York: Routledge, 1992.

Prentice, Richard. *Tourism and Heritage Attractions*. London: Routledge, 1993.

Press, Charles. *The Political Cartoon*. Rutherford, NJ: Fairleigh Dickinson University Press, 1981.

Price, Martin. "The Picturesque Moment." In *From Sensibility to Romanticism: Essays Presented to Frederick A. Pottle,* ed. Frederick W. Hilles and Harold Bloom. New York: Oxford University Press, 1965, 259–92.

Price, Uvedale. *An Essay on the Picturesque: As Compared with the Sublime and the Beautiful; And, on the Use of Studying Pictures, for the Purpose of Improving Real Landscape*. 3 vols. 1794; reprint, Farnborough, UK: Gregg, 1971.

Priest, William. *Travels in the United States of North America*. London: J. Johnson, 1802.

Priestley, F.E.L. "Newton and the Romantic Concept of Nature." *The University of Toronto Quarterly* 4 (July 1948): 323–36.

Quimby, George Irving. *Indian Culture and European Trade Goods*. Madison, WI: University of Wisconsin Press, 1966.

Ray, Arthur J. *I Have Lived Here since the World Began: An Illustrated History of Canada's Native People*. Toronto, ON: Lester/Key Porter, 1996.

Reed, Ishmael. *Flight to Canada*. New York: Random House, 1976.

Renzetti, Elizabeth. "Writers Opt for Bus, Not Barrel." The *Globe and Mail* (Oct. 31, 1996): C3.

Roberts, W. Rhys. *Longinus on the Sublime*. Cambridge: Cambridge University Press, 1935.

Robertson, Douglas, ed. *An Englishman in America, 1785: Being the Diary of Joseph Hadfield*. Toronto, ON: Hunter-Rose, 1933.

Robertson, J. Ross, ed. *The Diary of Mrs. John Graves Simcoe*. Toronto, ON: William Briggs, 1911.

Robinson, Sidney K. *Inquiry into the Picturesque.* Chicago, IL: University of Chicago Press, 1991.

Rose, Gillian. *Feminism and Geography: The Limits of Geographical Knowledge.* Minneapolis, MN: University of Minnesota Press, 1993.

Ross, Alexander M. *The Imprint of the Picturesque on Nineteenth-Century British Fiction.* Waterloo, ON: Wilfrid Laurier University Press, 1986.

Rothman, Ellen K. *Hands and Hearts: A History of Courtship in America.* New York: Basic Books, 1984.

Rousseau, Jean-Jacques. *Essay on the Origins of Languages.* Trans. John T. Scott. Vol. 7 of the *Collected Writings of Rousseau.* 1781; Hanover, NH: University Press of New England, 1999.

Royal Commission to Inquire into Alleged Abuses Occurring in the Vicinity of Niagara Falls. Toronto, ON: The Archives of Ontario, 1873. (RG 18–14).

Rudisill, Richard. *Mirror Image: The Influence of the Daguerreotype on American Society.* Albuquerque, NM: University of New Mexico Press, 1971.

Russell, Mary. *The Blessings of a Good Thick Skirt: Women Travellers and Their World.* London: Collins, 1988.

Russell, William Howard. *My Diary North and South.* 2 vols. New York: Harper & Brothers, 1863.

Sanders, Valerie. *Reason Over Passion: Harriet Martineau and the Victorian Novel.* Sussex, UK: Harvester Press, 1986.

Sawyer, K.E. *Landscape Studies: An Introduction to Geomorphology.* London: Edward Arnold, 1970.

Schama, Simon. *Landscape and Memory.* New York/Toronto: A.A. Knopf/ Random House of Canada, 1995.

Schiappa, Edward. "Burkean Tropes and Kuhnian Science: A Social Constructionist Perspective on Language and Reality." *Journal of Advanced Composition* 13(2) (Fall 1993): 401–22.

Schwartz, Seymour I. *The French and Indian War, 1754–1763: The Imperial Struggle for North America.* New York: Simon & Schuster, 1994.

Scott, Donald M. "Knowledge and the Marketplace." In *The Mythmaking Frame of Mind,* ed. James Gilbert et al. Belmont, CA: Wadsworth, 1993, 91–112.

Seaman, Patricia. *The Nightingales.* Toronto: Coach House Books, 2001.

Sears, John. *Sacred Places: American Tourist Attractions in the 19th Century.* New York: Oxford University Press, 1989.

Seibel, George A. *The Niagara Portage Road: 200 Years 1790–1990.* Niagara Falls, ON: The City of Niagara Falls, 1990.

———. *Ontario's Niagara Parks: A History.* 2nd ed. Niagara Falls, ON: Niagara Parks Commission, 1991.

———. *300 Years Since Father Hennepin: Niagara Falls in Art 1678–1978.* 2nd ed., with Addenda. 1978; Niagara Falls, ON: Niagara Falls Heritage Foundation, 1992.

Severance, Frank H. *Old Trails on the Niagara Frontier.* Buffalo, NY, 1899.

Shaftesbury, Anthony Ashley Cooper. *The Moralists: A Philosophical Rhapsody (1709). Republished as Treatise V of Characteristicks of Men, Manners, Opinions, Times, etc.* Vol. 2. Ed. John M. Robertson. London, 1900.

Shields, Rob. *Places on the Margin: Alternative Geographies of Modernity.* London: Routledge, 1991.

Shirreff, Patrick. *A Tour through North America; Together with a Comprehensive View of the Canadas and United States as Adapted for Agricultural Emigration*. Edinburgh: Oliver & Boyd, 1835.

Sigourney, Lydia Huntley. "The Hermit of the Falls." In *The Poems of Frances Ridley Havergal and Lydia Huntley Sigourney*. Chicago and New York: Belford, Clarke, 1885, 253–59.

———. "Niagara." In *Select Poems*. 4th ed. Philadelphia: Edward C. Biddle, 1842, 88–90.

Simonds, Merilyn. "Code of Arms." *Canadian Geographic* (Mar./Apr. 1996): 44–59.

Slotkin, J.S. *Readings in Early Anthropology*. London: Methuen, 1965.

Slotkin, Richard. *Regeneration through Violence: The Mythology of the American Frontier, 1600–1860*. Middletown, CN: Wesleyan University Press, 1973.

Smedley, Audrey. *Race in North America: Origin and Evolution of a Worldview*. Boulder, CO: Westview Press, 1993.

Smith, D.B. *Aboriginal Ontario: Historical Perspectives on the First Nations*. Toronto, ON: Dundurn Press, 1994.

Soyka, Fred, and Alan Edmonds. *The Ion Effect: How Air Electricity Rules Your Life and Health*. Toronto, ON: Lester and Orpen, 1977.

Spendlove, F. St. George. *The Face of Early Canada: Pictures of Canada Which Have Helped to Make History*. Toronto, ON: Ryerson, 1958.

Spencer, Joseph William Winthrop. *The Falls of Niagara: Their Evolution and Varying Relations to the Great Lakes; Characteristics of the Power, and the Effects of Its Diversion*. Ottawa, ON: Dept. of Mines, Geological Survey Branch, 1907.

Spurr, David. *The Rhetoric of Empire: Colonial Discourse in Journalism, Travel Writing, and Imperial Administration*. Durham and London: Duke University Press, 1993.

Staines, David, ed. *The Canadian Imagination: Dimensions of a Literary Culture*. Cambridge, MA: Harvard University Press, 1977.

Statistics Canada. *Canada Year Book 2002*. Ottawa, ON: Publication Sales and Services, 2002.

Stepan, Nancy. *The Idea of Race in Science: Great Britain, 1800–1960*. Hamden, CT: Archon Books, 1982.

Stevens, Victoria. "Lights Fantastic." *The Toronto Star* (Dec. 3, 1994), Sec. F: 1,8.

Stewart, Susan. *On Longing: Narrative of the Miniature, the Gigantic, the Souvenir, the Collection*. Baltimore, MD: Johns Hopkins University Press, 1984.

Stolnitz, Jerome. "Beauty: Some Stages in the History of an Idea." *Journal of the History of Ideas* 22(2) (Apr.–June 1961): 185–204.

Stowe, William W. *Going Abroad: European Travel in Nineteenth-Century American Culture*. Princeton, NJ: Princeton University Press, 1994.

Strickland, Carol. *The Annotated Mona Lisa: A Crash Course in Art History from Prehistoric to Post-Modern*. Kansas City, KS: Andrew T. McMeel, 1992.

Strickland, Walter George, ed. *A Dictionary of Irish Artists*. 2 vols. New York: Hacker Art Books, 1968.

Swingle, L.J. *Romanticism and Anthony Trollope*. Ann Arbor, MI: University of Michigan Press, 1990.

Table Rock Album and Sketches of the Falls and Scenery Adjacent. 1848; Buffalo, NY: Franklin Steam Printing House, 1862.

Taylor, Annie Edson. *Over the Falls: How the Horseshoe Falls Was Conquered.* n.p., 1902.

Tesmer, Irving H., ed. *Colossal Cataract: The Geologic History of Niagara Falls.* Albany, NY: State University of New York Press, 1981.

Thomas, Clara. *Love and Work Enough: The Life of Anna Jameson.* Toronto, ON: University of Toronto Press, 1967.

Thomas, Gillian. *Harriet Martineau.* Boston, MA: Twayne, 1985.

Tinkler, Keith J. "Canadian Landform Examples—2. Niagara Falls." *The Canadian Geographer* 30(4) (1986): 367–71.

———. "Déjà Vu: The Downfall of Niagara as a Chronometer, 1845–1941." In *Niagara's Changing Landscapes,* ed. Hugh J. Gayler. Ottawa, ON: Carleton University Press, 1994, 81–110.

———. *Field Guide: Niagara Peninsula and Niagara Gorge.* Hamilton, ON: McMaster University Printing Services, 1993.

———. "The Idea of a History and the History of an Idea." *Geomorphology* 1 (1987): 69–85.

———, et al. "Postglacial Recession of Niagara Falls in Relation to the Great Lakes." *Quaternary Research* 42 (1994): 20–29.

Tiplin, Albert H. *Our Romantic Niagara: A Geological History of the River and the Falls.* Niagara Falls, ON: The Niagara Falls Heritage Foundation, 1988.

Tovell, Walter. *Niagara Falls: Story of a River.* Toronto, ON: Royal Ontario Museum, 1966.

Trachtenberg, Alan. *Reading American Photographs: Images as History.* New York: Hill & Wang, 1989.

Travellers Accounts from the Clearwater Collection in the Niagara Falls (New York) Public Library. Collected by George A. Seibel. Microfilm #15. Niagara Falls, ON: Niagara Falls Public Library, 1982.

Trigger, Bruce G. *Natives and Newcomers: Canada's "Heroic Age" Reconsidered.* Montreal and Kingston: McGill-Queen's University Press, 1985.

Trollope, Anthony. *An Illustrated Autobiography.* 1883; Wolfeboro, NH: Alan Sutton, 1989.

———. *North America.* Ed. Donald Smalley and Bradford Allen Booth. 1862; New York: Alfred A. Knopf, 1951.

———. *North America.* Ed. J.W. Ward. 1862; Toronto, ON: Penguin, 1992.

Trollope, Frances. *Domestic Manners of the Americans.* Ed. Donald Smalley. 1832; London: The Folio Society, 1974.

Tuan, Yi-Fu. *Passing Strange & Wonderful: Aesthetics, Nature and Culture.* Washington, DC: Island Press, 1993.

———. "Surface Phenomena and Aesthetic Experience." *Annals of the Association of American Geographers* 79(2) (1989): 233–41.

———. *Topophilia: A Study of Environmental Perception, Attitudes and Values.* Englewood Cliffs, NJ: Prentice-Hall, 1974.

Turner, Arlin. *Nathaniel Hawthorne: A Biography.* New York: Oxford University Press, 1980.

Turner, Frederick Jackson. *History, Frontier, and Section: Three Essays.* 1891; 1893; 1925. Intro. Martin Ridge. Albuquerque, NM: University of New Mexico Press, 1993.

Turner, Jane, ed. *The Dictionary of Art.* 34 vols. London: Macmillan, 1996.

Turner, Victor. "Variations on a Theme of Liminality." In *Secular Ritual,* ed.

Sally F. Moore and Barbara G. Myerhoff. Amsterdam: Van Gorcum, 1977, 53–55.

Twitchell, James B. *Romantic Horizons: Aspects of the Sublime in English Poetry and Painting, 1770–1850*. Columbia, MO: University of Missouri Press, 1983.

Ulmer, Gregory L. "Metaphoric Rocks: A Psychogeography of Tourism and Monumentality." *Postmodern Culture* 4(3) (1993): 15 pp. Online. Internet.

Urquhart, Jane. *The Whirlpool*. Toronto, ON: McClelland and Stewart, 1986.

Urry, John. *The Tourist Gaze: Leisure and Travel in Contemporary Societies*. London: Sage, 1990.

Vachon, André. *Dreams of Empire: Canada before 1700*. Trans. John F. Flinn. Ottawa, ON: Public Archives of Canada, 1982.

———. *Taking Root: Canada from 1700–1760*. Trans. John F. Flinn. Ottawa, ON: Public Archives of Canada, 1985.

Valverde, Marianna. *The Age of Light, Soap and Water: Moral Reform in English Canada, 1885–1925*. Toronto, ON: McClelland and Stewart, 1991.

———. "The Love of Finery." *Victorian Studies* 32(2) (1989): 169–88.

Vidler, Virginia. *Niagara Falls: 100 Years of Souvenirs*. Utica, NY: North Country Books, 1985.

Von Mehren, Joan. *Minerva and the Muse: A Life of Margaret Fuller*. Amherst, MA: University of Massachusetts Press, 1994.

Walder, Dennis. *Dickens and Religion*. London: George Allen and Unwin, 1981.

Waldron, Holman D. *With Pen and Camera at Niagara Falls*. Portland, ME: Chisholm Bros., 1898.

Ward, Peter. *Courtship, Love and Marriage in Nineteenth-Century English Canada*. Montreal and Kingston: McGill-Queen's University Press, 1990.

Warkentin, Germaine, ed. *Canadian Exploration Literature: An Anthology*. Toronto, ON: Oxford University Press, 1993.

A Warning Cry from Niagara. London: J. Nisbet, n.d., 1–3.

Way, Ronald L. *Ontario's Niagara Parks: A History*. Niagara Falls, ON: Niagara Parks Commission, 1946.

Weiskel, Thomas. *The Romantic Sublime: Studies in the Structure and Psychology of Transcendence*. Baltimore, MD: Johns Hopkins University Press, 1976.

Weld, Isaac. *Travels through the States of North America...During the Years 1795, 1796, and 1797*. London, 1799.

Wells, H.G. *The Future in America: A Search After Realities*. New York and London: Harper & Brothers, 1906.

———. *A Modern Utopia*. London: Thomas Nelson & Sons, 1905.

———. *The War in the Air: And Particularly How Mr. Bert Smallways Fared While It Lasted*. London: George Bell and Sons, 1908.

Wells, Jennifer. "The Last Magic Show." The *Globe and Mail Report on Business Magazine* (Apr. 1994): 48–58.

Welty, Eudora. "The Key." In *The Collected Stories of Eudora Welty*. New York: Harcourt Brace Jovanovich, 1980, 29–37.

Wexler, Sanford. *Westward Expansion: An Eyewitness History*. New York: Facts on File, 1991.

Whalen, Dwight. *The Lady Who Conquered Niagara—The Annie Edson Taylor Story*. Brewer, ME: Edson Genealogical Association, 1990.

————. *Lover's Guide to Niagara Falls*. Niagara Falls, ON: Horseshoe Press, 1990.

Who Was Who in America. 4 vols. Chicago, IL: Mercer, 1960–67.

Williams, Edward Theodore. *Niagara—Queen of Wonders: A Graphic History of the Big Events in Three Centuries*. Boston, MA: Chapple, 1916.

————. *Scenic and Historic Niagara Falls, River, Rapids, Whirlpool and Frontier*. Niagara Falls, NY: n.p., 1925.

Williams, Raymond. *Keywords: A Vocabulary of Culture and Society*. New York: Oxford University Press, 1983.

Wilson, Leonard Gilchrist. *Charles Lyell: The Years to 1841—The Revolution in Geology*. New Haven: Yale University Press, 1972.

Wlecke, Albert O. *Wordsworth and the Sublime*. Berkeley, CA: University of California Press, 1973.

Wolfe, R.I. "The Changing Patterns of Tourism in Ontario." In *Profiles of a Province: Studies in the History of Ontario*. Toronto, ON: Ontario Historical Society, 1967, 173–77.

Wood, Denis. *The Power of Maps*. New York: The Guilford Press, 1992.

Wood, Susan Joan. *The Land in Canadian Prose, 1840–1945*. Ottawa, ON: Carleton University Press, 1988.

Woods, Nicholas A. *The Prince of Wales in Canada and the United States*. London: Bradbury and Evans, 1861.

Wordsworth, William. *The Prelude, or Growth of a Poet's Mind*. Ed. Ernest de Selincourt. 2nd ed., revised by Helen Darbishire. Oxford: Clarendon Press, 1959.

————. *The Prose Works of William Wordsworth*. Ed. W.J.B. Owen and Jane Worthington Smyser. Oxford: Clarendon Press, 1974.

Wright, Frances. *A View of Society and Manners in America: A Series of Letters from That Country to a Friend in England during the Years 1818, 1819 and 1820*. 2nd ed. New York: E. Bliss & E. White, 1821.

Yates, Gayle Graham, ed. *Harriet Martineau on Women*. New Brunswick, NJ: Rutgers University Press, 1985.

York, Lorraine M. "'Sublime Desolation': European Art and Jameson's Perception of Canada." *Mosaic* 19(2) (Spring 1986): 43–56.

Young, Gordon. "The Great Lakes: Is It Too Late?" *National Geographic Magazine* 144(2) (1973): 147–85.

Young, Robert J.C. *Colonial Desire: Hybridity in Theory, Culture and Race*. London and New York: Routledge, 1995.

Zack, Naomi. *Philosophy of Science and Race*. New York and London: Routledge, 2002.

Zaslow, Morris. *Reading the Rocks: The Story of the Geological Survey of Canada, 1842–1972*. Toronto, ON: Macmillan, in association with the Department of Energy, Mines and Resources and Information Canada, 1975.

Zeller, Suzanne. *Inventing Canada: Early Victorian Science and the Idea of a Transcontinental Nation*. Toronto, ON: University of Toronto Press, 1987.

Zimbardo, Rose A. *A Mirror to Nature: Transformations in Drama and Aesthetics, 1660–1732*. Lexington, KY: University Press of Kentucky, 1986.

Zwarg, Christina. "Footnoting the Sublime: Margaret Fuller on Black Hawk's Trail." *American Literary History* 5(4) (1993): 616–42.

Index

and industry/tourism, 129, 158;
as an influence, 80, 82, 90, 135;
and the quest-test, 128, 130–31,
155
Hall, Catherine, 139
Hamilton, Thomas, 133, 135; and the
quest-test, 118, 132, 151, 155–56;
silences another writer, 73, 157
Hancock, Robert, 18, 42–44
Harrison, J.B., 144
Hawthorne, Nathaniel, 76–77, 83, 90;
and the Burkean sublime, 62,
79–80, 110, 156; as an influence,
95; influenced by Hennepin, 78;
and tourism, 80; and the
Wordsworthian Romantic
sublime, 81–82
Henn, Edmund, 45
Hennepin, Louis, 20, 51, 55, 74, 143,
151, 167n15; descriptions of
Niagara, 17, 21–22; illustration
(attributed), 24–26, 67, 140;
professed inadequacy, 17, 39, 104,
153; influence on others, 18,
27–29, 33, 41, 51, 59, 78, 98,
153–59; called liar, 30–32, 34;
Indian name for Niagara, 2
Henry, Alexander, 86
Henry, Walter, 140–42, 152, 157
Heroic Age of Geology, 115–16
Hervieu, Auguste, 71
Hinton, John Howard, 46
Hipple, Walter John, 74
Hogarth, Mary, 92
Hogarth, Mrs. George, 92
Horseshoe Falls/Canadian Falls, 26,
27, 32, 45, 48–49, 51, 67, 76, 78,
129, 147, 159, 165n21
Hudson River School, 46, 50–51,
171n54
Hunt, Mrs., 65
Hunt, William Morris, 108
Hutton, James, 115
hydroelectricity, 120, 142, 147–51,
159
hysterical/sublimed, 57, 111–12,
140–42, 152, 157. See also
feminine aesthetic; sublime;
Burke, Edmund

Indian(s): in art/literature, 14, 41,
43, 56, 65, 108, 142, 159; anxieties
about, 93, 95–99, 154; as children
of nature, 37, 154; and intoxicants,
37–39; as inferior Americans, 46;
and naturalization 18; as Noble

Savage, 44–45, 47, 66, 154;
war-like, 95, 111; sublime, 42,
96; subservient, 38–40;
as threatening/uncivilized, 55,
154–55; victimized, 95, 154,
171n52; in the wilderness, 45;
word for, 166n47. See also
Five Nations; Neutral Nation;
Seneca Nation; Six Nations
industry/industrialists, 45, 48,
54–55, 104, 142–43, 149–52.
See also preservation/
preservationists
Irwin, William, 10

Jasen, Patricia, 11
James, Henry, 63, 104–109, 112
Jameson, Anna, 86, 104, 135, 156;
and the Burkean sublime, 62, 84,
87–89; as double-voiced, 85, 87,
156; as an influence, 95; and
mocking/parodic discourse, 87,
97, 110; and the New Woman, 85;
and Romantic recuperations, 157
Jameson, Robert Sympson, 85
Jesuits, 20, 43
John Bull, 55, 173n77
Johnny Canuck, 55, 173n78
Joliet, Louis, 20

Kalm, Pehr, 18, 27, 30, 113–14,
128, 133, 137, 151–52, 154–55;
description of Niagara, 31–34,
36–39; illustration (attributed),
34–36; influence on others, 43,
118
Kant, Immanuel, 9, 18, 56, 111, 144;
educated sublime, 62–63, 102,
104, 137; gendering aesthetics,
117; Indian as noble, 47; Indian
as sublime, 42, 96, 178n70;
theory of race, 44
Knight, Richard Payne, 8, 62

ladder: 36; aestheticized, 152;
Mrs. Simcoe's, 67, 122–23,
126, 133; representing traces
of the indigene, 123, 155;
tournament, 124–27, 133, 151.
See also masculine aesthetic
Langmuir, John W., 146
La Salle, René-Robert, Cavelier
de, 20–21, 30
LeClerc, Sebastian, 27
legend: drowning bird, 139–40;
healing spray, 20; Indian, 36–39,